About the Author

ED RUGGERO is the author of *Combat Jump: The Young Men Who Led the Assault into Fortress Europe, July 1943* and *Duty First: A Year in the Life of West Point and the Making of American Leaders*. He was an infantry officer in the United States Army for eleven years and is an experienced keynote speaker on leadership development. He lives in Wallingford, Pennsylvania.

THE FIRST MEN IN

ALSO BY ED RUGGERO

NONFICTION

Combat Jump

Duty First

(with Dennis Haley)

The Leader's Compass

The Corporate Compass

(with the Center for Army Leadership)

Army Leadership

FICTION

The Academy

Breaking Ranks

Firefall

The Common Defense

38 North Yankee

THE FIRST MEN IN

U.S. PARATROOPERS
AND THE FIGHT TO
SAVE D-DAY

ED RUGGERO

HARPER

NEW YORK · LONDON · TORONTO · SYDNEY

HARPER

A hardcover edition of this book was published in 2006 by HarperCollins Publishers.

THE FIRST MEN IN. Copyright © 2006 by Ed Ruggero. All rights reserved. Printed in the United States of America. No part of this book may be used or reproduced in any manner whatsoever without written permission except in the case of brief quotations embodied in critical articles and reviews. For information address HarperCollins Publishers, 10 East 53rd Street, New York, NY 10022.

HarperCollins books may be purchased for educational, business, or sales promotional use. For information please write: Special Markets Department, HarperCollins Publishers, 10 East 53rd Street, New York, NY 10022.

FIRST HARPER PAPERBACK PUBLISHED 2007.

Designed by Joseph Rutt

The Library of Congress has catalogued the hardcover edition as follows:

Ruggero, Ed.
   The first men in : U.S. paratroopers and the fight to save D-Day / Ed Ruggero.—
1st ed.
   p. cm.
   Includes bibliographical references and index.
   ISBN-10: 0-06-073128-1
   ISBN-13: 978-0-06-073128-1
   1. World War, 1939–1945—Campaigns—France—Normandy. 2. United States. Army—Parachute troops. I. Title.

D756.5.N6R84 2006
940.54'21421—dc22   2006040158

ISBN: 978-0-06-073129-8 (pbk.)
ISBN-10: 0-06-073129-X (pbk.)

08 09 10 11 ❖ / RRD 10 9 8 7 6 5 4

for

the fallen

Afghanistan
Iraq

I want to tell you what the opening of the second front in that one sector entailed, so that you can know and appreciate and forever be humbly grateful to those both dead and alive who did it for you.

—Ernie Pyle, *Brave Men*

CONTENTS

THE FIRST MEN IN

PROLOGUE

NORMANDY
JUNE 6, 1944
0230 HOURS

Captain Roy Creek had only seconds to look around after his parachute opened. In the distance, antiaircraft fire sparked upward at the fleet of aircraft droning over the peninsula, though none had hit his aircraft. Nearby, he could just see the mushroom shapes of other parachutes in the air around him. Below him was what looked like a meadow, flat and grassy, with no trees to grab his chute and, more important, no obvious sign of any German defenders. This was Creek's first combat and his first jump into enemy territory. So far, so good.

Then he hit the water.

He was immediately in over his head, the nearly hundred pounds of equipment strapped to his body pulling him down, the tangled swamp grasses grabbing his legs. His collapsing chute floated down on him like a shroud.

For Creek, who had grown up in arid New Mexico and had never learned to swim, this was a nightmare. The brackish water closed around him; his own warrior's gear pulled him down into the cold darkness. He thrashed at the water, felt the surface with his hands; it was above his head, but not too far. The trick was to stay calm.

Fighting panic, he grabbed at the knife strapped to the outside of his right boot. Thank God it hadn't come loose in his flailing. He whipped it out, fighting against the tangled risers, the long thin lines connecting parachute to body harness and now spread over him like a net. He sawed desperately at the thick harness, the leg strap, then the belly band around his middle. In his frenzy he cut every strap he could find, including (he later learned) the straps holding his equipment: the musette bag with his personal gear, his map case, his ammunition. His tommy gun, tied in behind his reserve parachute, also went down in the dark. He was free of the weight but still in danger of drowning.

He kicked and flailed and, by sheer luck, found some purchase in the mud and slimy grass, and he felt the bottom rise beneath him. Finally, his head cleared the water, and he sucked in cool air. Still terrified, he didn't stop fighting until he had pulled himself out and lay on a muddy bank, gasping for breath.

When he regained his wits, Creek realized he had narrowly escaped drowning in an area that was supposed to be dry.

Where did all this water come from? The drop zone of his unit, the 507th Parachute Infantry Regiment, part of the 82nd Airborne Division, was just west of the gentle—and narrow—Merderet River. In their map studies, the Merderet River looked more like a stream; an athletic young paratrooper could probably jump across it in most places. But Creek had hit the edge of a wide swamp, with water deeper than a man's head. Had they landed so far from their drop zone that he was in a lake that didn't even appear on their maps? Or had the American planners completely missed the fact that the river had flooded its banks?

Neither case looked good. If he was that far off the mark, he would have a difficult time figuring out where he was, gathering his men, and moving to their objective. If he was anywhere near the right place, but the planners had missed a large body of water right in the middle of their area of operations, what else might be wrong with the plan?

Best to think about that later. Focus on the immediate. An infantry captain in command of a company of nearly 150 men should not be lying on the ground, lost, soaked, and unarmed. It was an inauspicious start to his war.

Behind him, Creek could see his parachute floating on the surface, marking the spot where he had landed and where, he suspected, his weapon, ammunition, and equipment might be.

He could hear movement on the bank, and what might be the sounds of some other men struggling in the water, but there was no one in the immediate area to help him, and he wasn't sure he would admit losing everything even if a GI did appear. He realized with a sickening feeling that there was nothing to do but go back in the water a second time to retrieve his equipment.

In a test of sheer will, he waded in. Any misstep into an unseen hole or the river channel might be his last effort. His own parachute, floating on top of the water, was dangerous, a net waiting for some prey. He pushed the chute out of the way and bent over quickly, thrusting his arms in front, kicking his feet to search for his tangled gear. As soon as his fingers touched the webbing, he pulled it hard toward him, then backpedaled toward the bank he had just left.

Once back on dry ground, he took stock. He had his tommy gun and the canvas case of extra magazines. Somewhere under the water nearby were his gas mask and the musette bag containing all his rations, extra socks, raincoat, notebook, toiletries, all the items he had so carefully selected when he was packing in the staging area in England. He'd miss the equipment later, he knew, but for the moment he was glad to be alive.

Creek checked his weapon and his ammunition, then stood. He could hear small arms and antiaircraft fire in the distance but nothing close by. Overhead, planes were still crossing the peninsula. He heard movement in the grass, some sloshing at the water's edge. Walking toward the sound, he discovered his radio operator, and a few other figures in the darkness, and led them a short distance away from the flood.

When he heard movement behind some thick undergrowth, Creek halted, his tommy gun at the ready, then gave the challenge. "Flash."

"Flash, hell, this is Colonel Maloney."

The second in command of the 507th PIR, Lieutenant Colonel Arthur Maloney, stepped clear of the bushes. Creek was glad to see him.

Maloney was a big paratrooper, physically imposing and a dominating presence wherever he was.

"How are things going, sir?" Creek asked.

"Not so good," Maloney answered. "We haven't enough people assembled here to take our first objective."

Maloney guessed that the Germans had closed the locks where the Merderet and nearby Douve rivers drained into the Channel, which in turn flooded the flat valley where they'd just landed.

Maloney and Creek were just two of the more than fourteen thousand American paratroopers jumping into France in those first hours of D-Day. The mission of the U.S. 82nd and 101st Airborne Divisions was to land behind Utah Beach at the base of the Cotentin Peninsula, seize the important roads, bridges, causeways, and other choke points to secure the beach from German counterattacks, and pave the way for the U.S. VII Corps to move inland. The drop zones of Major General Maxwell Taylor's 101st Airborne Division described an arc extending from just north of the market town of Carentan to the long exit causeways behind Utah Beach. The 82nd Airborne Division, under Major General Matthew Ridgway, was to land in three drop zones north and west of the crossroads town of Ste. Mère Eglise and seize the town and the critical bridges at La Fière and Chef du Pont.

The 507th PIR (of the 82nd Airborne) was one of two regiments slated to land west of the Merderet River, secure the area, then move south to assist in the capture of the important bridge at La Fière. American commanders expected German counterattacks across the bridge and so had planned to capture it with simultaneous assaults at each end, the 505th on the east bank, and the 507th on the west bank.

Roy Creek and the fifty or so men who had emerged from the darkness were not far from their objectives, as it turned out, but had nowhere near the manpower or, more important, the organization to get on with their mission.

Maloney was starting to piece together a picture of what had happened, and whenever he ran into a small group of troopers, he became more convinced that the regiment was not only badly scattered but mixed in with other units as well. In fact, there were men from all three parachute regiments of the division, and even some troopers from the 101st, wandering around the west side of the flooded Merderet.

Confusion and frustration were compounded by Maloney's inability to communicate. The radios were either water damaged or lost at the bottom of the marsh, and without them, he could talk only to the men immediately around him. Even if he wanted to use runners to carry messages, he didn't know where to send them or what news they might carry. He had only a vague grasp of the situation, and that didn't sit well with him.

Captain Roy Creek's worries were on a different scale. Maloney told him to begin organizing what men they did have into some sort of defensive position. German doctrine called for immediate counterattacks, and the Americans knew from their intelligence briefings that one of the enemy units in the area, the 91st Air Landing Division, was specifically trained to fight paratroopers.

Creek put the men into a line, a small arc facing away from the flooded area. This was their first combat, and—thanks to the scattered drop—the men were strangers to one another. In the darkness, positioning them was mostly a matter of "Hey, you," and "Go there," but the men responded, moved out, went where they were told to go. *That's a good sign*, Creek thought, *perhaps the first of this day*.

A few hundred yards away, Brigadier General Jim Gavin wasn't satisfied with the way the men were responding.

The thirty-eight-year-old Gavin was the Assistant Division Commander of the 82nd Airborne Division, making him one of the youngest general officers in the theater. Gavin was already well known throughout the Army for his exploits the previous summer, when he had led the first large-scale airborne invasion mounted by the U.S. Army, as part of the assault on Sicily. The drop there had been monumentally fouled up, with his thirty-four hundred troopers scattered over nearly a thousand square miles of the island. But Gavin and his subordinate commanders had pulled things together and, with several key victories, had managed to help speed U.S. troops off the beach. Their success, which was a near thing, kept the airborne concept alive. What the airborne commanders had learned in Sicily and in the later jump into Italy helped them prepare for this much larger parachute assault into occupied France. But for those first hours in Normandy, it didn't look to Gavin as if this drop had gone any better than the fiasco in Sicily.

Gavin commanded the three parachute infantry regiments of the 82nd, which had been designated Force A and consisted of just under sixty-four hundred men.[1] Like Creek, Gavin had landed on the west side of the Merderet, although he had an easy landing in an orchard several hundred yards from the edge of the water. The young brigadier sent out patrols to reconnoiter the area and quickly determined that there were several things wrong with the drop. First of all, the color-coded assembly lights of the 507th and 508th, tiny battery-powered lights on poles meant to give the troopers a rallying point, were east of the Merderet—the wrong side. Gavin also quickly discovered the wide lake that now separated them from whatever parts of the division were east of the Merderet. He sent his aide, Captain Hugo Olson, across the marshy ground to find out what was happening on the far side and to get information that would help Gavin determine his exact location.

With Olson gone, Gavin and the men around him tried recovering some of the equipment that had fallen into the water. Gavin knew they would desperately need the ammunition, bazookas, radios, and mines that had been wrapped in bundles and dropped from the bellies of the airplanes on big cargo chutes.

It is a peculiar feature of airborne operations that generals sometimes find themselves doing work that would, in other units, be done by sergeants. But paratroopers, who could land anywhere and suddenly be alone, did not have the luxury of such class distinctions. Until the men were organized and the sergeants and lieutenants and captains took over the smaller units, Gavin had to be concerned with even the smallest details. So the general was supervising from the edge of the flooded area when Lieutenant James H. Devine volunteered to wade back into the water to find the important bundles of weapons and equipment.

Devine peeled off his clothing before going in. Gavin worried that the lieutenant's pale skin was easy to see in the dark, and that some German sniper might spot him. Devine made it in and out safely, but with no good news about the equipment. They could spot the large cargo parachutes floating on the water's surface, but getting the heavy bundles out of the mud and grass was going to be difficult, if not impossible. For the moment, they'd continue to look for bundles on dry ground and leave the more difficult recovery work for later.

Gavin moved along the edge of the marsh and found foxholes already dug; apparently the Germans had prepared positions throughout the area to give them some flexibility in their response. It was another indication to the young general that they were facing an experienced, professional foe that had no intention of giving up anything without a fight.

Command along this portion of Hitler's Atlantic Wall had passed, in January 1944, to Field Marshal Erwin Rommel, a legendary combat commander. Rommel's arrival in France gave new life to German defensive preparations. There was plenty of work being done that was apparent to the Allies and their photo reconnaissance planes: minefields and trenchworks, antiglider and beach obstacles, prepared positions for everything from artillery to individual riflemen. Since Rommel was a superb professional, his presence meant that enemy commanders would have rehearsed their counterattack plans. Rommel did not get to be Germany's most famous general by using a lackadaisical approach.

Olson, Gavin's aide, returned in about an hour and told his boss that the water was nearly a thousand yards wide and shoulder deep in many places, but it could be crossed. More important, he had found a railroad on the far side; the track bed was well above the level of the water.

This was the major rail line that ran south from the port of Cherbourg and passed west of the critical crossroads town of Ste. Mère Eglise before continuing to Chef du Pont and, eventually, to Paris. Now Gavin knew where he was.

Olson had run into elements of the 508th PIR on the eastern bank. That regiment was also supposed to have dropped west of the Merderet. In true paratrooper style, they weren't waiting around for instructions, but had set out to attack the enemy at the nearest critical point: the bridge at La Fière.[2]

As he waited for the first light to appear over the eastern side of the Merderet, Gavin had between 100 and 150 troopers with him, but the general was frustrated. In spite of the efforts of leaders like Roy Creek and Arthur Maloney, the soldiers remained, as far as Gavin could see, largely disorganized.

Because the drops tended to scatter units and separate soldiers from their leaders, paratroopers had to be self-sufficient and eager to accomplish the mission. Gavin expected even the lowest-ranking troopers to show great initiative, but he found the opposite among the green soldiers of the 507th and 508th he encountered early on D-Day.

Gavin learned just that morning that the men of the 507th had covered up the insignia of rank on their helmets. Leaders, especially officers, were favorite targets of snipers; the insignia gave them away.[3] In the darkness, moving among men they didn't know, with no insignia of rank visible, the soldiers felt anonymous and so were not all that quick to respond to orders. Gavin found it difficult to get the men organized as quickly as he wanted.[4]

Many of the soldiers lying amid the hedgerows in those hours just before dawn had started out, like Roy Creek, in the water. Like him, they were soaked, their uniforms leaden, their boots soggy, their T-shirts and underwear chafing them. Most of them were cold, as the temperature dropped into the low sixties and cool winds brushed across the peninsula from the Atlantic.

Creek kept warm by moving about, searching for men from his own unit, E Company of the 507th. Twelve hours earlier he had stood on the departure airfield in England and looked out over the nearly 150 men of his command. He had trained them, prepared them as best he could, and had expected to lead them in combat. They were a team, a sophisticated weapon, and their readiness gave him confidence. Now they had been scattered over the countryside. He worried about his soldiers and wondered how he'd perform leading the ad hoc group collected on the bank.

Around 0415, about an hour before first light, the men heard the engines of another flight of C47 transports, and they watched the sky just above the tree line. The planes were towing the first wave of hundreds of gliders that would come into Normandy, and the only ones scheduled to make a dangerous landing in darkness. The gliders carried Batteries A and B of the 80th Airborne Antiaircraft Battalion, armed with 57 mm antitank guns, as well as communications men of the division artillery, some signal elements, headquarters staff, and some jeeps and trailers full of ammunition.

The sound of the planes drifted away, but shortly afterward the big gliders started appearing in their eerie, silent approach. They made no sound until they hit. Many of them crashed, their delicate wings torn off by the brush, by the stakes the Germans had planted in so many open areas (poles driven into the ground, some topped with mines, and dubbed "Rommel's Asparagus"). Some splintered against trees or crashed into the thick hedgerows. They wobbled and rolled, dived into the water, bumped over embankments at a hundred miles an hour. The paratroopers on the banks cringed as they watched and thought about the glider troops inside the fragile birds.

Creek watched one of the canvas-sided American-made Waco gliders land in the flooded area just 150 yards from his perimeter. As soon as the glider stopped moving, the men inside began to leap out; they had been trained to clear the craft immediately and seek cover.

Creek and his men had not encountered any enemy and were not aware of any Germans nearby, so they were surprised when automatic weapons opened up on the glider from the tree line to their north. The enemy fire tore through the canvas, made water spouts in the flood, thumped into the mud and, horribly, into the glidermen.

Creek ordered his little band to open fire on the distant woods, hoping to make the German gunners take cover so the glider troops could get clear of the open area. But the covering fire could not completely suppress the Germans, and many of the newly arrived glidermen went down, falling dead or wounded into the water. Finally, the survivors made it to the safety of the hedgerow where Creek and his men had taken cover.

Creek's green troops were starting to get a picture of what combat was going to be like. During the night, some of them had jumped at shadows or been spooked by noises beyond their own positions, but none of them had actually seen any evidence of a strong German presence. They still hadn't seen any clear targets—just muzzle flashes amid the green brush and leaves—but they had seen evidence of what the enemy could do to GIs caught in the open.

With the daylight, Creek had a better view of their situation, but it was not promising. Their key weapons—the automatic rifles and mortars and light machine guns—were at the bottom of the marsh or scattered across the countryside. They knew nothing of what was happening to anyone outside their own small group. There was no tactical cohesion, no real unit to speak of, no supporting artillery, and the Germans seemed to be all around them. They were, as Creek would say later, "just a group of invaders who were wondering what happened to all their thorough planning."[5]

Creek did receive one piece of what he considered good news: a runner told him General Gavin was somewhere nearby on the west side of the flooded plain. Creek was glad to hear it, as Gavin was a legend in the division, a fighting general. Creek also knew that Gavin's presence nearby meant they would be attacking somebody soon.

A sergeant who had survived the glider crash and made it to Creek's position told the captain that a nearby airframe contained one of the precious 57 mm antitank guns. Creek sent a message to Maloney about the gun, and Maloney sent word back that Creek should recover the weapon.

This would be Creek's first combat patrol, the first move that would take him into contact with the enemy. He would make the move not with the men he had trained and who had come to trust him, but with men trained by someone else, to whom Creek was just some captain, an unknown entity.

Creek selected twelve GIs and one other officer, then divided the small force into a recovery team and a fire support team, the latter to provide covering fire for the men who waded out to the aircraft. Creek set his fire support team in position to watch over the rest of the patrol in case the Germans should suddenly appear. He figured there was a good chance that the Germans might be watching the wrecked glider, waiting for GIs to recover the equipment on board, but all was quiet. Creek led the recovery team himself and made it to the crashed aircraft without incident. The men even managed to get the gun—a British-made, two-wheeled field-piece meant to be towed behind a jeep—clear of the glider. But the heavy piece quickly sank into the mud and grass, making it impossible to move.

Just then, German infantry on the banks opened fire, wounding two men. Creek's patrol returned fire, though it was almost impossible to spot the enemy. The captain ordered the breech block pulled from the gun, making it unusable for the enemy, and the little band struggled back. The incoming fire did not let up, and two more men were hit before they made the safety of their own position. One of those troopers died of his wounds.

Creek's first mission was a failure, and he felt the disappointment deeply; he would do better next time. Creek sent a runner to Maloney, reporting that they had secured only the breech block, at the cost of one man killed.

Shortly after daylight, Gavin learned that another glider had landed in the swamp a short distance away. The general was keen to find one of the 57 mm antitank guns that would be crucial to the paratroopers' survival. Gavin sent a patrol under Lieutenant Thomas Graham, a combat veteran of the 505th Parachute Infantry Regiment (whose regiment was east of the river), to see about recovering the weapon.

But the appearance of the gliders had roused the Germans in the surrounding areas, and they had the entire landing area under fire. Graham reported that the only way to reach the glider would be to launch a deliberate attack on the German positions, which would mean organizing a cohesive force and then pinpointing the enemy. Gavin couldn't afford to wait indefinitely; he had to get his small force moving toward the bridges. But neither could he afford to walk away from the weapons in the scattered bundles and crashed gliders. Gavin told Maloney to make the men available to Graham, who would try to secure the gun.

Graham and his patrol manhandled the jeep and gun out of the glider, but they both sank quickly in the mud, and no amount of pulling would free them. Graham removed the breech block from the gun and destroyed the jeep with explosives.

Throughout all of this, the German fire hitting Gavin's position increased to the point where he worried he would soon be pinned down and unable to move. Gavin trotted up to the firing line to see for himself what was happening. The troopers of the 507th, who were in combat for the first time, seemed more interested in avoiding incoming fire than in shooting back at the Germans. Gavin was furious. They were supposed to move forward, to find better firing positions, to close with the enemy; yet even after months of training, they clustered behind cover and fired blindly. The general moved about, hoping to inspire—or shame—the men to act. Striding along behind the undergrowth, Gavin saw something whiz by his face (he would later say it looked like the taillight of a truck); the Germans were firing tracer ammunition at him. He ducked but continued to move, trying to stir the troopers to action.[6]

Gavin was supremely frustrated. All the efforts of his men to retrieve weapons and equipment from the gliders and the flood had failed. The men who were with him on the western bank were not taking the fight to the enemy, and the junior leaders did not seem to be taking charge.

If the Merderet had been the timid little stream they had expected, the water obstacle would not have caused them much difficulty. But now he faced a marsh a thousand yards across that had swallowed up critical combat gear: radios, jeeps, antitank guns, ammunition, and food. As far as he could tell, the Merderet split his larger force and had thrown the entire division plan into disarray. He had no way of knowing how many of his men were on either side, but he did know he had to consolidate his forces before he could capture his objectives.

Since they were already west of the flood, Gavin wanted to sidestep south and attack La Fière from the west (the original mission of the 507th). But he didn't think his disorganized band could make that move, fight through German resistance, and attack the causeway. He still did not know the full extent of the flooding, and he had no clear picture of enemy strength on his side. He knew only that he was cut off, out of contact, and surrounded by men who were not yet in any shape to fight.

Gavin decided his best move was to take his little band across the flooded plain and link up with the 505th PIR (the only American parachute regiment, of the six dropped on D-Day, that had combat experience). He hoped the 505th had landed near its drop zones and was already accomplishing its missions. But even if he found the same kind of disarray on the eastern side, he had more options over there.

Gavin and his boss, Major General Matt Ridgway, had discussed what they would do if the jump was badly executed and they wound up hanging on until relief came. The plan was to circle the wagons around Ste. Mère Eglise and wait for the beach forces. Gavin was unable to contact his division commander, but figured he could cross to the east side and attack the bridge at La Fière alongside the veteran 505th PIR. If that proved impossible, he would move to the fallback position of Ste. Mère Eglise.

Checking his equipment after the jump, Gavin found that the only piece of his personal gear he'd lost was his wristwatch. This seemed somehow symbolic, for as he watched the sky lighten and listened for the sounds of battle on the far bank, he was keenly aware that they had no time to spare in getting his men organized and moving on the objectives. Farther to his east, along nearly fifty miles of the Norman coast, assault waves of Allied troops churned through a choppy sea toward the invasion beaches.

●　　●　　●

Around 0900, Lieutenant Colonel Edwin Ostberg, commander of the 1st Battalion of the 507th, called Roy Creek and the other officers together and said he'd come from Gavin's command post with orders: they were moving across the flood again, to hit the railroad on the far side, turn right, and head south toward Ste. Mère Eglise and the bridge at La Fière.

Roy Creek was going back into the water for the third time.

They made the wounded and injured as comfortable as possible, ensuring that they had water and food nearby. The paratroopers all knew that, in an airborne invasion behind enemy lines, men who could not move might be abandoned, as the troopers had no jeeps or ambulances to evacuate them, or, for that matter, any place to evacuate them to. The men being left behind tried to be optimistic, tried to convince themselves that they'd be rescued by advancing American units once the assault forces cleared the beaches. Even the most upbeat among them must have felt a cold dread as they watched their comrades walk away, as they listened for the first sign of an advancing enemy. And if the Germans found them first, they hoped to be treated humanely, or at least not shot to death where they lay—though that was always a possibility.

Creek made his plan for pulling out—always a tricky move. Although they were not in constant contact with the enemy, Creek was mindful of the Germans who had appeared when the gliders came in. If that force was still in the area and decided to attack the paratroopers in the midst of their withdrawal, things could get ugly. Creek worried that the Germans who had fired on the glider were still around or had even been reinforced. He worried that he might lose control over the men if they came under fire, as he hadn't established a strong chain of command and was working with noncoms he didn't know. He also worried that he would step into deep water and drown.

He could see the first troopers moving out, and Creek, trying to appear confident, trying to look as if it made perfect sense to step out into a sunlit open area that had, an hour earlier, been sprayed by German fire, moved to the edge of the water, his boots still squishing from his earlier dunkings. He waded in, feeling the cold water move up his legs, over his waist, up his chest.

Around him, the men pushed through the water and the tangled grass. Many of them had lost equipment; others threw away heavy gear that threatened to drown them.

Bill Walton, a correspondent for *Time* magazine who had jumped with Gavin's force, was particularly concerned with what good targets he and the others would make once they cleared the concealment offered by the woods and hedgerows. The wide floodplain in front of him was brightly lit, and everyone moved slowly. A Signal Corps captain, whose team had been sent to photograph the invasion, struggled with his heavy equipment. Walton offered to help by carrying two movie cameras, but when he reached the deep water and saw that the equipment might drown him, he tossed the expensive cameras aside. The captain let out an audible moan.[7]

The troops were further burdened by their jumpsuits, which were impregnated with a chemical meant to repel poison gas but which had the effect of making them water repellent. Water rushed in at the neck, wrists, ankles, and waist but could not drain quickly, so the men carried even more weight.

As they had feared, the GIs were still under observation from the bank, and they had no sooner set out than the Germans opened fire. Most of the shooting was from a great range and not particularly effective, but that was small comfort to men who could hear the rounds zip by. Creek could see the occasional geyser as a bullet hit the water, but the incoming fire was only part of his concern.

The water came up to his neck, then to his chin. Every bit of training he'd had as an officer told him his job was to take care of his soldiers, but out in the open, where invisible holes and unseen channels threatened to drown him at any moment, he could do nothing for them except put one foot in front of the other and hope for the best.

Following their general, Creek and the paratroopers pressed ahead, moving east toward their objectives, marching to the sound of the guns.

THE GATHERING HOST

The soldiers crowded onto the late-night train watched their reflections in the windows as the ancient cars, smelling of tobacco and sweat, rocked through the night and the Northern Ireland countryside. Some of the young men headed for infantry companies looked out at the rain and thought about the field problems that would be coming up, all the nights they'd spend marching around in the dark and cold. On good nights, they'd get to come back to small, overcrowded tents, where they'd attempt to dry their wet clothes beside the finicky coal stoves. But there'd be lots of other nights they'd spend maneuvering around the damp countryside, practicing their soldier skills, digging foxholes, and manning machine gun positions and listening posts, all the thousand details that went into becoming competent infantry soldiers.

Some, like Fred Caravelli, a twenty-six-year-old from Philadelphia, were conscious that they had a long way to go to catch up with the veterans they would join at the end of the train ride. Caravelli was a replacement slated for the 82nd Airborne Division, which was already famous for its exploits in Sicily and Italy. In fact, it was the reputation of the airborne forces that had put Fred Caravelli on that train.

Before he received his draft notice, Caravelli was in a movie theater with his wife, Marie, when a newsreel showed British paratroopers and told of their tough training and their esprit. Caravelli leaned over in the dark and whispered to Marie, "That's what I'm going to do."

In early 1943 Fred's draft notice finally arrived. He had not enlisted before then because he felt an obligation to stay with Marie and his mother, who was living with them. But once the draft board decided for him, he felt a sense of relief: the waiting at last was over. When it came time for Marie to put him on the train headed west to basic training, Fred was in an upbeat mood. This son of an Italian immigrant thought of himself as thoroughly American, and he wanted to do something for his country. Now he would get the chance.

Caravelli wound up in the infantry, training at Camp Robinson, near Little Rock, Arkansas, one of the hundreds of military bases that grew like weeds around the country as America put millions of civilians into uniform to fight a global war.

His previous job, working in a uniform factory, had been demanding, but basic training toughened him up in new ways. Fred was never a big guy—on entering the service he measured five foot six and 132 pounds—but he was determined to stick with even the toughest field problems. In doing so he set an example for the other men. One GI even told him, "I look at you, and I figure if a little SOB like you can do it, I can too."

The long road marches, all the hours of running up and down the low hills, all the mucking around the countryside loaded down like a pack mule with the tools of a modern infantryman turned Fred into a tough physical specimen. When he showed up at Fort Benning, Georgia, for airborne school and its famously grueling physical training, the program turned out to be easier than he expected.

After his infantry training and four weeks of jump school, Fred was assigned to the 541st Parachute Infantry Regiment at Camp McCall, North Carolina. But he was tired of shuttling from one stateside post to another, and so when the call went out for volunteers to go overseas, Fred put his name in and soon received orders for the 82nd Airborne Division.

When his group of replacements went north to New York, the port of embarkation for all GIs headed to Europe, Fred got a short pass, and he and Marie arranged to meet at Jack Dempsey's nightclub in New York.

Later, Fred noticed the hotel staff looking at them as if he was just another GI shacking up with a young woman, but it hardly mattered to him. What mattered was that Marie was close once again. He had no way of knowing when, or even if, that would happen again, but neither of them talked about the possibility that this hurried meeting might be their last.

Like a lot of young men in uniform who had never seen how terribly random war could be, Caravelli was convinced that he was one of those who would come back. Yet, in spite of his optimism, in spite of his sincere desire to do his part, when he took Marie to Penn Station and found the platform for the train to Philadelphia, it was almost more than he could bear. He would not see her again for two years.

The troop train finally pulled into a darkened Irish station, and the men could hear the sergeants calling them to get up, grab their gear, and move out onto the platform. It was pouring rain, and they were told to fall into ranks. Caravelli had stood in enough Army formations to know that this kind of waiting around was an open-ended deal: they could be outside in the downpour just long enough to do a quick roll call, or they could be standing around for the better part of an hour. All they could do was hope for a covered place to stand.

Caravelli took his place in the ranks—out in the open—and decided, after a few minutes of waiting with no idea what was going on, that this was just more Army *chickenshit*, the all-purpose term that described the vast inefficiencies to which they were subjected: the lines, the waiting, the march-there-and-back-again mistakes that ate up their time and made them uncomfortable. But chickenshit was most disturbing because it sent a message that the soldiers' time was not valuable, that no one cared if the private was inconvenienced or soaking wet, or hungry, or had gone without a beer or a woman or a letter from home in a long time. Those men plagued with an active imagination might even worry that the same inefficiencies, and the same blind spot for their suffering, might carry over into combat. If their time was worthless, their discomfort not something for those in charge to consider, might the same thing be true of their lives?

There was movement along the line, and before he knew what was happening, Caravelli was looking up into the face of a tall two-star general. The man had a narrow, hawklike face, but Caravelli thought he had a fatherly look about him. Maybe it was his voice, low and unthreatening; maybe he was even genuinely interested in the soldiers who had joined him in this dreary, rainy corner of Ireland.

"What do you do?" he asked when he got to Caravelli.

"I'm a rifleman, sir," Caravelli managed.

"Good. We need riflemen," the general said before moving on to the next man.

As conversations go, it wasn't much. A brief exchange, circumscribed by rank. It wasn't as if Caravelli was free to ask the old man a question, like "Who the hell are you?" But it wasn't lost on the private that the general had gotten himself out of bed on a miserable night to welcome a handful of new paratroopers.

By the time the sergeants gave them the order to move, Caravelli had a good first impression of the 82nd Airborne Division and its commander, Major General Matthew Ridgway.

The 82nd traced its beginnings to Camp Gordon, Georgia, where it was formed on August 25, 1917. Since its soldiers represented all forty-eight states, the unit was nicknamed "the All Americans," and the red, white, and blue shoulder insignia it adopted was marked with a double A.

Deployed to France in the spring of 1918, the 82nd Infantry Division fought in three major campaigns. One of its soldiers, a Tennessee sharpshooter and former hell-raiser turned Sunday school teacher named Alvin York, became the division's only Medal of Honor recipient. York's feat—he took command of a decimated patrol of fewer than ten men and captured 132 enemy soldiers—made him famous in the United States. Gary Cooper won an Oscar for portraying York in the 1941 movie *Sergeant York*.[1]

Demobilized after World War I, the division was reactivated on March 25, 1942, at Camp Claiborne, Louisiana, under the command of Major General Omar Bradley. In August of that year, the 82nd became the first airborne division in the U.S. Army and reorganized under Matt Ridgway.

Soldiers who wanted to become paratroopers had to attend the Army's new jump school. Soldiers who did not volunteer to become parachutists—all jumpers are volunteers—had to be replaced. There were enormous growing pains as Ridgway and his subordinate commanders sought experienced officers and noncoms who had completed airborne training or were willing to give the rigorous and dangerous training a shot. General George Marshall, the Chief of Staff of the Army, was an early believer in the concept and so lent his support to the efforts to find quality soldiers.

Marshall, and many other American commanders, looked to the German use of paratroopers in the invasion of Crete as evidence that the concept of *vertical envelopment* worked. In May 1941, a German force of nearly twenty-five thousand troops came down on the British-held island in the Mediterranean. The attackers included parachutists, glider troops, and some infantry that came in by air on runways captured by the paratroopers.

But Allied code breakers gave the defenders advanced warning, and the attackers suffered nearly 44 percent casualties, including nearly three thousand killed and another eight thousand wounded. Nevertheless, the Germans—whose casualty figures were not known to the Allies—captured the island, so it looked to Marshall and the Allies as if the German airborne attack was a success.

Up to that point in the war, Hitler's forces had not suffered such appalling losses. (Barbarossa, the invasion of the Soviet Union, was months away.) Even as Marshall decided that Crete showed the utility of an airborne assault, Hitler and his generals concluded that large-scale airborne assaults were too costly. "The days of the paratroopers are over," Hitler declared.[2] But the Allies were unaware of this conclusion.

The Allies' first opportunity to use a large-scale airborne force to spearhead an invasion came in Sicily, in July 1943. A shortage of aircraft dictated that Matt Ridgway could send only one parachute regiment, augmented with a battalion from another regiment, into battle. Ridgway gave the job to Jim Gavin, then a thirty-six-year-old colonel who built and commanded the 505th Parachute Infantry Regiment.

Gavin, an early proponent of the airborne concept, worked tirelessly to prepare his men, even though much of what he taught them about jump techniques, assembly, organization, and loading was untested theory. Gavin, commanding the 505th Parachute Infantry Regiment, and Reuben Tucker, commanding the 504th PIR (there were only two parachute regiments in the division in the summer of 1943), created a culture of tough, aggressive risk takers who were confident in themselves and their leaders. The soft-spoken Gavin admonished newly arrived junior officers that "around here, being a lieutenant means you're last one in the chow line and first one out the aircraft door."[3]

This was more than just advice on day-to-day living; it was the kind of leadership Gavin demanded of himself and his subordinates. Gavin believed that his officers, particularly the lieutenants who were closest to the troops, must be able to do everything the soldiers could do. What's more, they must always lead by example. If the company marched fifteen miles, the officers might cover twenty, taking into account the fact that they were constantly moving up and down the column, checking on the soldiers. When hot chow was delivered to the field and the men lined up, mess kits in hand, the officers were at the tail end of the line. If there wasn't enough food to go around, it was the officers—not the privates—who missed a meal.

On July 9, 1943, the 505th Regimental Combat Team (Gavin's regiment plus the third battalion of Tucker's 504th PIR) made the first large-scale parachute assault in the history of the U.S. Army. Their mission was to jump into the hills just inland from the invasion beaches (at Gela and Scoglitti) and block the enemy counterattacks. The plan began to fall apart even before they left the departure airfields, when Gavin received reports that winds across the drop zones were far in excess of the fifteen miles per hour considered safe for parachutists.

Things went downhill from there. Instead of landing in a couple of tight drop zones, Gavin's thirty-four hundred troopers were scattered over nearly a thousand square miles along the southern coast of Sicily. Some landed almost sixty-four miles from where they were supposed to be. Many of the men were lost and couldn't find their buddies, their leaders, or their equipment. Gavin was among the most isolated and greeted the morning of D-Day, July 10, 1943, with only five troopers under his control.

Yet over the next three days, the troopers would display a remarkable degree of creativity and aggressiveness. Disorganized and under-equipped, the GIs took on the German and Italian defenders and even stood toe-to-toe with German armor units. (Allied intelligence knew there were German tanks on the island, but kept that information from the assault troops in order to protect the source of the information.) Still, their successes were scattered, and on a smaller scale than Ridgway and Gavin had hoped for. Dwight Eisenhower remained unconvinced that it made sense to drop large parachute units behind enemy lines; perhaps it would be better to use the men as guerrillas, to disrupt enemy movement and communications. But George Patton, who commanded the U.S. troops in the Sicily invasion, gave the paratroopers credit for speeding his move off the beaches by as much as two days.

In September of 1943, the 82nd Airborne Division was called upon to help Mark Clark's beleaguered forces hang on to their foothold at Anzio on mainland Italy. In the early-morning hours of September 13, the 504th Parachute Infantry Regiment jumped into the beachhead and immediately went into action to shore up the defensive line. They were joined the next night by Gavin's 505th, and the two regiments (later reinforced by the 325th Glider Infantry Regiment) turned back the German attacks and eventually expanded the beachhead.

The jump into Italy marked the first use of pathfinders, who jumped some thirty minutes ahead of the main body to mark the drop zones for the follow-on pilots. Under command of Captain Jack Norton, the Americans, in cooperation with British Airborne, refined their techniques for getting these specially trained troops to the right place. The

pathfinders—all of whom volunteered for the hazardous mission—
would play a big part in the upcoming invasion of France.

The veterans of the 505th PIR were in pretty good spirits when they
boarded the USS *Funston* for their movement from the Mediterranean
theater, in November 1943. The *Funston*, a large attack transport, was
designed, from the keel up, to accommodate a large number of soldiers.
There was a bunk for every man, adequate latrines, and even a sit-down
mess where the troopers enjoyed some of the best food they'd had since
leaving the States, including fresh-baked bread, with cakes and pies for
dessert.

Berge Avadanian, who worked in the intelligence section of the 2nd
Battalion of the 505th PIR, found it hard to fathom how the Navy had
managed to leave shore with only one movie on board. For weeks, the
troops watched Humphrey Bogart and the incomparable Ingrid
Bergman in the 1942 release *Casablanca*. The movie was projected on a
large piece of sailcloth suspended on an exposed deck. Since the light
went through the cloth, the troopers alternated sides, watching the
movie from one side on one night and the opposite side the next night.
It wasn't much, but the movie looked a little different, with movements
and sets reversed. Before long, the men knew the lines as well as the
actors.[4]

After a stop in North Africa, the *Funston* and its convoy left for the
open sea on December 1, and the troopers engaged in that old soldiers'
pastime of rumormongering. The most popular stories were built
around the regiment's alleged return to the States. Rumors of what they
might do there ranged from helping to train new airborne units to—
surely the most fantastic—traveling around with Hollywood starlets to
sell war bonds.[5] The rumors got a boost as the *Funston* continued to
steam west after clearing Gibraltar. But morale took a nosedive once the
ship turned north and the troopers knew that the other rumors, those
that had them preparing for the invasion of the Continent, were most
likely true.

Their December arrival off Belfast came with some pleasant surprises. The weather was cold, but that was a change from the months they'd spent in Africa and Italy. And the landscape was an incredible green. The 505th had spent most of the last year baking in North Africa, where daytime temperatures reached 120 degrees, then campaigning in Sicily and Italy, which were only slightly less hot and slightly more civilized.

After debarking, the troops moved into march formation and began their walk through Belfast. The streets were soon lined with children, and Avadanian strained to understand what they called out to the GIs. It sounded to him like "Gotnigumchum?"

The paratroopers were not the first Americans the Irish children had seen, and they had gotten used to handouts of candy and gum from the GIs. They were calling out, "Got any gum, chum?"

The troops were trucked from Belfast to Cookstown, where they were happy to learn that they'd be living in Quonset huts, which gave much better protection from the weather than tents. They also soon learned that the Irish were friendly and welcoming.[6] Soon nearly every soldier had befriended an Irish family with whom they could spend some of their free time. The luckier among them made friends with young women, whom the American soldiers delighted in calling "lasses."

Avadanian noticed a change in mess hall fare that seemed directly proportional to how close the GIs became to their Irish neighbors. During the first part of their stay, Sunday dinner (the midday meal) in the troops' mess was baked chicken. As the weeks went by and more and more soldiers found their way to Sunday dinner in Irish homes, the menu changed. Instead of baked whole chickens, the mess served chicken dishes and casseroles, and there was noticeably less chicken per serving. It didn't take a detective to figure out that the GIs were giving chickens as gifts to the locals.

In Northern Ireland, as in the rest of the United Kingdom, food shortages had become a way of life as the nation struggled with the effects of war and the burden of keeping its armed forces supplied. And since nearly half the food consumed in Britain had to be imported, the war at sea, which went so badly for the Allies for so long, had a direct effect on the paucity of food on British tables. An entire generation spent its childhood without a glimpse of an orange or a lemon. Rationing began in earnest in January 1940 and continued in some way until 1954, nine years after the war's end.[7]

But the privations didn't keep the soldiers from enjoying themselves while they could. Fred Caravelli's run of good luck continued when he was assigned to C Company of the 505th. When he got to his squad tent, his new squad leader asked him when he last had a pass. It had been a while, Caravelli reported.

"Well, they should have given you a pass. I'm going to get you a pass to go to Belfast," the sergeant said.

"Thanks," Caravelli answered, genuinely touched. "But I really can't use it, because I don't have any money."

To Caravelli's great surprise, the squad leader took up a collection among the men and came back with one hundred dollars, a month's pay for a paratrooper. Caravelli was nearly overwhelmed. More important, he was convinced that he had landed, by sheer dumb luck, in the best squad in the Army. He took the money and had a good time.

Mark Alexander, the executive officer and second in command of the 505th PIR, rented accommodations for his unit's headquarters in an old castle near Cookstown, some twenty-five miles inland from Belfast. Alexander and his officers befriended the family that continued to occupy part of the house, and follow their normal rituals, in spite of the presence of so many houseguests. The heir to the castle marked midnight by climbing the parapet and playing a bagpipe, its eerie notes rolling out across the damp, cold darkness.

The entire family enjoyed talking about the history of the place, in particular the great hunters who had lived in the castle. Alexander, who had grown up in Kansas with a hunting rifle in his hand, was impressed with one trophy room, where plaques noted the prodigious numbers of ducks taken by family hunters. Then one day he was shown a photograph of the family scion, who posed with a small cannon. It turned out that the nobleman filled the cannon with grapeshot (making it, in essence, a very large shotgun), then opened fire on flights of ducks as they landed on the lake nearby.

For Dennis O'Loughlin, who had grown up in Montana, the time in Ireland was a chance to examine his own ethnic roots. Training was not particularly rigorous, and the conditions were better than in North Africa before the Sicily operation. Northern Ireland wasn't too cold, though a fine rain fell almost constantly. O'Loughlin expected the Emerald Isle to be green but was surprised that nearly everything, from houses to fence posts, was covered in some kind of damp moss.

Like many of the troopers who had been in North Africa, O'Loughlin had suffered a bout of malaria and was still fairly weak. His First Sergeant found him light duty: KP at the officer's mess. But O'Loughlin soon learned that the job also entailed doing personal services, like shining shoes and laundry. The proud GI told his friends he'd opt for the guardhouse before he'd "go pimping" for the officers.[8]

Instead, he took the job of latrine orderly, because he figured no one would bother him very much as long as he did a good job. Another benefit was that he would finally have some time alone. The young Montana native, who had spent years working alone as a trapper and woodsman, found the crowds, close quarters, and complete lack of privacy of Army life oppressive, even after two years in uniform. He was always looking for ways to escape the crowds, even for short breaks. When he was in basic training, he was marched into a crowded auditorium to hear a recruiting pitch from some airborne noncoms. He wasn't particularly impressed with the paratroopers and didn't think that jumping out of airplanes sounded like such a great idea. But when O'Loughlin saw how few men raised their hands to volunteer, the thought occurred to him that he could trade this big, smelly, unruly group for a smaller one, so he raised his hand. It hadn't worked out exactly as he'd hoped, but that didn't stop him from looking for further opportunities.

Latrine duty turned out to be one of those jobs that gave him some solitude. The chief benefit of doing the job no one wanted was that, as he predicted, the young soldier got out of a lot of inspections and other nonsense. He also managed to get a key to the coal shed and so always had fuel to heat water for the showers, which made him popular with his fellow GIs.

The preparations for the invasion of France presented all sorts of challenges for Jim Gavin, but those busy months in 1943 and '44 were also heady times for the young general. His 505th Parachute Infantry Regiment had fought brilliantly in the Sicilian and Italian campaigns, and Gavin was intensely proud of what his men had accomplished. His early faith in this new arm, the Airborne, had been vindicated.

Gavin was promoted to brigadier general on October 10, 1943, in a small ceremony in front of the Questrua, the Naples city police station, which the 505th had been using as a headquarters. As he looked out at the ranks of combat-hardened troopers assembled in the ancient square, he couldn't help but think that he'd come a long way from his humble beginnings.

Born to Irish immigrant parents in New York on March 22, 1907, Gavin was orphaned before he was two years old, which left him stranded in a Catholic orphanage. Adopted by Martin and Mary Gavin of Mt. Carmel, Pennsylvania, he grew up in the hilly coal country, though he was determined to stay out of the mines.

Gavin showed signs of his ambitious nature even at an early age. At ten he was already selling newspapers on the corner of Third and Oak streets, the main intersection in town. By thirteen he was the local agent for three out-of-town newspapers and had other boys working for him. An avid reader, he worked his way steadily through the holdings at the Mt. Carmel library.

Like many working-class parents, the Gavins thought education was a luxury, and one they could not necessarily afford. Jim Gavin left school after the eighth grade and went to work to help support his family, although he managed to stay out of the mines.

On the day he turned seventeen, Gavin left for New York City, armed with a sharp mind, a keen ambition, and little else. His goal was straightforward, if not easy: he had to find a way to educate himself. On April 1, 1924, he enlisted in the U.S. Army, passing himself off as an eighteen-year-old. His first duty station was Panama, but he was there only a short time when he learned that he was eligible to take the entrance exam for West Point, which was offered to all enlisted soldiers. In spite of the fact that he had only an eighth-grade education, Gavin managed to win an appointment, and he graduated in the top half of his class on June 13, 1929.

A little more than four months later the stock market crash marked the beginning of the country's long slide into the Great Depression and the formative period for the generation that would fight World War II. The Army suffered with the rest of the country during the Depression, with Congress frequently cutting both its strength and pay. There was little chance for promotion, and even veterans of the Great War were often reduced several pay grades as cutbacks rolled through the ranks. Yet Jim Gavin had found a home. The Army served him as it did so many young men from modest—or, in Gavin's case, less than modest—means. It gave him an education, it gave him respectability, and it gave him opportunity, if not for promotion, then at least for travel and the chance to work with talented leaders. Gavin continued to read widely, especially in military history, and he worked on his writing skills as well. By 1940 he had published several articles in professional journals and was making a name for himself as a thinker and innovator.

Things started moving quickly for Gavin, as for all the officers of his generation, after the German invasion of Poland in September 1939. To the professional military men, it looked less and less likely that the United States might sit this one out.

In the winter of 1940–41 Gavin was a captain stationed at West Point, a member of the Tactical Department, and responsible for overseeing the military development of cadets. He kept up with the widening war and made sure his cadet charges did, too. He had already decided that the U.S. Army should field an airborne force. The Germans had used airborne troops in the early campaigns of the war, but Gavin thought the Americans should take the concept even further. He and some other thinkers in the Army believed that it was possible to send in, by parachute and glider, an entire combined arms team of infantry, artillery, engineers, signal and medical units, everything needed to fight a sustained battle for several days.

Gavin remained a tireless promoter of the airborne concept, and he put everything he had into preparing himself and, later, his men for the challenge. He proved himself as a thinker and, in Sicily, as a combat commander. When Chief of Staff George Marshall told Ridgway he needed an "able officer with vision and combat experience" to advise the London planners about airborne operations in the upcoming invasion, Ridgway recommended Gavin.

"He, more than any other [officer] I know in my division or out," Ridgway wrote, "has vision, combat experience, professional knowledge and personality for this assignment." But Ridgway, who didn't want his second in command disappearing into some headquarters job, added, "I want him back."[9]

In mid-November 1943 Ridgway briefed Gavin on the landings that were to take place in France the following spring. Planning for the invasion had begun in London in March 1943, and the initial design called for a large contingent of paratroopers and glider troops. Gavin was to go to London to take part in the planning. Although it was an honor to be selected, Gavin worried that he might disappear into the huge headquarters and planning staff being built up in England, but Ridgway assured him that he would return to the division in time to take part in the fight.[10]

The airborne portion of the invasion, code-named Operation Neptune, would dwarf anything the Allies had done to this point in the war. Using more than thirteen hundred transports and thirty-three hundred gliders, the Allies would launch an airborne army of nearly fourteen thousand paratroops and glidermen—one British and two American divisions—behind the beachheads in France to secure the breakout routes for the forces landing on the beaches.

Even as he tackled the massive planning challenges, Gavin looked for ways to improve the performance of the airborne formations. He had a broad mission: get the right men with the right training and the best equipment to the exact spot on the battlefield from which they could have the greatest influence.

Gavin had been especially focused on improving weapons and tactics since the end of the Sicily campaign. He had fought on the front line at Biazza Ridge in Sicily, where the shortcomings of American antiarmor weapons, in particular, were spelled out in the casualty lists. The principal American antitank weapon, the bazooka (officially the 2.36-inch rocket launcher), had proved all but useless against German armor, especially the big, heavy-plated tanks the Germans continued to field. The soldiers who had been on Biazza Ridge would not soon forget the sight of GIs who had been crushed under the treads of enemy tanks, their shattered bazookas pulverized with their bodies.

Gavin also oversaw the training of the pathfinders, who would jump twenty to thirty minutes ahead of the main body and mark the drop zones with a combination of visual signals (various lights were developed for the purpose) and radio directional equipment. There was a great deal of cooperation in this area between the British and the Americans, who freely shared ideas and techniques. This sharing was in stark contrast to the animosity rampant in almost every other area where British and American planners were supposed to work together. Major Jack Norton, recently promoted to operations officer of the 505th PIR, was convinced that the paratroopers in both armies identified with each other too closely to let petty differences get in the way of cooperation that would save lives.

Until he left for London, Gavin's daily concerns were about soldiers and teams of soldiers, and how best to prepare them. All of that changed when he reported for duty in the war-scarred capital of England. Shuttling amid the various headquarters, Gavin entered a world of very senior officers who, though they were making life-and-death decisions for the paratroopers, had never jumped from an airplane.

In Gavin's final meeting with Ridgway, the division commander warned Gavin that he'd run into a hornet's nest of politics when he reached London. In particular, Ridgway told Gavin to keep an eye out for Lieutenant General F. A. M. "Boy" Browning, the senior officer in the British Airborne. Although Browning had not commanded a division, his three stars outranked all the American airborne officers. (Ridgway, the senior American paratrooper, wore the two stars of a major general.) Thus Browning would be the commander if the British and American airborne forces were combined.[11] Ridgway warned Gavin that he was not to give in to any pressure to let Browning gain overall control of all the airborne forces.

There was already bad blood between Ridgway and Browning, dating back to the run-up to Sicily and Operation Husky. The shortage of aircraft for that invasion had both American and British planners scrambling for the lion's share of available troop lift. Ridgway believed that Browning planned to use his status as Ike's principal adviser to gain control of all the airborne forces, which would give him authority to shift transports from the American to the British.

Early in 1943 Browning had appeared at Ridgway's headquarters at Oujda, French Morocco, to discuss the upcoming invasion of Sicily. Browning laid out his plans, and Ridgway's suspicions were confirmed: Browning was making a power play, and the American general had no doubt that his troops were about to be cut out.[12]

When Browning, in turn, asked to see Ridgway's plans, the commander of the 82nd Airborne balked. "I don't have a plan," Ridgway told Browning. "Not until General Patton, my army commander, has approved . . . do I have a plan."

It was not an auspicious beginning to the relationship, and before the Sicily campaign was over, the situation worsened. It got so bad at one point that Ike's Chief of Staff, Major General Walter Bedell Smith (known, inevitably, as "Beetle"), called Ridgway in for a dressing down. Ike insisted that his subordinate commanders get along and cooperate with each other, and he brooked no parochialism. As Ridgway remembered it later, Smith told him he could get in line and cooperate or he "might as well start packing up, for he was going home."[13]

Neither Gavin nor Ridgway ascribed Browning's behavior to anything sinister. It was simply in keeping with the general British attitude that the Americans were amateurs and their best role would be to provide the logistic support to the more experienced British. This condescending attitude, Gavin would later write, "fired the flames of mistrust and misunderstanding among the U.S. planners and . . . commanders of the battles that were to follow."[14]

This attitude infuriated Ridgway and scores of other commanders (including the fiery George Patton) more than any sinister design might have. Indeed, it might have been better for Allied relations if Browning had been simply a glory monger who wanted the laurels for himself. It galled the Americans that the British were simply dismissive.

Gavin left Naples on the morning of November 16, 1943, and stopped in Palermo, Sicily, to meet with the leaders of the Troop Carrier Command, the arm of the U.S. Air Corps that delivered the paratroopers to the battlefield. Close coordination with Troop Carrier was essential, in training as well as in combat operations, and Gavin used the visit in Sicily to check on the progress of the new pathfinders. The experiments were going well enough that they planned to begin large-scale training of pathfinders once the units reached England.

From Palermo, Gavin flew to Algiers, then to Marrakech, where he boarded a four-engine cargo plane that flew well out over the Atlantic to avoid any German interceptors based in France. The aircraft was crowded, and Gavin and the other exhausted passengers stretched out on the cold aluminum flooring to get some sleep. The plane landed in Scotland the following morning, and Gavin left immediately for London, arriving around 1600 on November 18, after more than two days of almost nonstop travel. Gavin went to the Grosvenor House (near the site of the modern U.S. embassy in London), where billets were provided for visiting officers.

In late 1943 London still showed signs of the tremendous suffering of the Blitz, when the Luftwaffe destroyed scores of thousands of buildings and killed tens of thousands of Londoners. But the city was also coming back. While there was still a strict blackout enforced at night, people moved about, and the visiting Yanks could enjoy at least some of the attractions of one of the world's most cosmopolitan cities. (The temptations of London night life, which could distract officers who were supposed to be focused on their work, would lead Eisenhower to move most of his staff out of the city proper after he arrived in early 1944.)

On his first day in London, Gavin walked east through the city to St. James Square, a tidy rectangle dominated by a huge equestrian statue of William III. There, in Norfolk House, he found the office of Major General Ray Barker, the American Deputy Chief of Staff of COSSAC (Chief of Staff Supreme Allied Command), which was the planning cell and initial headquarters for the invasion. By the end of 1943 COSSAC was a headquarters waiting for a commander.

Barker took the paratrooper to meet the Chief of Staff, British Lieutenant General Frederick E. Morgan, who had a quiet, scholarly demeanor and had proved to be an excellent choice for an overwhelming job.[15] Morgan told Gavin that he was to be the senior airborne adviser to COSSAC. This was quite a responsibility for the young brigadier, who had just pinned on his first star. But Gavin had a reputation for a quick mind, he had combat experience, and he had an incredible appetite for hard work.

While Morgan and Gavin were discussing the American brigadier's new responsibilities, Lieutenant General "Boy" Browning joined them. This was the first meeting between Gavin and Browning. Browning had a thin face and a neat mustache, dark hair combed straight back from a widow's peak, and a narrow chin. Gavin, the junior officer, stood as Browning entered. This was the man Ridgway had warned him about. In the midst of their very first conversation, Browning made a cutting remark about Ridgway's decision, in the Sicily invasion, to go in by ship instead of by parachute. He implied that Ridgway was a coward.

Gavin kept his cool but defended Ridgway's decision to travel aboard Patton's command ship. The airborne force in Sicily was a regimental combat team (Gavin's regiment plus a battalion of Tucker's 504th). It would have been inappropriate for the division commander to come along, as it would have undercut Gavin's authority as commander. Ridgway, Gavin insisted politely, did the right thing. Browning demurred, but Gavin had already marked him—as Ridgway had warned him—as a man to be watched.

As Gavin saw it, Browning had a two-stage plan for a British takeover of the airborne forces. First, he proposed that all Troop Carrier commands be combined under one commander. Then, he would propose a similar arrangement for the airborne soldiers themselves. The concept had a solid grounding in military theory—unity of command is one of the principles of war.

But Gavin and Ridgway weren't the only officers who were suspicious of Browning's motives. When Browning proposed the formation of a single Troop Carrier Command, Lewis H. Brereton, commander of the U.S. Troop Carrier Force, agreed in principle, provided that the overall commander was an American. Brereton argued that since the vast majority of assets would be American, it made sense that the commander be a Yank also. As Brereton well knew, this arrangement was unacceptable to the British, and Browning was stymied for the moment.

Gavin's introduction to the politics of the London planning staff was followed by a more enjoyable meeting when he visited Lieutenant General Omar Bradley's headquarters in Bryanston Square. Bradley was an enthusiastic supporter of the airborne forces, and, along with Patton, had been one of the few senior U.S. commanders to credit them with helping the Sicily campaign. Bradley (who had commanded the 82nd Infantry Division in 1941, before it became an airborne division) thought the airborne assault in France was an essential part of the invasion, and his certainty would only grow as the plans for what was now called Operation Overlord took shape in the coming months.

The two Americans talked about the plans COSSAC had developed, and the fact that the plans would probably change once a commander for the invasion was named. The plan for Overlord, as it existed in November 1943, called for three infantry divisions, two British and one American, to land on the coast of Normandy, north of the city of Bayeux (on what eventually became landing beaches Gold and Omaha). These three divisions would be followed by two more. The two U.S. airborne divisions, the 82nd and the untested 101st, were to land just south of the city of Bayeux to block German forces attempting to counterattack the beach. The British 6th Airborne would land north of Caen to seize the important bridges in the area and to attack, from behind, the formidable coastal artillery batteries.

Gavin saw immediately what Bradley already knew: the plan was too miserly, the planned beachhead too small, the forces committed not enough to hold the lodgment. A single German artillery battery positioned near Bayeux would be able to sweep the entire beachhead.[16] The Allies had to start thinking bigger.

The changes began with the naming of a commander for Overlord.

In the summer of 1943, in a series of meetings in Quebec and at President Franklin Roosevelt's home in Hyde Park, New York, the British Prime Minister, Winston Churchill, became convinced that the Americans had a legitimate claim to the command slot. It was generally assumed that Roosevelt would pick his most talented soldier for the job. George Marshall was the Chief of Staff of the Army and the architect of America's amazing comeback from a third-rate (or even fourth-rate) military, in 1939, to one of the preeminent powers of the war. But even as the invasion forces gathered in Britain and Allied planners pored over maps of France, Roosevelt made no official announcement. When the president tried to engage Marshall in a conversation about who should command the invasion, Marshall refused to participate. That was a decision for the commander in chief, and Marshall, who was nothing if not a model of integrity, would not lobby for the job. He indicated to Roosevelt that he would serve where he was called.

As late as the autumn of 1943, Eisenhower was not even under consideration for the job.[17] Ike figured Marshall would get it, and that he would be sent back to Washington to replace the Chief of Staff, a prospect he did not relish. Ike's long-standing aversion to politics and politicians would make the job a nightmare, he thought. "They'll have to carry me up to Arlington [National Cemetery] in six months," he predicted.[18]

But on December 7, 1943, the second anniversary of the attack on Pearl Harbor, Roosevelt joined Eisenhower in Tunis and told him, "Well, Ike, you are going to command Overlord." The president later told George Marshall, "I feel I could not sleep at night with you out of the country."[19]

Eisenhower was recalled to Washington at the end of 1943 for a series of meetings, but also because Marshall, who had seen how haggard Ike had become in the Mediterranean, wanted the fifty-three-year-old Eisenhower to get a rest before taking on the huge job ahead of him. Ike asked Field Marshal Bernard Law Montgomery, the Brit who had been named to command the ground forces in Overlord, to represent him, Eisenhower, in the planning meetings until Ike returned to London. The two men had worked together and understood and respected each other.

On January 2, 1944, Montgomery arrived in the British capital. He was a famous man in Great Britain, and crowds followed his moves around the capital. Some American officers who had served with him, Gavin among them, had their doubts about Montgomery's fighting spirit, though they recognized he was a thorough planner. The American officers also knew that Eisenhower, who would arrive in London shortly, did not countenance backstabbing, gossip, or lack of cooperation among his American and British staffs. If Ike thought an officer was being recalcitrant and that the alliance—and by extension the troops—might suffer, the man could quickly find himself shipped back to the States.

Montgomery immediately started tinkering with the plans. The principal reason for the small scale of the initial three-division plan was not the lack of available troops—Britain was groaning under the weight of Allied troops training for the invasion. It was the shortage of landing craft to move the troops. Of all the millions of tons of material and equipment assembled for the vast invasion, it was this constant shortage of landing craft that most plagued the Allies in opening the second front in northwest Europe. American shipyards were operating at full capacity. The U.S. Navy wanted the available steel to build warships, not landing craft. In the Pacific, Douglas MacArthur also clamored for landing craft. The shortage became the single biggest logistic bottleneck in the months leading up to the invasion and prompted Churchill, befuddled by the lack of planning and the confusing acronyms for the various craft, to comment that "the destinies of two great empires seem to be tied up in some god-damned things called LST's."[20]

When Ike decided to expand the assault force from three to just over five divisions, the shortage of landing craft became so acute that the Allies postponed an amphibious invasion of southern France in order to free up the resources.[21]

Ike's expansion of the invasion force also meant a wider invasion front, and the American sector now included the base of the Cotentin Peninsula. Omar Bradley, who would command the U.S. ground forces, wanted to cut that peninsula at its base, thus isolating and eventually capturing the important port of Cherbourg. Bradley and Gavin agreed that the airborne forces could give the Americans a decisive advantage in their efforts to cut the thirty-mile-wide peninsula.

Gavin jumped wholeheartedly into his job as the chief airborne planner. As with all military operations, planning began with the objective, and early on in the process Gavin and his colleagues were told that the objective of the landings (from which Gavin would derive the objectives for the U.S. airborne forces) was to establish a firm lodgment that the Allies could hold against counterattacks by the German forces known to be in the area. Another of Bradley's principal objectives was the rapid seizure of Cherbourg, which was to serve as the Allies' main port for the tons of supplies that would sustain the armies.

Bradley's primary mission, establishing the lodgment, would be made considerably easier if the Allies could keep the Germans from using all the available forces in France to oppose the landings. The way to achieve this end was to convince the Germans that the landings in Normandy were a feint, a secondary attack meant to draw attention away from the main landings, which would occur elsewhere. This simple need grew into one of the most sophisticated and successful deceptions in the history of warfare: Operation Fortitude.

The Germans knew, of course, that the Allies would invade France at some point, and a straightforward study of weather and tide tables helped German intelligence officers make educated guesses as to when the attack might come. The only real questions that remained for the Germans were the exact time and location of the assault. To divine Allied plans, the Germans used aerial reconnaissance to spy on preparations in England. These efforts were severely hampered as the Allies gained complete air superiority in the theater. Enemy intelligence also relied on intercepts of radio transmissions, but the Allies took a series of steps to limit what might be gleaned by anyone listening in. The simplest measure was to use telephones rather than radios, and the fact that the Allies were all located on an island made communications security easier.

Allied counterintelligence sections stressed the need for secure transmissions. The millions of Allied soldiers who used radios in training learned to avoid giving information "in the clear." Instead, they used code words (which changed often) for training locations, units, command, and anything else that might be of interest to German intelligence officers trying to build an order of battle (a schematic that showed best estimates of units, their strengths, armaments, and commanders).

The Allies decided, early on, to take advantage of some assumptions the Germans made about Allied intentions.

The Germans knew, for instance, that the Allies needed to capture a fairly large port on or shortly after D-Day, to handle the millions of tons of supplies that a vast, modern army consumes in offensive operations. The Germans also believed the Allies would want the invasion beaches close to England and the protective umbrella of Allied airpower. Since the ultimate objective was Berlin, the Germans believed that the Allies would take the shortest route to Hitler's capital. Finally, the Germans expected that once they started launching the V-1 buzz bomb rockets from the Pas de Calais area (the strikes were to begin in June 1944), the Allies would aim the invasion at those bases rather than suffer more civilian casualties in London.

All of these assumptions led the Germans to believe that the landing area would be near the Pas de Calais, the point on the continent closest to England. Allied soldiers headed for the Pas de Calais would spend as little time as possible getting seasick on landing craft and would arrive in better condition to fight. The coastline had useful ports and was close to the British ports at Dover and Folkestone, which would enable quick resupply of ammunition, fuel, and reinforcements across the narrowest part of the Channel. Ships making this crossing would have minimum exposure to the testy Channel weather. Finally, the Pas de Calais was also close to the airfields in Kent, meaning Allied planes could spend more time over the battlefield and less time (and fuel) getting there.

To the Germans, the Pas de Calais seemed the obvious target for the coming invasion, and the Allies did what they could to reinforce that notion without obviously showing their hand.

Allied counterintelligence efforts also enjoyed remarkable success. Spies in England working for the Abwehr, the German intelligence service, had been identified and turned by Allied agents. By early 1944 they were being used by the British to funnel misinformation to their handlers on the continent. One of these, a Catalan code-named GARBO by the British, not only developed an entire notional network of operatives but received hefty expense payments from the German high command to run the string of nonexistent spies.[22] These "spies" fed faulty intelligence to the Germans through GARBO.

Coordinating all this misinformation was a critical task, because the British had to ensure that the Germans did not receive conflicting reports that aroused suspicion. This task fell to the London Controlling Station, or LCS, headed by Colonel John Bevan and manned by a group of imaginative and very thorough officers who set out to fool the entire German security apparatus.

The plan was audacious, and it capitalized on what had been a personal and professional disaster for George Patton, Ike's outstanding combat commander. In August 1943 Patton, visiting casualties in Sicilian field hospitals, had come across at least two soldiers hospitalized for combat stress. Patton considered these men nothing more than malingerers and cowards, and he slapped two of the soldiers (in separate incidents in two hospitals) and ordered them thrown out of the ward that held men wounded in combat.

Several correspondents approached Eisenhower with a completely unethical offer: they would keep the incident quiet if Ike fired Patton. Ike, who did not at first realize the danger the incident posed, instead issued Patton a severe rebuke and directed that he change his behavior and address the problem. He also suggested that Patton apologize, in person, to the affected troops.

The journalists, who detested the blustering Patton, kept the story out of the papers at home, and Patton dutifully trudged from one Seventh Army unit to another until he had apologized to every command. But in November 1943, the muckraking columnist Drew Pearson gave the American public a sensationalized version of the events in his weekly radio show, and the public clamor for Patton's scalp began. Ike stood by his man and his decision, because he believed that George Patton, by sheer dint of his ability as a commander, could shorten the war and thus save American lives.

But Patton would miss Overlord. Instead, Ike used him as part of Operation Fortitude, in which Patton became the commander of the fictional First U.S. Army Group (FUSAG), stationed in southeast England (nearest the Pas de Calais).

The Germans thought, as Ike did, that George Patton was the best combat general the Allies had, and they would never have believed that the Americans would sacrifice such a resource simply because he had slapped a private soldier. Once again, the Allies used the Germans' assumption to their advantage. As Patton moved around England in his duties as commander of this notional army, his signature style and high profile made him a favorite subject for British journalists. The Allies knew full well that those British newspapers were read by Axis spies in Ireland, Portugal, and Spain. As far as the Germans were concerned, the best American general commanded the invasion army closest to where the Germans expected the blow to fall.

Allied intelligence worked to strengthen this assumption. While FUSAG did not have any troop formations, it did have radio traffic. Stations were set up throughout the FUSAG "training areas" in England, mimicking—in message volume and content—the kind of radio traffic an entire army might generate. Vehicle parks were constructed, with wooden and canvas trucks, aircraft, tanks, jeeps, and boats. Huge piles of fake supplies, entire tent hospitals, as well as ammunition and fuel dumps, some created by the British film industry, were scattered throughout the area. Ships that were unfit for service were docked in nearby Dover and spruced up to look serviceable. Entire road systems were built, and at night the dirt roads were plowed to make it look as if heavy armored vehicles had been maneuvering in the area.

Finally, the Royal Air Force was directed to leave some holes in the air defenses, so that a few German reconnaissance flights could get through and photograph the massive buildup of FUSAG.[23]

Convincing the Germans that the main landings would be at the Pas de Calais was only part of the intelligence plan; the other part was in denying them information about the real location and timing of the invasion.

Eisenhower petitioned Churchill to ban all visitors from the popular coastal areas of southern England, where huge staging areas for equipment were overflowing with military assets, and where large-scale training exercises were hard to keep out of public view. Churchill refused at first, saying he did not want to further disrupt the lives of civilians. But when Montgomery made a similar request of the Prime Minister, and Eisenhower reiterated his concern that they should do everything in their power to protect the lives of Allied soldiers, even if it did mean a massive inconvenience, Churchill relented. The Prime Minister also gave in to Eisenhower's request that diplomatic pouches from the London embassies of neutral countries be subject to search. There was enough of a hue and cry in the diplomatic community that Hitler learned of it in Berlin.

In April Eisenhower also had to make a tough call in the interest of security. One of Ike's West Point classmates, Major General Henry Miller, was overheard at Claridge's, the popular London hotel, talking about the supply problems he faced as chief of logistics for the U.S. 9th Air Force. But, he added, his problems would all be over by June 15, at which point the invasion would have occurred. Challenged on this point, Miller offered to take bets.

Eisenhower learned of the incident by the next morning, and in spite of the pleas of his classmate, he demoted Miller to his permanent rank of colonel and shipped him back to the States in disgrace. Miller suffered further ignominy when the story and his photo ran on the front page of the *New York Times*.

Fortitude was one of the great investments of manpower and resources the Allies made in Operation Overlord. The Germans remained convinced that their initial assessments were correct, that the landings in Normandy were a diversion and the main thrust would be against the Pas de Calais. Efforts to make the force look bigger than it was were also successful. At the end of May German intelligence indicated an Allied strength in England of eighty-nine divisions, when there were only forty-seven. Significantly, the Allies had managed to convince the Germans that they had sufficient landing craft to lift twenty divisions in the first wave, when British and American logisticians were scrambling to find the lift for five assault divisions.

Even after the actual landings, Allied counterintelligence continued to bolster the German assumption that the main attack was still to come and would fall on the Pas de Calais. At 2330 hours on June 9, D+3 in Normandy, a teletype printer at Wehrmacht headquarters printed out a message from the German spy the British knew as GARBO.

After personal consultation on 8th June with my agents Jonny, Dick and Dorick, whose reports were sent to-day, I am of the opinion, in view of the strong troops concentrations in South-East and Eastern England, which are not taking part in the present operations [in Normandy], that these operations are a diversionary maneuver designed to draw off [German] reserves in order then to make a decisive attack in another place. In view of the continued air attacks on the concentration area mentioned, which is a strategically favorable position for this, [the main attack] may very probably take place in the Pas de Calais area, particularly since in such an attack the proximity of the air bases will facilitate the operation by providing continued strong air support.

A German intelligence officer underlined in red the phrase "diversionary maneuver designed to draw off reserves in order then to make a decisive attack in another place." This, he added, "confirms the view already held by us that a further attack is to be expected in another place." The message was eventually passed to Hitler, who remained convinced that the attack in Normandy was a diversion, and that the main Allied assault was still to come.[24]

TRAIN THOROUGHLY

Train thoroughly while you have the opportunity. Remember it is good to be brave but better to be smart and less painful to those around you.
—Colonel Mark Alexander,
505th Parachute Infantry Regiment

During those late winter and early spring months, while the Fortitude cells were working their magic on German intelligence, Gavin and the assault planners studied enemy troop dispositions in Normandy, using aerial photographs and, when available, reports from the French underground. They studied the construction of man-made obstacles and the reinforcing of natural obstacles, which picked up after Rommel's arrival in France in January 1944.

The landing beaches in the original plan, north of Bayeux, had worried Gavin. Although the area offered plenty of level drop zones for the paratroopers and open landing zones for the glider troops, the wide-open country was also excellent terrain for counterattacking German tanks. Gavin preferred the terrain at the base of the Cotentin, which was mostly orchards and small farm fields divided by hedges. There was high ground around the port itself, but the southern part of the peninsula was low-lying ground drained by the Douve River and its principal tributary, the Merderet. The entire valley of Douve was a broad alluvial plain subject to flooding, while the higher ground was used for mixed agriculture, including orchards and pastures. The fields tended to be small and bordered by the hedgerows, but the road network was good. There was no wet or dry season to speak of, and the soil tended to hold water, meaning the ground was often thoroughly soaked. It was not a place to drive vehicles off-road. High temperatures from May to July averaged in the mid-sixties (Fahrenheit). At night, all the moisture caused low-lying clouds and ground fog that could cut visibility to zero.

It was in this terrain analysis that Allied planners made a faulty assumption for which the fighting troops would pay dearly. The analysts assumed that the hedges in Normandy were like the hedges in England—easily passable for men and vehicles; they were not. This was *bocage* country, where Norman hedgerows were often ten to fifteen feet thick at the base, a mass of tangled tree roots and stone, sometimes reaching up twenty or thirty feet. In many places the only way in or out of one of these fields was through a well-worn and well-marked entrance, which the German defenders covered with automatic weapons fire. Fighting in the bocage would turn out to be like fighting in a maze or in a huge building with lots of small rooms. The fields themselves were also too small for glider landings, which would play havoc with the reinforcements for the paratroopers. Except for the fact that the low-lying Cotentin was crisscrossed by streams and rivers, which made it less likely that the Germans could launch large-scale armored counterattacks, the landscape favored the defenders.

Although they blundered when it came to seeing the hedgerows, Allied intelligence proved quite adept at pinpointing German units and determining which ones were armored and which ones were not. The photo interpreters knew, for example, that the Norman French had practically no automobiles; they used carts and, for personal transportation, bicycles. Therefore any autos that appeared in the photos were most likely German staff cars. The Germans also had a habit of digging shelters into the banks of the roadways to protect these vehicles from Allied air attack. When viewed from above, these revetments looked like the chevrons on a soldier's sleeve, and a dense collection of these diggings indicated a headquarters.

The Germans usually chose large châteaus for their headquarters. The sequence was predictable: a German commander would choose a headquarters, then the digging would start, with revetments for vehicles appearing in the surrounding area. Then came the emplacements for antiaircraft guns ringing the headquarters. As quickly as the Germans built and reinforced their command posts, maps spread throughout the "war rooms" of Allied planning cells in England with little markers indicating the locations of enemy headquarters.

In late December Gavin met with Omar Bradley, who would command all American ground forces in the invasion, to discuss the use of the airborne divisions. The expansion of the invasion front had pushed Bradley's area of operations so that it now included the base of the Cotentin Peninsula (also called the Cherbourg Peninsula, after the port city at its northern tip). Cherbourg, at the far western end of the invasion area, and Caen, at the far eastern end, were the only port facilities in the immediate area, and the Allies needed to seize a port capable of handling the thousands of tons of supplies flowing in to keep the war machine supplied with everything from bullets and plasma to gasoline and engine parts.

Montgomery planned to seize Caen by the end of D-Day, and there were artificial harbors (ingenious combinations of old ships sunk as breakwaters plus floating piers) being prepared for both the American and British beaches. Bradley was charged with grabbing Cherbourg early in the campaign. To do that, he wanted to cut the peninsula at its base, thus sealing off all the German units from escape, and move north to capture the port in the first week of the battle.

Bradley showed Gavin some of the aerial photos of the Cotentin, and Gavin was happy to see that the Germans had flooded at least some of the farmland by blocking the mouth of the Douve River and closing locks along the Douve and Merderet rivers. To Gavin, this meant that the Germans did not expect to use armor there. His lightly armed paratroopers would be on a more even footing with the enemy infantry they would face. (Allied photo interpreters failed to see how extensive the flooding was. In many areas, tall marsh grasses thrived in the shallow waters, which made the flood harder to see in aerial photographs. It was this resulting flood that caused Gavin and others so many problems on D-Day.)

Bradley was considering stringing the drop zones of the two airborne divisions across the breadth of the peninsula, in essence using the paratroopers as a blocking force to keep the Germans from either escaping to the south or reinforcing to the north. Gavin thought this plan would put the airborne units on the western side of the peninsula too far from the landing beaches and the relief that had to come across those beaches.

Later, Gavin and Bradley agreed on a plan that answered both of the commanders' goals: the 82nd Airborne (which had the largest number of combat veterans) would drop just west of St. Sauveur le Vicomte, secure that city, and move west to cut off the base of the peninsula. Maxwell Taylor's unblooded 101st Airborne Division would land farther south, near Ste. Marie du Mont, and move toward the causeway exits of Utah Beach. In this plan, the 101st would help speed the beach forces toward the relief of the 82nd.

Even as he dealt with the tremendous responsibility of being chief planner for two U.S. airborne divisions, Gavin had other weighty concerns. One of his most critical challenges was to standardize procedures throughout the airborne force and between the paratroopers and the Troop Carrier Command.

Airborne and Air Corps planners had to agree on such details as how planes were loaded, warning and jump signals, flight formations (which determined how troopers were scattered on the ground), and even terminology to be used in this relatively new business of delivering soldiers by parachute.[1]

Also of concern to Gavin was the fact that Troop Carrier Command had only recently been organized in Britain, with nowhere near the required number of aircraft, and with many inexperienced pilots. Demands on the Air Corps were so great that it was difficult to secure training time for the pilots.

The 505th PIR, which had fought in the Mediterranean, had developed its own procedures for all the million details of getting an airborne force to the right drop zones. And because of their status as combat vets, these men thought their procedures were beyond improvement by the inexperienced 101st Airborne or even by the British paratroopers.

The Allies could not even agree on the aerial formations for the jump aircraft. The British preferred to use "bomber stream" formations for their troop planes, which meant planes flying in a randomly formed stream. (They believed that antiaircraft gunners had an easier time hitting planes flying in predictable patterns.) The American paratroop commanders wanted the planes in a "V of Vs" formation, with three aircraft in each V, and each three-ship formation occupying a spot in a larger V. The Americans believed this formation gave airborne commanders better control over dispersion on the ground.

American and British planners used different terms in planning, which led to some confusion. The British referred to the selected target as the *drop zone*, whereas the Americans referred to it as the *jump area*. Such minor distinctions became critical when dealing in a high-stakes, high-pressure venture with thousands of soldiers, many of them with comparatively little experience.

Gavin, who knew personally many of the key planners from the 101st Airborne Division, worked to standardize American airborne practices, publishing a "Training Memorandum on the Employment of Airborne Forces" before the end of 1943. He followed quickly with a document meant to standardize practices in both the British and American forces. Aided by a Royal Air Force Wing Commander named Duglad McPherson, Gavin spent a great deal of time traveling to various far-flung headquarters, where every staff officer and commander wanted, in his words, to "discuss, alter, criticize, and contribute" to the plan. Although his patience was tried, Gavin knew it was important that all commands participated. The more closely they adhered to standardized procedures, the more flexible and responsive the airborne forces would be. The British could fly in American transports, and American troops could fly in British gliders.

Throughout the first two months of 1944, the plans for Overlord and Neptune (the airborne component) were in a state of flux, as the generals tried to hammer out the best way to employ the airborne divisions. There was even some question as to whether it was a good idea to use the airborne divisions at all. No one doubted the courage of the individual paratroopers, but Eisenhower and his chief for air operations, Sir Trafford Leigh-Mallory, were not convinced that using massed formations of paratroopers was a good idea.

Leigh-Mallory was concerned that there wasn't sufficient lift to deliver the troopers to the battlefield with enough combat power to accomplish their missions. In addition, the newly redesigned 82nd and 101st Airborne Divisions now each had a regiment of glider infantry, representing one fourth of their combat power. But getting gliders to a contested battlefield was so risky that it nearly made parachuting behind enemy lines look easy.

Although gliders had been around for a while, neither the British nor the Americans had used them in large-scale combat operations before World War II. There were advantages to gliders: they delivered fully loaded combat troops to point landing zones behind enemy lines. The glider soldiers came in silently and were ready to fight as a team as soon as they cleared the aircraft. Paratroopers, by contrast, were scattered in their drops and needed time, often a great deal of time, to regroup and form units that were ready to fight.[2]

The gliders themselves could be mass-produced cheaply (about twenty-five thousand dollars on average for the smaller U.S. version), and it was easier and less expensive to train glider troops than it was to send paratroopers to a four-week course. Glider troops also did not receive the hazardous-duty pay of fifty dollars a month that paratroopers merited, although many of the paratroopers acknowledged that riding into battle in a glider was as hazardous, if not more so, than parachuting in.[3]

For all their advantages, the short history of the gliders in World War II was already full of horror stories. In the assault on Sicily, some British gliders were cut loose early and dropped into the sea, drowning many of the troops on board. In August 1943, at a demonstration in St. Louis, Missouri, where many of the Waco gliders were made, five thousand people watched as the wing fell off a glider carrying the mayor of St. Louis and nine other civic officials, dropping the craft like a rock from two thousand feet and killing all on board.[4]

The troops, of course, had the clearest view of the dangers involved, as evidenced by the nicknames they gave their aircraft: "flying coffins" and "towed targets." The gliders were unarmed, unarmored, and power-less to do anything but land once they were cut loose from their tow planes. The light aircraft were extremely vulnerable to wind shifts and in their approach flew so low over enemy positions that they could eas-ily be engaged by small arms fire from the ground. In fact, their only de-fense was their stealthy approach; the first gliders in any wave were often past before defenders realized what was happening. But follow-on echelons made slow, fat targets.

The two types of glider available for Operation Neptune were the British Horsa and the American Waco. The smaller Waco gliders had canvas skins stretched over an aluminum tube frame, while the Horsa was made completely of wood, even down to the pilot's joystick control. The Horsa, especially, tended to break up in crash landings, which were common. Because of the dangers of landing, glider troops in the Amer-ican airborne divisions—who had never made a glider assault in com-bat—got very little training. Instead of practicing the entire operation, they simulated landings and concentrated on the battle drills they'd need once they dismounted.

Then, weeks before the invasion, some of the American glider troops, who made all their preparations on the Waco gliders, were told they would use the big British-made Horsas instead. The glidermen had created their manifests, organized their units, and learned to configure their loads for the Waco payload of 3,750 pounds. Now they had to re-draw their plans to handle a mix of Wacos and Horsas, which had an enormous payload of 6,900 pounds. The equipment used to lash the loads weighed nearly three hundred pounds, and everyone had to re-learn his job.

There was another challenge with the Horsa: it took a lot longer to unload. The command modified the aircraft, installing an explosive charge that was designed to safely blow the tail section off so the men and equipment could pour out of the larger opening that was left. But there was no getting around the fact that the American pilots had almost no experience flying the much larger, ungainly Horsa. (One major drawback to the Horsa was that the tricycle landing gear, which was located under the pilot, had a tendency to push through the deck of the aircraft on landing and then rip back through the length of the glider.)

The glider regiments faced significant challenges just getting to the battlefield, but the paratroopers needed the quick reinforcements and infusion of equipment and supplies. Risky as it was, the glider assault remained part of the invasion plan.[5]

Major General Matt Ridgway traveled from Ireland to London to participate in the high-level meetings where airborne strategy was worked out. Ridgway had a great deal of respect for Omar Bradley, and vice versa, which gave Ridgway some latitude in pressing his views forcefully.

As the plan existed in early 1944, Ridgway and his troopers were part of VII Corps, which was commanded by Ridgway's West Point classmate "Lightning Joe" Collins. (The ambitious Ridgway had served under another classmate, Mark Clark, in the Mediterranean; he was quite conscious that his former peers had surpassed him, though he served them faithfully.) Collins earned his nickname in the Pacific theater for the aggressiveness and speed his 25th Infantry Division showed in action against the Japanese. (The division still bears the nickname "Tropic Lightning.")

Collins was a great organizer and an inspiring leader. If Ridgway had any reservations about serving under him, they would only have sprung from the feeling that the war, the promotions, and the chances to command larger formations were passing him by. Ridgway had firmly hitched his prospects to the notion that large airborne formations were possible. If George Marshall, with his affinity for the paratroopers, had been given command of Overlord, Ridgway might have been promoted to Corps Commander over both the 82nd and 101st. But Ike, who was unsure as to what contributions the paratroopers could make, was in charge. And Leigh-Mallory, who had serious doubts about Neptune, was Eisenhower's principal adviser for air operations.

Leigh-Mallory's chief complaint was that there were not enough troop carriers available to deliver both U.S. airborne divisions as well as the British 6th Airborne. He argued that German fighters and the extensive antiaircraft installations scattered around Normandy would shoot down a large number of aircraft and gliders. He further insisted that the terrain on the Cotentin, with its smaller fields bordered by hedges and its water obstacles, was unsuited for glider landings.

When Bradley continued to develop his plan to use the two American airborne divisions to cut the Cotentin, Leigh-Mallory became more vocal in his objections. He thought the 82nd Airborne Division, in particular, would be in a dangerous position on the western side of the Cotentin, far from the relief that would have to come over Utah Beach.

Leigh-Mallory was blunt with Bradley, telling him, "I cannot approve your plan. It is much too hazardous an undertaking. Your losses will be excessive—certainly far more than the gains are worth."[6]

Leigh-Mallory speculated that the airborne forces could suffer 70 percent casualties: nearly eight thousand young men killed, wounded, captured, or missing on the enemy-held peninsula. Eisenhower could well imagine what failure would look like: lightly armed paratrooper units running out of food and ammunition miles behind enemy lines, his assault forces bottled up on the beaches and unable to reach their comrades inland, German formations slicing into the paratroopers' defensive positions.

If Ike's Air Marshal proved right, the entire assault on the Cotentin could turn into a huge disaster, with a heartbreaking loss of life among the glidermen and paratroopers. Eisenhower asked Bradley to explain his position, and Bradley conceded that there was a risk of large casualties, but his troops could be easily bottled up on Utah Beach unless the airborne divisions secured the exit causeways.

At this point Omar Bradley cast his lot with the paratroopers. He told Eisenhower that he would not invade Utah Beach if he did not have the paratroopers to secure the beach exits and block the expected counterattacks. If this was a bluff, it was an effective one. The landings at Utah were an essential part of the plan and had been since early January when Eisenhower decided to expand the invasion area. The lodgment would not be big enough without Utah Beach, and the Utah Beach assault would fail without the paratroopers. Finally, Ike agreed that the potential losses were worth risking. He overruled Leigh-Mallory. Planning for Operation Neptune continued at a feverish pace.

The most difficult aspect of the planning for glider assault was timing. The airborne commanders wanted the glider troops to land with or immediately after the paratroopers, not only to provide reinforcement but because the gliders carried important weapons and equipment, such as antitank guns, jeeps, ammunition, and artillery. Since the paratroopers would jump by moonlight, hours before the beach forces hit, glider operations would have to be conducted at night as well. Even if the gliders were scheduled to land at dawn (one of several plans floated during the search for a compromise), that would mean that the tricky takeoffs and the hazardous over-water flight would be conducted at night. The British had used gliders at night during the invasion of Sicily the previous summer, with disastrous results: many of the gliders never even made the coastline, and scores of soldiers were drowned. Given that experience, the British were opposed to any plan for glider operations during the hours of darkness.

In an attempt to win concessions from Leigh-Mallory and the British, American planners staged a demonstration of a dawn landing by glider. Forty-eight gliders of both types were assembled and the tow pilots carefully rehearsed. Still, the demonstration was a disaster. One glider crashed, killing some of its occupants, and twenty-three others had extremely hard landings that injured passengers and damaged equipment.

Leigh-Mallory won that round. There would be no mass landings of gliders at dawn, though the parachute forces would be allowed to use some gliders for a predawn delivery of the antitank guns, ammunition, communications gear, and medical supplies needed early on D-Day. The major landings of glider infantry, who would reinforce the parachutists, would take place later on D-Day.[7]

•   •   •

While planning for the invasion was taking place in London, Chief of Staff George Marshall tried to persuade Ike to use the paratroopers in a different, much more dangerous mission.

In the fall of 1943 Marshall, working with the Air Corps Chief Henry "Hap" Arnold and a small planning staff in Washington, devised an audacious plan for the use of the Allied airborne forces that would have changed the entire thrust of Overlord. Instead of using these forces to lend aid to the beach landing forces, Marshall and Arnold wanted to drop them deep inside France and give the beach landing forces the mission of linking up with them.

Marshall's plan called for four or five airborne divisions to be dropped at Evreux, near Paris, where they would establish the airborne equivalent of a beachhead—called an "airhead." The parachutists and glider troops would commandeer all vehicles in the area and make contact with the French underground. Meanwhile, reinforcements would land by aircraft at captured fields inside the airhead, reinforcing the perimeter and consolidating the gains. The two generals in Washington thought that the beach landing forces, with their heavy armor and artillery, could dash inland fast enough to relieve the paratroopers before the situation became untenable, before the Germans could smash the paratroopers.[8]

There were some merits to the plan. Marshall believed that the Germans, faced with a strong enemy force so far behind their lines and so far from where they expected to do battle, would be unable to mount an effective defense. Forced to fight at the beaches and far inland, their efforts in each area would be piecemeal and ineffective.

When British General Frederick E. Morgan, the COSSAC Chief of Staff, came to Washington in October 1943, Marshall showed him the plan. Morgan was stunned. He expressed his skepticism, and then the two-star general, facing two four-star generals who had conceived the plan and seemed to believe in it, immediately cabled London for support.

Leigh-Mallory, the air chief for Overlord, was the first to respond. Rather than take on Marshall and Arnold on the wisdom of putting so many lightly armed troops so far behind enemy lines, he argued that there would not be sufficient lift to move that many airborne troopers. In fact, he worried he might not have sufficient lift to deliver even one full division by the spring of 1944. With landing areas so deep behind enemy lines, the vulnerable cargo planes and even more vulnerable gliders would have to run a gauntlet of still dangerous German fighters. The attrition of Allied air assets, already stretched thin at the start, would make supplying and reinforcing the airhead more difficult as the days went on. Finally, the target areas were so far from the beaches that any number of things could delay the relief and imperil the thousands of airborne troopers.

Marshall, who had dedicated huge sums of money and some of his most talented leaders to the development of the airborne divisions, was not dissuaded right away. He set the plan aside for the time being but kept open the option of carrying out the plan using just American troops.

The end of Marshall's plan came about after Eisenhower was named Supreme Commander for Overlord. Ike and his most senior people, Deputy Commander Arthur Tedder, ground force commander Bernard Montgomery, American First Army commander Omar Bradley, and British Second Army commander Miles Dempsey, agreed with the initial plan to use the airborne forces near the beaches and looked askance at Marshall's.

Still, Marshall wrote to Ike in February 1944, urging him to consider the plan. Marshall was too much of a professional to overstep his bounds and force Ike's hand, but he tried his best to be persuasive.

This plan appeals to me because I feel it is a true vertical envelopment and would create such a strategic threat to the Germans that it would call for a major revision of their defensive plans. It should be a complete surprise, an invaluable asset of any such plan. It would directly threaten the crossings of the Seine as well

as the city of Paris. It should serve as a rallying point for a considerable element of the French underground. In effect, we would be
opening another front in France and your [amphibious] build-up
would be tremendously increased in rapidity.

The trouble with this plan is that we have never done anything
like this before, and frankly, that reaction makes me tired. Therefore I should like you to give these young men [the briefing officers Marshall sent to England to sell his idea] an opportunity to
present this matter to you personally before your Staff tears it to
ribbons. Please believe that, as usual, I do not want to embarrass
you with undue pressure. I merely wish to be certain that you
have viewed this possibility on a definite planning basis.[9]

Because of the great respect Eisenhower had for Marshall, he was
very careful in letting the boss know that he didn't think the deep thrust
into France was a good idea. "I agree thoroughly with the [strategic]
conception but disagree with the timing," Ike wrote. His first job was to
get a solid hold on a piece of France, then capture Cherbourg so that he
could feed his war machine. The airborne troops must be used to support
these objectives, not to alter completely the objectives of the invasion.

When Jim Gavin took over as chief airborne planner for Overlord, he
was surprised to hear what Marshall had proposed. The Chief of Staff
wanted an important strategic role for the airborne divisions—which is
what Ridgway, Gavin, and the other airborne commanders had been
seeking all along. But the paratroopers' inadequate antitank weapons
and chancy resupply plans made Marshall's plan too risky.

Gavin had seen, from a foxhole on Sicily's Biazza Ridge, how poorly
armed the paratroopers were for battling tanks. He carried with him the
mental image of soldiers crushed by enemy tanks, remnants of their
mangled bazookas mixed with the gore.

The antiarmor weaponry in the U.S. Army was inadequate for the
job. Missiles from the shoulder-fired rocket launcher, called the
bazooka, often bounced off German tanks. (The small rocket could

penetrate the rear and, if it hit right, the side armor of some panzers, but that required the gunner to get close, to crawl past the tank or let the tank pass him.) The U.S.-made 37 mm antitank gun was also not powerful enough. The Americans tried getting their hands on as many British-made 57 mm antitank guns as they could, but these had to be delivered by glider, which brought its own set of problems. Once linkup with beach forces took place, of course, the paratroopers had access to much larger antitank weapons, but no one could guarantee when that linkup would occur.

Gavin could see, in his mind's eye, the airhead near Evreux torn up by German armor long before the beach forces could arrive. The chief's plan, Gavin would write later, was "an interesting example of how a concept can be postulated by those who look on combat as a theoretical exercise." For all Marshall's compassion and concern, when viewed from Washington, the war still looked too much like a map board exercise.[10]

The shortage of highly qualified commanders was a problem every division commander faced, but it was particularly acute in the airborne regiments. There was simply no deep pool of jump-qualified candidates for command. Add to that the rapid growth of the new arm—five new parachute regiments would participate in the Normandy invasion—and Ridgway simply had to settle for what was available and try to develop those commanders he had. By far the biggest concern was posed by the man Gavin had chosen to replace him as the commander of his beloved 505th PIR, Colonel Herbert Batcheller.

Batcheller had been Gavin's executive officer, his second in command, at the formation of the 505th at Fort Benning in July 1942, and had served with Gavin through the train-up and overseas deployment, as well as in the campaigns in Sicily and Italy. Although his courage on the battlefield was unquestioned,[11] he did not inspire the kind of confidence that Gavin did, and there were occasions when his behavior in garrison was indefensible.

At Fort Bragg, home of the regiment for the first part of 1943,

Batcheller kept a motorcycle stashed outside the reservation. In the evenings, he frequently slipped off post, an offense that would get an enlisted man thrown in the stockade, and rode his motorcycle to visit his wife. Even when he was present during the training day, he did not strike the staff officers who worked for him as a decisive commander. Jack Norton, who served as the executive officer of a battalion in Sicily and Italy, noticed that Batcheller often fell asleep during meetings in which critical details of an upcoming operation were being hashed out. But it was in Ireland that Batcheller completely lost the respect of the men and junior officers.

Batcheller took command of the 505th in Italy, after Gavin was promoted to brigadier general. Batcheller was in the unenviable position of taking over from a man who had enjoyed not only tremendous success as a combat commander but also the near fanatical loyalty of his soldiers. Mark Alexander, a gifted combat commander who was moved to regimental executive officer to shore up Batcheller's command, thought that taking over the 505th from Gavin was about as tough an assignment as a man could draw.

The new commander was simply "not very impressive in demeanor," in the way he carried himself, in the way he acted around subordinates. He did not act like a commander. But his real troubles started when he began keeping company with an Irish widow who lived near the regimental area. Incredibly, with the invasion only months away, he neglected his duties and spent almost every afternoon with her; what's more, he did little to hide his actions.

Batcheller had a big U.S. Army staff car, painted olive drab with a white star, which he left parked in front of the woman's home just outside the gate. The soldiers didn't even have to leave the post to see that their commander, conspicuously absent from training, was shacking up. Some of the men were bothered by the fact that Batcheller, a married man, was flaunting this behavior. But what really bothered everyone was his taking advantage of his rank to enjoy privileges other men didn't have. It was antithetical to Gavin's admonition about leaders being "last in the chow line."

This kind of behavior at the top pretty soon had an effect on the entire outfit. Even the soldiers noticed a slide in discipline. Dennis O'Loughlin, the Montana native who had volunteered for latrine duty, noticed that the guardhouse in Ireland was always full of soldiers who had missed curfew or had shown up drunk and disorderly. Discipline was so lax that even the guards assigned to watch the restricted men spent a good bit of their time sleeping.[12]

By far the biggest problem was with soldiers going AWOL—absent without leave. The situation was rampant in the division, and nowhere more so than in the veteran 505th PIR. Mark Alexander placed some of the blame on the division leadership, which had not made arrangements for the men to have sufficient leave time. The 505th had deployed from the United States in April 1943, then spent two months in training under miserable conditions in North Africa before launching their first combat operation. The Sicily invasion was followed quickly by another combat jump into Italy and a longer campaign to help the Allies break out of the beachhead at Salerno. Although the men were given short passes when the unit was pulled off the line, most men got no more than a couple of days off. By the time they reached Ireland in December 1943, they felt they deserved a break. But even the relatively generous leave and pass policy adopted in Ireland didn't provide enough of a break for the weary soldiers. Batcheller did nothing to address the problem, even as AWOL rates soared.

The fact that the training in Ireland wasn't all that demanding only seemed to convince the paratroopers that the division could spare them for a week at a time—a week when a man could get away from the constant crowds of other men, maybe enjoy a conversation with a young woman, or at least with a civilian, and sit in a pub or a restaurant to savor a meal and a cigarette without some sergeant hurrying everyone along.

Although Mark Alexander believed that the division's poor leave policy contributed to the problem, it was his duty to enforce military discipline. The stream of paperwork continued even after he became sick with jaundice and the side effects of malaria medication. Confined to bed, too drained to move, he still had to process the courts-martial of AWOL soldiers. Alexander was angry with the men, who were shirking their duty, and he was angry with his boss, because Batcheller ignored the problem while he played house with his Irish girlfriend.

Batcheller's frequent absences put Alexander in an awkward position with Ridgway, the division commander. One day, Ridgway visited the regiment while Alexander was working through a stack of courts-martial paperwork. Finding no sign of Batcheller, Ridgway asked, "Where's Colonel Batcheller?"

Alexander was able to say, "Sir, I don't know," which was an honest, if not a complete, answer. After the division commander made several visits without finding Batcheller, Alexander warned his boss.

"The general has been looking for you," he said. "You'd better make yourself available."[13] But Batcheller did not change his ways.

Lieutenant Bob Fielder was present when Gavin visited the command post of the 505th during a field exercise. Gavin quizzed Batcheller about the disposition of his battalions, and it was clear even to Fielder that Batcheller had no idea what was going on with the field problem.

Overall, conditions in Ireland were far from ideal for training. First, the AWOL rate remained high, and Ridgway knew he'd soon have to do something about Batcheller. Valuable training time was being wasted on disciplinary action, and soldiers confined to the guardhouses were not getting the training they needed. The short days and long nights in Ireland also limited daylight training time. The move to England in February 1944 promised to alleviate some of those problems: there would be more training, fewer passes, more restrictions on the soldiers' time. But Matt Ridgway inherited new problems, too.

On a reconnaissance of the area in which his troops would be billeted, near Leicester, England, Ridgway noted the large number of support troops, many of whom were, in the vernacular of the time, Negro units. These men had been billeted in the area for a while and had established friendships with the local populace. Of particular concern to Ridgway was the sight of black soldiers dating white Englishwomen.

Such practices weren't all that remarkable in England, but many of Ridgway's soldiers had grown up in the land of Jim Crow. They had trained in Georgia and North Carolina, had spent their off-duty time in towns where black citizens stepped off the sidewalks to make way for white people, even for the lowly white soldier. Ridgway was concerned that when his troopers arrived in Leicester and saw white English-women with black GIs, trouble would ensue. He was right.

On the first night of liberty for his men after they arrived in Leices-ter, a paratrooper was stabbed in a fight with Negro soldiers. He didn't die, but the rumor that swept through the division area claimed that he did. Fueled by rumor and racism, the incident threatened to engulf the division and distract the soldiers from the tasks that needed attention.

Ridgway immediately visited every one of his units bivouacked in the area and, as he put it later, "laid down the law." He told the officers that the Negro troops in the area wore the same uniform the paratroopers wore, that they were under the orders of competent authority and were performing tasks just as essential to the war effort as the work the para-troopers did. The men would comport themselves like soldiers and con-centrate on getting ready for combat. Ridgway acknowledged the racial problems at home but decided it was not the responsibility of the 82nd Airborne Division to sort things out on the other side of the ocean.

Ridgway also met with town officials and promised them that he and his commanders would do everything they could to keep the peace. He doubled the MP patrols and personally rode and walked through the streets at night to keep his eye on things. If the truce forced on the men was uneasy and unnatural, it was effective. The soldiers got into fights from time to time (for which they were restricted to their regimental areas), but there were no more stabbings and no murders.[14]

The other challenge that faced Ridgway on his arrival in England was the task of incorporating all the new units assigned to the division for the upcoming invasion. Until February 1944, the 82nd Airborne Divi-sion consisted of the 505th Parachute Infantry Regiment, the 504th

PIR (which was still in Italy and would miss the Normandy invasion), and the 325th Glider Infantry Regiment. By the time the division headquarters closed on Leicester, Ridgway had two more brand-new parachute regiments, already in England but not yet assigned to a division. He drew the 507th and 508th PIRs (while Major General Bill Lee's brand-new 101st Airborne Division drew the 501st and 502nd). Ridgway put Gavin, recently returned from his job at the planning headquarters and happily away from the political scene in London, to work on standardizing the training among these regiments.

This meant that the commanders, staffs, and soldiers of those units had to learn how the 82nd Airborne did things, what the procedures were for everything from requesting resupply to conducting a night movement to launching an attack. Of the four regiments that made up the division at the beginning of 1944, three had commanders who were relatively new to the responsibilities at this level.

The 507th Parachute Infantry Regiment was commanded by George V. "Zip" Millett Jr., a West Point classmate of Gavin's. The Class of 1929 graduated only 299 men, so it is likely that Gavin and Millett knew each other as cadets. Millett graduated fourth from the bottom of the class, while Gavin, who had not attended high school, graduated two-thirds of the way down the class list. As fellow infantry officers in the tiny prewar Army, they had crossed paths on enough occasions that, in his letters home, Gavin referred to Millett as "Zip."

Gavin would write later that he was "not overjoyed" with Millett or Roy E. Lindquist, the commander of the 508th PIR. Gavin thought Millett was overweight and soft for a field soldier, not in shape "physically or mentally for what he was going into."[15]

While he wasn't a zealot about combat training, Millett was committed to the regimental sports program. In the peacetime Army, competitive sports served to promote both physical fitness and the competitive spirit. During those prewar years, when there was not much money for adequate training exercises, sports also gave the men something constructive to do. The emphasis on sports lessened as the Army went to war, but there were still elaborate programs.

Millett lavished attention on his sports program, which would not have been a problem except that he neglected the field training of his solders to do it. Even some of Millett's own subordinates had questions about his fitness for combat command. One battalion commander (there were three battalions in each regiment) thought Millett was a "good ol' boy, laid back, [but] totally committed to sports" at the expense of combat training.[16]

For his part, Roy Lindquist of the 508th PIR was a "hell of a good administrator," in Gavin's opinion, and "kept records like I've never seen before." But he was not the dynamic combat leader that would be needed once the bullets started flying. In Ridgway's eyes, any regimental commander—especially one who had not been in combat (the case with Millett and Lindquist)—would suffer by comparison with Reuben Tucker of the 504th and Gavin, who had commanded the 505th.

Gavin believed that the key to success and survival in combat was tough, unrelenting training. He had demonstrated this in the two months he spent in North Africa as commander of the 505th in the lead-up to Sicily. Conditions in the desert were miserable, with temperatures routinely over one hundred degrees, the troops suffering from poor food, worse water, and dysentery, and all the while plagued by insects, infections, and an ever-present fine grit of sand that clogged weapons, equipment, and bodies. Yet Gavin had kept up a relentless pace of training. The payoff was that many of his troopers found that, at least as far as the physical demands went, combat was in some ways easier than training under Gavin.

The young brigadier, now entrusted with the combat training of the entire division, set out to replicate the conditions that would prepare his men for combat in France. He was especially hard on the leaders, the men—at every level of the chain of command—whose decisions would most influence the battle and would determine whether or not lives were wasted.

On all training maneuvers, Gavin demanded that leaders be able to make quick, accurate decisions and be ready to plan new operations on the run. A typical field problem might begin with an overnight march, eighteen to twenty miles with full combat equipment. When they stopped and the men expected a rest, another mission came down, and the officers jumped into their planning mode while everyone else prepared to move out again. Daylight hours were filled with combat drills and force-on-force maneuvers. Dusk brought orders for another forced march, which could last for hours. Around midnight, word came down to halt and disperse (in case of an air raid), and the exhausted troops stumbled to find a dry place to rest. Gavin let them sleep for an hour or so, which was "just enough to cause them to lose their sense of orientation to events and environment." Then runners went around and prodded the sleeping commanders, who were given a new set of orders calling for immediate movement leading into an attack. And all the while Gavin watched and evaluated and critiqued, looking to develop the leaders he needed for the invasion: tough, smart, ready for anything.

Gavin called the training "exacting," and it gave him "an opportunity to get to know a lot about them and for them to learn much about themselves."[17]

As difficult as the training was, Gavin knew it did not come close to the rigors of combat, and especially could not replicate the shock of going into battle, which for the paratrooper happened not in a long move toward the battlefield by truck or by foot, but in the short time—sometimes measured in minutes—between the green light and the landing.[18]

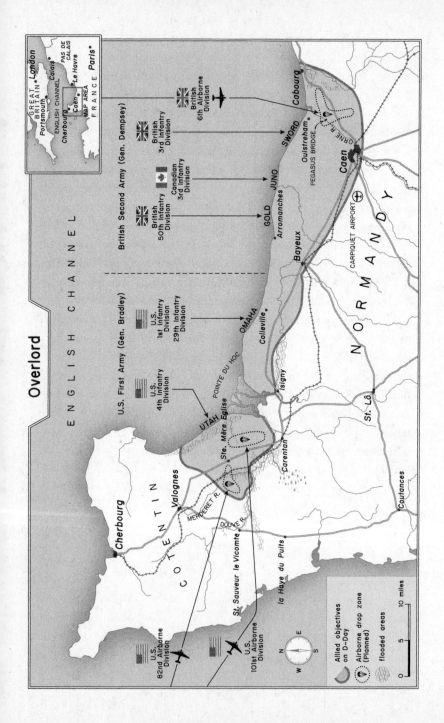

Overlord

OPERATION NEPTUNE

By March 1944, with the likelihood of a spring invasion looming over the rainy tents and Quonset huts in England, the command situation in the 505th PIR reached a breaking point. Ridgway and Gavin decided that Herbert Batcheller had to be replaced.

For many of the officers in the regiment, the choice of a new commander could not have been clearer. Mark Alexander, who had taken over command of the 2nd Battalion weeks before the Sicily jump, had proven himself an outstanding combat commander, in spite of his relative lack of experience.

Alexander was a graduate student at the University of Kansas in 1940 when he befriended the son of the university's ROTC commander, Colonel Ed Renth. One evening, Alexander joined the Renth family for dinner, and the colonel told Alexander that the United States would definitely get involved in the war that had already engulfed Europe and Asia.

"When war comes," the colonel counseled, "you want to be an officer."

Alexander asked how such a thing might happen, and the old soldier told him to enlist in the Kansas National Guard as a private. The colonel would provide him with the various manuals he needed to study for advancement. When the need for officers in a rapidly expanding Army became acute, the Army would give written exams to determine who might be officer material. Alexander, who had already proven himself as a student, stood a good chance of being selected.

In October 1940 Alexander enlisted in the Kansas Guard. Soon after, just as Colonel Renth had predicted, the Guard gave written tests to identify potential lieutenants. Alexander passed, though he later grew concerned at the poor state of training in his Guard unit, the 35th Division. He began looking to get into a unit that would be better prepared when they came face-to-face with the enemy. That led him to the 505th PIR of the 82nd Airborne.

By June 1943 Alexander was a major, serving as the executive officer of the 2nd Battalion as they trained for the invasion of Sicily. When his battalion commander, James Gray, went missing from the regimental area in North Africa for three successive days, Gavin called Alexander in and asked where Gray was. There was no sign of Gray, not any word about what might have happened to him. Finally, with the days until the invasion ticking by, Gavin put Alexander in charge of the six hundred men of the 2nd Battalion, 505th Parachute Infantry Regiment. Alexander wasn't sure what to make of the new appointment, and he certainly hadn't expected to find himself in command of an elite combat unit before he'd even had time to wear out a couple of pairs of GI boots. When Mark Alexander climbed aboard his aircraft in Tunisia on July 9, 1943, to lead a battalion into combat, he had been in the Army two years and nine months.

Yet beginning with his service in Sicily, Alexander had proven to be a good choice. He was steady and fearless in combat, hardworking and thorough in training and in garrison. When Herbert Batcheller took command of the 505th PIR, Alexander was promoted to regimental executive officer. Now, with Batcheller on the way out, Alexander seemed the natural choice to succeed him.

Yet Ridgway surprised everyone by going outside the unit to find its next commander, pulling the executive officer of the 508th PIR, Lieutenant Colonel Bill Ekman, over to Gavin's old regiment.

Ekman was a talented officer and an absolutely dedicated professional, but there were some problems with his appointment. He was not a combat veteran, and he was an outsider. Everyone, including Ekman, expected he would have a tough time coming in to take over the 505th, which had already been through two campaigns and had, in the words of one of its soldiers, "felt as if they had single-handedly moved the war forward toward victory."

To some of those involved, it looked as if Ridgway was just taking care of another West Pointer. (Batcheller, also a West Point graduate, didn't leave the division but was given command of the 1st Battalion, 508th PIR. This was a demotion, but also an astounding second chance.)

But Mark Alexander thought Ekman was a good choice. He had almost twice the time in service that Alexander had, and he had Ridgway's confidence. The important thing, Alexander insisted, was getting the troops ready.[1]

Ekman knew that the unit he was taking over, though it already had a storied reputation in the Army, had some difficulties that had to be addressed quickly. Discipline had lapsed during Batcheller's tenure, and training was not where it should be. Ekman worried about the many replacements the regiment had absorbed, and whether or not they knew their jobs well enough to make a contribution. The discipline problems, sloppy uniforms, failure to salute and observe other military courtesies, the high rates for both AWOL and venereal disease were all indicative of a unit that was sliding downhill.

Ekman decided that when he introduced himself to the troops, he'd put his concerns right up front. Just to make sure he didn't miss any of the points he wanted to make, he typed the notes for his speech on small cards.[2]

This was a tremendous opportunity for the thirty-one-year-old Ekman. He was about to take command of an experienced and famous parachute regiment on the eve of a tremendous invasion in which they would play an important part. He was charged, by Ridgway and Gavin, with getting a handle on discipline in the unit, because discipline was important to success on the battlefield.

Some of the men were veterans of two campaigns; some of them had just shipped in from the replacement depot. In spite of the widespread discipline problems, all of them were intensely proud of their unit and keenly aware that their combat experience set them apart. They also all knew that Ekman did not have that combat experience, which meant he had something to prove to them.

Ekman planned to start his first speech to the troops by acknowledging that his success as a leader depended, in part, on their acceptance of him. He hinted at how much he stood to learn from them, and how he needed their cooperation to fix what was broken in the regiment. He wanted to do all that from a position of strength, maybe even with a little humor, and he practiced as he wrote out the speech.

"Men, I thought we'd get together so that we could have a meeting of the minds on certain vital subjects and so that all of you could see what your new Regimental C.O. [Commanding Officer] looked like."

Good opening. Next he gave credit to the 505th PIR for what they'd already accomplished. When he read the lines out loud, he said "five-oh-five," as everyone did.

"I can't begin to tell you how proud I am to be given the chance to command this outfit. I know the 505 of old, and back in the States we watched every newspaper report for news of the 505—and were not disappointed. You really showed everyone what the U.S. paratroops could do in combat. And how good they could do it."

Satisfied with this opening, Ekman got down to the essential facts around why the men were getting a new commander just before the expected invasion.

"But—being a good outfit in combat alone is not enough—a fine reputation gained in combat can be lost in damned short order after combat if the members of an outfit don't toe the line. . . . There are a few incidents which have occurred which might build up to serious proportions if we don't watch our step. I realize that there are only a comparatively few individuals who are causing this trouble, but the reputation of the entire unit suffers from it and I know that you don't like it—I know I don't."

Ekman looked back on his work. He thought appealing to their pride was the best way to gain their cooperation. He listed the problems that were affecting the unit: lost training time because of AWOL and disciplinary cases, race trouble with the support troops in the area, stealing from the Red Cross, venereal disease, and even jump refusals.

Then, in plain English, came an acknowledgment that his power was limited.

"Now I know I can't keep you in camp at night if a man makes up his mind to get out but I can make it damned hard for everyone caught. But I don't want to take such action—I want to stop it before it starts— so I'll try to make you want to stay in camp by providing as much entertainment as possible."

He talked about movie nights and reading rooms and clubs where the men could enjoy a beer after hours. The command could sponsor dances and swimming and athletics, all things designed to give the men a way to relax, something to do in their limited free time. He also planned to make passes available, as well as transportation for the men to get into town.

Near the end of his notes he talked about the invasion everyone knew was coming. They would be among the first to land, and the nation would be watching.

It was a good talk, he concluded, surveying his notes. It gave the men their due but left no doubt as to what he expected of them. He appealed to their pride and reminded them that they were, once again, about to take center stage in a great historical drama. Satisfied with his plan, he tucked the neatly typed cards into his pocket. When the time came for him to speak to the regiment, they were drawn up in formation, and all eyes were on him, waiting to hear what the new commander had to say.

Unfortunately, the first words out of his mouth were "Men of the five-oh-eight . . ."

Ekman's gaffe was met with jeers and hissing.

This is the oh-five, not the green oh-eight!

Even the noncoms and officers, who tried to quiet the troops and restore discipline, were amused at the mistake. Mark Alexander, Ekman's executive officer, simply thought, *The poor guy.*

• • •

Like many young commanders who take over a unit, Ekman was dis-
posed to be tough at first, because it's always easy to loosen up later. For
Ekman and his fellow leaders, professionals trying to make fighting men
out of citizen soldiers, it was a straightforward matter: disciplined soldiers were more likely to succeed, more likely to come home alive.

Men who didn't perform in training or inspections lost their pass
privileges. GIs who were insubordinate, who failed to follow orders
promptly, who lost or destroyed government property were liable to
more serious actions, up to and including time in the stockade. Ekman
even paid attention to the small things: uniforms and military courtesy.

To the soldiers, Ekman's approach looked misguided. How important
was a salute in a unit preparing for combat? To the men, it just looked
like more Army chickenshit.

Ekman stayed on course, and he worked hard to make sure the stan-
dards were enforced. Unlike Batcheller, he spent his time at training,
and he also watched over the men when they were on pass. When he
visited nearby Leicester, Ekman had to deal with the inconvenience of
the blackout, which was meant to thwart German bombers. There were
tiny lamps on the corners that threw only enough light to act as guide-
posts, but not enough to illuminate the area. The soldiers and civilians
had grown accustomed to making their way around in the darkness.

Ekman came to a church square that had a few tiny marker lights
shining down on the sidewalk. As he reached the corner, he heard
someone say, "Colonel Ekman?"

Ekman said, "Yes?"

As he turned around, a fist came out of the dark and hit him in the
eye, knocking him down to the pavement. He heard feet running away
and then someone call back, "I just wanted to be sure!"

The next morning, Ekman sported a black eye.

"Bill, what the hell happened to you?" Alexander asked.

Ekman told him the story. It wasn't as if he could hide the evidence,
and he was sure that every soldier in the regiment had heard the story

by that morning and was waiting to see what the old man would do. Would he ignore it? Take it as a warning? Ease off on his approach to discipline?

All of those things looked like surrender to Ekman, and he wasn't about to surrender to anyone. He had been challenged in a crude sort of way, so he responded in kind. At a regimental formation, he challenged whoever had hit him to meet him behind the mess hall to settle things man-to-man.

Of course, no soldier stepped forward. Maybe it was the fact that striking an officer was a court-martial offense that could lead to serious jail time. Maybe it was the young colonel's demeanor, which clearly indicated that he was going to fight for command of the regiment.

After the formation, Mark Alexander said to his boss, "Bill, if you think any of those guys are going to admit to hitting you in the eye, you're dreaming."

But Ekman had made his point.

For all his reputation with the 505th, Ekman was anything but a by-the-book martinet. At West Point, his spirited antics frequently got him in trouble, and he became a "centurion," meaning that during his cadet career he walked in excess of one hundred hours of punishment tours in the barracks area.[3]

One night Ekman and his roommate, Ward Ryan (who would later become chief of staff of the U.S. Air Force), crossed the frozen Hudson to see Dick's Folly, a half-finished mansion visible on the hill just across from the academy. But their plans were not airtight, and their escape route was torn up by an ice-breaking ship working to keep the channel open. Ekman and his friend, both wearing dress uniforms, ran all the way to the Bear Mountain Bridge, which crossed the river miles south of West Point. Once on the west shore, they hitched a ride with an early morning delivery truck. The driver, once he heard their amazing story, brought them all the way to the academy gate. They ran another mile to the cadet area and arrived, sweat-soaked and sleep deprived—but on time—just as the rest of the corps of cadets formed up for breakfast and accountability formation.

Although he left those kinds of antics behind when he became a senior officer, Ekman was still unconventional and creative when it came to taking care of his men.

As the Christmas season approached in 1943, the 508th Parachute Infantry Regiment, with Ekman as the executive officer, was wrapping up its stateside training before deploying to the European theater for combat. Even the most naive trooper knew that for many in their ranks, this would be the last Christmas at home for a long time, and for some, the last Christmas they would ever see. The regimental leadership made every effort to get the maximum number of men on leave to enjoy the holiday with family and friends, or at least in some setting more hospitable than an Army post.

But among the men who wanted to travel home, only three hundred or so had saved enough money to travel. When Ekman saw the paperwork on the numbers of men who were going and the number staying behind, he started talking to the regiment's noncoms. Most of those stranded, he learned, had places to go and wanted to go, but were simply short of cash for train fare.

Ekman went to the train station and talked to the station manager, pleading the case for his soldiers. The manager wasn't without compassion, but he did have a business to run, so he struck a deal with the young lieutenant colonel. The manager agreed to issue tickets to the men, who would pay him on the first payday after the holiday, if Ekman signed a note taking responsibility for any unpaid fares. When the two men figured out the numbers, the amount was a staggering twelve thousand dollars. Ekman signed the note, the men shook hands, and he went back to spread the news about the deal. He did not publicize his own involvement or risk, because he had decided that he was not going to tell his wife, Iris, what he had done. Instead, he was going to trust that the men would do the right thing.

After the holiday pass was over, Ekman nervously watched the reports come in from the companies and battalions about who had not made it back. The first head count revealed that twenty-three troops were missing, but some of these had difficulty traveling because of winter weather in various parts of the country. As payday approached, with its deadline for paying the station manager, ten men were still missing, and they looked like AWOL cases. Ekman had to come up with eight hundred dollars—two and a half months' salary—to cover his debt. He had given his word, and there was no doubt he would do it. He also had to tell his wife.

But the regiment's noncoms had been keeping a close eye on things, and they knew the colonel had put himself at risk for the soldiers. The next morning, when Ekman came to work, there was a paper bag in his desk, and inside was twelve hundred dollars in cash. Ekman paid the station manager and used the remaining money to host a beer bash for the troops.

Throughout his time in Britain, Gavin kept up a practice he'd started with his deployment from the States in April of 1943, writing frequently to his young daughter, Barbara. The letters were also for his wife, Peggy, and so he included things that might be beyond a nine-year-old's comprehension. But he also knew that Barbara would most likely read the letters someday as an adult.[4]

On Christmas Eve 1943, Gavin received a package from Barbara, with some candy he'd asked for. On Christmas Day, with the division still in Northern Ireland, Gavin's aide arrived in London and delivered four letters from Barbara, which made the thirty-seven-year-old father feel more connected to, and no doubt more homesick for, his family. He wrote her later that he had enjoyed Christmas dinner with a "very nice" British family, who, in spite of food rationing, went out of their way to serve a traditional dinner. There was even a plum pudding, carried into the room aflame.

In several letters Gavin told Barbara how British civilians were caught up in the war effort, not just in an involuntary way brought about by the rationing and shortages, but in a willful way.

"These British people are doing a wonderful job of regulating their lives and way of doing things towards winning the war. Everyone is doing something and regardless of their station in life everyone pitches in."[5]

On January 6, 1944, he wrote, "Today is an unusually nice day here with the traditional fog conspicuous by its absence. Although most Americans dislike England because of the fog, or no hot dogs, or no coca cola or something like that all of the boys coming up with me [from Italy and Sicily] think that it is wonderful. Even the cold and fog is much more like America than anything in the Mediterranean area. There are movies also, and shows if one can get the time or opportunity. Everyone here, all of the civilians here I mean, are doing their bit to help win the war. Compared to what I remember of the States it is very marked here. If people through their own efforts are ever worthy or deserving of victory these people certainly are."

Gavin's letters praised the British, whom he admired, and by comparison found fault with what was going on among American workers at home. He was particularly offended by news of strikes at defense plants that held up production while his soldiers waited for the equipment they needed to take into battle.

"The best thing the people in the states can do to save the lives of the boys over here or on any other front is not to worry but to work and save. Stop the strikes and give the youngsters the things they need to finish the job in a hurry and get home. Every strike and delay in production means more lives lost and more days of fighting. . . . Such things as the strike I read of yesterday when workers on invasion barges struck for more wages because they were given spray guns instead of paint brushes [thus reducing manpower needs] are pretty hard for soldiers to understand."[6]

Gavin's workdays got longer after Eisenhower's January arrival in England and the vast expansion of the plan for Overlord. Following American custom, Gavin was usually at work by seven-thirty or eight in the morning. His British counterparts wouldn't appear until nine-thirty or so but would remain at work until seven or eight in the evening. Gavin usually wound up staying from the beginning of the American workday until the end of the British workday, which left him little time for recreation or even exercise. He was able, from time to time, to go for a run, joking in his letters that he might have to chase, or he might get chased by, some "fleet-of-foot kraut."

He also filled his letters with references to Barbara's schoolwork and vacations, although the slow delivery of mail made it difficult to keep up with things that were happening in her life. When he heard about her experience in camp or her report card, it was usually long after the fact. As the gray winter wore on and he worked ever longer hours, he sometimes let weightier concerns slip into his writing, details about life insurance policies and bank accounts. Inevitably, he followed the pragmatic advice with comments about why Barbara shouldn't worry, how he had plenty of good "bounces" in him to get him through the upcoming jumps.

He was careful never to be maudlin, but he did want her to know he was thinking of her. "This being Feb. 14th it is fitting and proper that you, the young lady of my esteem should be inquiried on the possibility of being my valentine," he wrote. Gavin sent Barbara numerous gifts, sometimes in the mail, sometimes in the care of other officers (including Ridgway) who traveled back to the States on official business. Gavin found her stamps from throughout the British Empire, as well as coins and military insignia from Allied nations. The combat general even went shopping for a kilt for his daughter, an enterprise that included getting her sizes and gathering the right number of clothing coupons.

As the training intensified during the wet spring, as the young troopers sharpened their boot knives and bayonets and Gavin hustled to ensure that every unit in the division was as ready as he could make it, he thought more about his daughter.

April 24

As I believe I have told you on past occasions, never worry about my well being. My jumps are somewhere beyond the fifty mark now and I am sure that I have a lot of bounces left in me. My past experiences have convinced me . . . of the great virtue of digging a

deep hole fast. It will be a fleet-of-foot kraut that will catch
pappy. . . . This all sounds silly and I suppose it is. Actually I don't
know what to say. As I recall, I didn't seem to be exactly inarticulate
before Sicily or Italy. Maybe I didn't know any better then. Anyway
it will be a real clambake and I wouldn't miss it for anything.

Detailed planning for the landing and subsequent fighting went on at a
rapid pace all through the spring of 1944. While the rifle companies
practiced maneuvering through the foggy hills and fields around Leicester in the English Midlands, officers and noncoms on the various staffs
pored over the maps and the aerial photos that came in every day.

In February the missions of the 82nd's parachute regiments were
handed out. The division was to land in three drop zones west of the
city of St. Sauveur le Vicomte, then fan out from there to seize the
town, block German reinforcements from moving north onto the Cotentin Peninsula, and block enemy counterattacks headed toward the
rear of Utah Beach.

Gavin, who would command the three parachute regiments, was especially interested in the very challenging mission given the untested
508th PIR, which was to land on a dominant piece of terrain marked on
Allied maps as Hill 110. The development of the plan for Hill 110
shows the typical attention to detail and the harsh calculus of determining "acceptable" casualties.

Hill 110 is so named because it rises to a height of 110 meters. It is a
clear height with no woods, located about five kilometers west of
Sauveur le Vicomte. On a clear day, the hill provided a view all the way
to the east and the Channel, and to the much closer Atlantic on most
days. The airborne troops were to seize the hill and clear it of defenders.
German artillery spotters left unmolested on such a vantage point
would play havoc with American movement in the area.

The hill's slopes were too steep for gliders, but there were no large
trees or boulders that would hinder a parachute landing. Colonel Roy
Lindquist, commander of the 508th PIR, had some reservations about

landing there, but Gavin pointed out the hill was at least as good as the drop zones in Sicily and Italy. Those operations had suffered high numbers of injuries—broken legs, arms, and backs—but the cost was considered "acceptable."

As Gavin's and Lindquist's staffs studied the photos that came in from aerial reconnaissance over a period of a few weeks, they noticed changes taking place. First, they saw the telltale chevron emplacements, which the Germans dug to protect their vehicles from Allied bombing. The large number of these indicated that a headquarters of some size had been located in the area. Then, about three weeks before D-Day, there appeared on the slopes large numbers of black dots, in regular, geometric patterns. Every day the black specks spread over the hill, until soon the whole drop zone was covered with them. American intelligence officers figured they were holes, since they cast no shadows in the early morning photos, as objects that stick out above the ground would.

Gavin and his planners knew about *Rommelspargel*, or "Rommel's asparagus," which was being used throughout Normandy. These were poles, six to twelve inches in diameter, which were sunk in holes in the ground, creating fields sown with tightly packed fence posts. In some places, the Americans knew, the Germans had strung wire connecting the tops of the poles and had even placed land mines or artillery shells on a number of them.

The American planning staff watched the holes and then watched them fill with poles. They couldn't determine, from the photos, if the wire and mines were in place. More alarming was the fact that the Germans had apparently figured out that Hill 110 was a likely drop zone, as it had clearly attracted the attention of the German engineers and construction battalions charged with building up the Atlantic Wall.

Now, it appeared, the Germans would be waiting for them, and the fight for Hill 110 would be costly. More frightening was the prospect that the enemy had somehow been tipped off to the Allied plan—why else this intense concentration on the exact American drop zone? Clearly, such a development would have disastrous results all along the coast.

As the planning staffs focused on Hill 110, they made some difficult decisions. The *Rommelspargel* were designed to stop gliders. Certainly, paratroopers would be seriously injured and even killed jumping into a field of thick fence posts, but Gavin and his subordinate commanders had to do the grim math: could they jump and still have enough men to complete the mission? Gavin reasoned that if they didn't jump onto the hill, they would have to take it by assault, which would delay the overall plan and might prove even more costly. So as German engineers and civilian construction workers kept up their preparations, the mission of the 508th PIR remained the same.

From the Pas de Calais to Brittany, German commanders were working to shore up their defenses. Rommel had stepped up the pressure on local commanders, demanding more mines, more *Rommelspargel*, more concrete emplacements. The Field Marshal maintained a brutal pace of inspection visits all through the spring. He left his headquarters by 0600 nearly every day, driving from one site to another across the stretch of France that faced England. In this, he was a mirror of his counterpart, Dwight Eisenhower, who also spent long days driving from one training event to another, inspecting troops and meeting with commanders. But Rommel traveled in order to intimidate lazy local commanders into greater efforts in building defenses. He left his headquarters each morning determined to stir things up along the Atlantic Wall, and he succeeded.

Eisenhower, on the other hand, had standing orders that no troops were to be kept standing around waiting for him to arrive. They were to keep training, use every available hour to hone their skills. Like Rommel, Eisenhower also chewed out subordinates, but only those unfortunate staff officers who couldn't manage the schedule well enough, who interfered with the soldiers' training to put on a show for the Supreme Commander.

But no commander can be everywhere at once, and German efforts along the Atlantic Wall varied from place to place. The American airborne planners spent untold hours trying to divine some message in why certain fields were planted with *Rommelspargel* and others were passed over. Later they learned from interviews with captured German commanders and civilians that the numbers of *Rommelspargel* planted depended on whether or not the local commander was dedicated or lazy.[7]

Though the efforts to plant obstacles were impressive (one of Rommel's reports noted a single division that had managed to emplace three hundred thousand stakes), it was not the only counterparatrooper measure the Germans took. In April the German high command in the west published a soldier's handbook titled *What Every Soldier Should Know About Airborne Troops*.[8] Illustrated in color, it was intended to familiarize German defenders with the men, units, and equipment they could expect to face in their battles behind the lines. The 243rd Division, which would tangle with the 82nd throughout its fighting in Normandy, published additional memos about airborne obstacles and about the most effective tactics for fighting paratroopers. The 243rd was diligent, establishing static sentinel posts and lookouts for early warning, running regular patrols to keep an eye on the countryside. They held alerts and exercises to practice their response to an airborne invasion.

In mid-May the German high command took another step to protect the base of the Cotentin. The 91st Infantry (also called the 91st Air Landing Division, because it was configured to fight paratroopers) was moved to the vicinity of St. Sauveur le Vicomte. This put an entire German division right on the drop zones of the 82nd Airborne Division; the complex plans, the fruit of months of work, had to be redrawn. On May 26, D – eleven, the 82nd Airborne got new orders, moving the division's drop zones farther east, toward the Merderet River.

Down at division level and below, preparations were frantic. Seen from Eisenhower's headquarters, the bigger plan had taken on definite dimensions by the middle of May. The scale of the undertaking, from the marshaling of forces in the United Kingdom to the planned assault, was fantastic.

During the buildup to D-Day, 7 million tons of supplies were delivered by sea from the United States to the United Kingdom, including 448,000 tons of ammunition. Civilian contractors and military engineers put in 400 million man-hours to construct 126 airfields for the

U.S. Army Air Corps, 270 miles of railroads, 43 million square feet of hardstand storage space, and 19 million square feet of covered storage space.

By D-Day Allied medical commands had gathered eight thousand doctors and had amassed six hundred thousand doses of the new drug penicillin, one hundred thousand pounds of sulfa, and eight hundred thousand pints of plasma. Many of these resources would be afloat just offshore from the invasion beaches on fifteen hospital ships.

During the period from April 1 to June 5, Allied air forces flew fourteen thousand sorties in their successful bid for complete air supremacy over the landing area. For this effort—which gave a tremendous boost to Allied chances of success—some twelve thousand airmen were killed or captured.

Operation Overlord finally involved nearly 2 million Allied soldiers, sailors, airmen, and civilians. At the point of the spear were more than 156,000 men who would go ashore in the first twenty-four hours. (There were thirty-nine U.S. combat divisions scattered throughout the United Kingdom and earmarked for the follow-up campaigns.)

Most of the combat power would move by sea, and the Allies had amassed an armada of nearly seven thousand vessels that included twelve hundred warships and fifteen hospital ships to treat the wounded. This vast fleet required 195,000 naval personnel.[9]

The first combat formations in France would land by glider and parachute and included most of the U.S. 82nd and 101st Airborne Divisions and the British 6th Airborne Division. The three combined divisions would number more than 23,000 thousand men. Following them by just a few hours would be the 75,000 British and Canadian troops of the British 3rd Division (Sword Beach), the Canadian 3rd Division (Juno Beach), and the British 50th Division (Gold Beach). Some 54,400 American GIs would come ashore on D-Day, comprising the U.S. 1st Division plus a regiment of the 29th Division (Omaha Beach) and the U.S. 4th Division (Utah Beach).

There had never been an amphibious invasion like this one. (And thanks to the development of nuclear weapons, which made large concentrations of men and equipment too dangerous, there will never be another.) Failure was utterly unthinkable yet entirely possible.

The 82nd Airborne Division would send 11,770 men into combat in Normandy. For the invasion, the division was divided into two main groups, Force A, under the command of Brigadier General Jim Gavin and Force B, under the command of Major General Matt Ridgway.

Force A contained the main parachute elements of the division: the 505th, 507th, and 508th Parachute Infantry Regiments, the combat engineers of B Company, 307th Airborne Engineers, some command and signal elements of division headquarters, signal and artillery units, and the U.S. Navy Shore Fire Control Party—Navy men who jumped in and were ready to call for naval gunfire. (During the fighting in Sicily, accurate naval gunfire had saved the paratroopers on several occasions by smashing German armor formations.)

The glider infantry constituted the bulk of Force B, under Division Commander Matt Ridgway. Fifty-two gliders, carrying all-important artillery and heavy machine guns, were to land in darkness just two hours behind the paratroopers. More of the division's firepower came in with Force B, including the 319th Glider Field Artillery (75 mm pack howitzers) and 320th Glider Field Artillery (105 mm snub-nosed howitzers), and the 80th Airborne Antiaircraft Battalion, which was armed with the versatile, British-made 57 mm antitank gun. (The British gun had a narrower wheel base than the American-made antitank gun, and so was easier to load into a glider.)[10] The rest of the division would come in beginning the morning of D+1. Three battalions of the 325th Glider Infantry Regiment, which would constitute the division reserve, were scheduled to come in beginning at 0700 on June 7.

Gavin's Force A was, in the division's official mission statement, to land "astride the MERDERET River," which, under normal springtime conditions, would not present a problem to vigorous soldiers used to moving rapidly on their own power. The drop zones of the three parachute regiments formed a triangle. The veteran 505th PIR was to land farthest east, on a drop zone centered just a thousand yards north and west of Ste. Mère Eglise, which was the D-Day objective. The 505th was also to establish a blocking position along the N13 highway at the tiny village of Neuville au Plain, about fifteen hundred yards north of Ste. Mère Eglise, and seize the eastern ends of the bridges at La Fière and Chef du Pont.

The 507th PIR, going into combat for the first time, would land on the most northern point of the triangle, west of the Merderet and north of the village of Amfreville, secure the local high ground, and seize the western end of the bridge of La Fière.

The 508th PIR, landing in the lower left of the triangle, was centered near the junction of the Douve and Merderet rivers. From there they would block enemy advances toward Ste. Mère Eglise (and beyond that, Utah Beach), and seize the western end of the Chef du Pont causeway and bridge.

The men of the 325th Glider Infantry Regiment, also veterans of the fighting in Italy, would come in on D+1 in the area just south of Ste. Mère Eglise and would constitute the division reserve for the anticipated move to cut the Cotentin Peninsula.

Ridgway's plan was complex, and it relied on the cooperation of many different commands and services, from the transport pilots who would haul his men to the battlefield to the fleet that would deliver the division support elements. Ridgway and Gavin had doubts about a few of the regimental and battalion commanders, but they had tremendous confidence in the vast majority of company-grade officers and noncoms. These men, down near the end of the chain of command, worked hard to train the individual soldiers in the skills they'd need to prevail against an experienced and determined enemy.

COUNTDOWN

Arthur "Dutch" Shultz, a twenty-one-year-old private from Detroit, had worked out a pretty good deal in England. He had volunteered for the boxing team as soon as he was assigned to C Company, 505th PIR, because he had learned, early in his enlistment and service in the antiaircraft artillery, that sports teams, boxing in particular, were a great way to avoid the monotonous training that most soldiers had to endure.

Schultz went into Leicester every afternoon to train, and he and his fellow boxers were delighted to discover that the gymnasium set aside for their use shared a building with a pub. In the evening, after their training, the young troopers simply went downstairs and drank beer until it was time to return to base. Despite this unorthodox approach to conditioning, Schultz managed to win the welterweight championship of the 505th PIR. Besides the accolades that distinction brought him, it all but guaranteed that he'd keep his spot on the team and his access to the warm beer served in Leicester, far from the meddling of the noncoms or the tedious combat training.

When his mother signed the papers allowing Schultz, then just seventeen, to enlist, she wanted him to learn a skill that would sustain him later. Things weren't working out quite the way his mother might have wanted, but Schultz was still pretty happy with his assignment in the 82nd Airborne Division.

Schultz had graduated from a Catholic high school in the spring of 1941, and by the end of the year, the United States was at war. Schultz had already decided that he would enlist in the Marine Corps, because his father had been a Marine in World War I. But Schultz's mother, who had served as an Army nurse during the Great War, had other ideas. She told her oldest son that he'd be better off in the Army, because he'd have a better chance to learn a trade.

Schultz was underage, and so needed his mother's signature to enlist, but he was totally opposed to joining the Army. He asked if he could join the Navy, but his mother was against that plan as well. The newspapers had been filled for several years with stories of lost battles at sea, and Mrs. Schultz felt that the enemy simply "sunk too many ships out there."

Finally, mother and son compromised on the U.S. Coast Guard, and Schultz went down to the recruiting station in Detroit. After taking his physical and a battery of tests, he was told to go home for a week, as the in-processing team was giving priority to those who had been drafted.

Schultz returned to his neighborhood and told all of his friends that he had enlisted, thus becoming the first member of his high school class to join the service. His friends took him out to celebrate that Saturday and generously picked up the bill. The following Monday, Schultz reported to the recruiting station again and again was told to come back in a week. His buddies repeated the Saturday night ritual, but to Schultz's disappointment, on his third trip to the station he was told there was a backlog of selective service people and that he should come back again in another week. By this time Schultz's friends were becoming suspicious and wondered if he had actually joined the service at all.

This third delay was the last. Schultz went to his mother and said, "OK, I'll join the Army."

Mrs. Schultz, not content with just getting her way, accompanied her son to the Army recruiter, where she talked to the sergeant and got assurances that Arthur would be sent into the antiaircraft artillery, which she thought would be relatively safe. In just two days he was on his way to basic training and from there to the antiaircraft course at Fort Bliss, on the hot Texas panhandle. His orders following school sent him to Norfolk, Virginia, where an Army unit was assigned to protect the vast Navy base in the unlikely event of a transatlantic air raid.

Schultz dealt with the boredom by volunteering for the boxing team. He had done some fighting back in Detroit at the CYO, the Catholic Youth Organization, and had even fought in a Golden Gloves competition. But even though boxing got him out of some of the most boring duty, Schultz soon grew restive babysitting a Navy base. It didn't help that when his younger brother wanted to enlist in the Marines, he had persuaded Dutch's father to sign the paperwork. The younger Schultz was already fighting in the Pacific while Dutch sat around with a bunch of sailors in tranquil Virginia.

When airborne recruiters visited the base, asking for volunteers for the paratroops, Schultz raised his hand and was soon on his way to Fort Benning, Georgia. In December of 1943 Schultz boarded a ship somewhere in the Chesapeake, bound for the European Theater of Operations. Crossing the North Atlantic in winter was a miserable experience on a small ship, and Schultz spent his time thinking he would die either from seasickness or from a U-boat attack. There were constant alarms, in which case the men would have to appear at their stations ready to abandon ship, but none of the ships in the convoy was sunk. Schultz's berth was far below the waterline, and every time the alarm went off he joined in the mad dash to get on deck with his life preserver. Hundreds of men struggled up the steep ladders as the ship rolled and pitched beneath them. Perhaps, he had reason to think, his mother had been right about the Navy.

Schultz's routine of boxing and beer drinking was interrupted one day when his company commander, Captain Anthony M. Stefanich, approached him. "Captain Stef," who was well liked by his men, had been telling them for weeks that it was a great privilege for the 82nd Airborne to spearhead the assault on Fortress Europe.

"Dutch, you know there's a possibility that you won't be able to make the jump," Stefanich said. "We're a little short of space."

Many of the companies were over strength in anticipation of heavy casualties in France. When the command doled out the limited space on the transport aircraft, there wasn't enough to go around. Some paratroopers would have to come across the beach with the division's logistics tail.

Schultz did not react to the news but simply looked at the officer. Stefanich thought he saw something in Schultz's eyes, and it made him stop in midsentence.

"Well, wait a minute," Stefanich said. "I'll see what I can do for you."

It was obvious that the captain thought Schultz was disappointed, and to some extent that was true. But Schultz honestly didn't know if the captain was doing him any favors by trying to get his name on the jump manifest. He had trained as a paratrooper and had expected, in spite of his relative lack of field training, to accompany his buddies. He supposed that would be better than coming in by boat, but it looked like the decision was out of his hands.

Four or five days later, Schultz ran into Captain Stefanich on the company street. The captain looked to be in a good mood.

"Dutch, we made it," he said. "We made it. You're going to be able to make the jump."

Schultz thanked the captain, as military courtesy required.

Like a lot of soldiers in the lead-up to the invasion, Schultz thought more and more about religion. In particular, the former altar boy wondered if he was being hypocritical to make deals with God and the Blessed Mother to keep him safe. He figured that if he did live he'd probably start sinning again, but that didn't stop him from going to Mass every day as the invasion approached.

Schultz also went to confession as often as possible. According to Roman Catholic doctrine, the absolution offered by a priest in confession put a soul in a state of grace. A man who died in this state—with his sins forgiven—went to heaven. A man who died with his sins unconfessed went to hell. It was a fairly straightforward proposition, but it required a degree of vigilance. One didn't want to spend too much time walking about with the black mark of sin, especially since the private soldiers like Schultz had no idea when they would be called to the airplanes.

On one occasion Schultz went to confession with a visiting British priest, and the young soldier duly confessed his sin of fornication, stressing that he was sorry for all six times. The priest chewed him out, Schultz thought, as well as any sergeant ever had.

At one Mass in the regimental area, Schultz saw Majors Frederick Kellam and James McGinity serving as altar boys for Father Matthew Connelly, one of the two chaplains assigned to the regiment. Father Connelly was a veteran of the Sicily and Italian campaigns, as was McGinity, who had been with the 505th from the beginning. All three officers seemed very old and experienced to young Private Schultz.

James McGinity was a handsome former wrestler from West Point's Class of 1940. He was twenty-nine years old, with a thick shock of dark hair and chiseled features. McGinity had been a company commander in Sicily and Italy, and had moved over to become the 1st Battalion's Executive Officer in the early spring. He gave off an air of quiet competence, and he had the experience and tactical sense to back it up.

Frederick Kellam was also a West Pointer, Class of 1936. Assigned to the division when it was in North Africa, he was disciplined for violating an off-limits zone and for being drunk and disorderly. By early 1944 his time in the doghouse was over, and he was given a chance to redeem himself when the talented commander of the 1st Battalion, Walter Winton, was injured on a practice jump. Ridgway used Winton's injury as an excuse to grab the young officer for duty in the division headquarters, where Winton was assigned to the operations section. Winton's injury and Ridgway's need for him at division headquarters created an opportunity for Kellam.

Kellam was a pleasant man, capable but untested. He could strike a balance, as the best commanders could, between being kind, understanding, and compassionate, while demanding great efforts from his men as they went through training that would determine the success of the invasion and their own chances of living to tell their grandchildren about it.

Like Ekman, Kellam, and the others who were not combat veterans, Schultz was keenly aware of his status. He did not wear the Combat Infantry Badge—a Kentucky Long Rifle on a blue rectangle, surrounded by a wreath—worn by those who had been in combat. He was also near the very bottom of the hierarchy, and certainly a long way down from Kellam and McGinity. So he was a bit surprised to see the two most senior officers in the battalion, men who had his life and the lives of hundreds of his comrades in their hands, kneeling as altar boys for the service. He found the sight comforting and was happy to know the officers felt themselves accountable to God.

There was no church, but the men were used to attending Mass wherever Father Connelly could set up: on the hood of a jeep, a folding table, in a mess tent. The congregants were in uniform; many of them were hard men who had seen hard things. They bowed their heads as the priest prayed and the servers gave the prescribed answers in Latin.

Many of the men in the crowd had developed the churchgoing habit as a result of their recent experience with sudden, violent death. Others had attended Mass regularly in civilian life. Some had been altar boys and could recite the prayers Kellam and McGinity said. Some of them, good Latin students, might even know the translations and would find comfort in the familiar supplications. The dead language made it feel like a secret conversation with God: a man could kneel in prayer, his eyes closed to all the martial trappings around him, and make his own fervent plea.

Judica mea Deus, et discerne causam meam de gente non sancta: ab homine iniquo et doloso erue me.

Judge me, O God, and distinguish my cause from the nation that is not holy; deliver me from the unjust and deceitful man.

Some among them must have thought of their counterparts across the Channel, Lutherans and the Catholics who wore a different uniform but prayed to the same God for deliverance. Many had seen the belt buckles on dead Germans, with the legend "Gott mit uns." God is with us.

Quare tristis es anima mea, et quare conturbas me?

Why art thou sad, O my soul, and why dost thou disquiet me?

Schultz worried about breaking the commandment against killing, and whether any amount of absolution could clean him of that mark. Around him were other men who had already killed and who had set aside their concerns. There were also men who had decided they would not survive.

Connelly, who had administered last rites to the dying, to the horribly wounded, prayed for the men kneeling before him.

Aufer a nobis, quaesumus Domine, iniquitates nostras: ut ad Sancta Sanctorum puris mereamur mentibus introite. Per Christum Domi-inum nostrum. Amen.

Take away from us our iniquities; we beseech Thee, O Lord, that, being made pure in heart we may be worthy to enter the Holy of Holies. Through Christ our Lord. Amen.

And then the soldiers, led by their altar boy commanders, began the plea for forgiveness.

Confiteor Deo omnipotenti . . . . Quia peccavi nimis cogitatione, verbo, et opera: mea culpa, mea culpa, mea maxima culpa.

I confess to Almighty God . . . that I have sinned exceedingly in thought, word, and deed: through my fault, through my fault, through my most grievous fault.

On May 30, 1944, the 82nd Airborne Division began its move from the training areas around Leicester to holding areas at the departure airfields. For the parachute regiments, these were strung in a north-south line in the green countryside east of Leicester. The place-names were musical: Fulbeck, Barkston Heath, Folkingham, Saltby, Cottesmore, and Span-hoe. Farther to the south, the glidermen moved to other fields west of London: Membury, Welford, Ramsbury, Greenham Common, Reading.

The men got off the buses and trucks in what looked like an over-sized stockade, with barbed wire all around and armed guards walking outside the perimeter. Once they were isolated, they would learn more details of the invasion. They were locked in to keep the secrets from getting out. Some of them suspected that the fence was also there to ensure that every man in the unit would be present for duty when it came time to suit up for combat.

The companies had been beefed up since the Sicilian campaign nearly a year before. Back then they'd gone into the fight with two rifle squads and one weapons squad per platoon, for a total of 119 officers and men in each rifle company. For the Normandy invasion, a third squad had been added to each platoon, bringing the rifle company strength to 158 men. Many of the rifle platoons had two lieutenants. Matt Ridgway expected his officers to lead from the front, which meant a high rate of casualties among leaders. Many young officers went into battle with their own replacements right beside them.

The camp, though temporary, was well equipped, and the men slept in pyramidal tents or on cots jammed into empty hangars. The cooks dished up plenty of hot chow from the mess tents, and the Special Services troops managed to find fairly new first-run movies to show the men in the evenings. They settled into an easy routine, resting, playing cards, reading, writing letters home. Some men studied the little paperback books of French phrases. They all took their place in line to exchange whatever English money they had for French francs, called "invasion currency." They talked over their missions, memorized details of the objective area, cleaned and oiled their weapons. Among the many items of issue were cigarettes, two cartons per man. Because they were cut off from the civilians outside the gate, the men couldn't trade their new wealth, and even the most dedicated smoker could pack only so many cigarettes in his kit. Valuable cartons were simply dumped in piles in the tents and hangars, and more than one GI thought about the rear area troops and British civilians who would clean up the base, who would turn the windfall into cash as other men went into battle.

While some of the men spent the time relaxing, there was also a sense of urgency. Officers hurried to and from meetings, and the intelligence people were out of sight in their war rooms, where the maps and terrain models were set up.

Berge Avadanian, who had memorized the lines to *Casablanca* on the trip from Italy, was one of those locked down as the invasion approached. Avadanian, an intelligence sergeant in the 505th PIR, had rebuilt the war rooms in a frenzy of activity after the division's drop zones were changed in late May. Because Avadanian and his colleagues knew the terrain models showed the countryside in Normandy—and because this was the critical piece of information that every German intelligence officer wanted to know—anyone with this knowledge was kept locked away. Avadanian spent his days in one tent, updating the models and maps according to the latest intelligence from aerial photos. Even the chaplains had an armed guard to keep an eye on them when they traveled among the division's separate airfields.

Major Jack Norton, the operations officer of the 505th PIR, was concerned about the resistance they expected to meet in France, which would be worse than anything they'd yet faced. A veteran of two campaigns, Norton was beyond the first-time jitters he'd experienced in Sicily. He knew that a certain amount of fear was healthy and perfectly normal; the only thing he worried about was whether he had done all he could to help prepare the regiment.

When Norton and the other staff officers had a moment to catch their breath, when they stepped back to look at the array of enemy forces depicted on the battle maps, they could only shake their heads in amazement at what they were about to undertake. Norton was not by nature a worrier, even though back in Sicily he'd come close to getting machine-gunned in his first hour on the ground (the bullets clipped his shoulder strap and helmet). He was pragmatic and philosophical about the prospect of death, no more or less worried than any of the other veterans. But when he saw the aerial photos of the enemy defenses and the fields of "Rommel's asparagus," when he looked at the plots of known enemy units and concentrations of armor, he couldn't help but marvel at the sheer audacity of what they were attempting. This was going to be the big one, Norton thought, and a lot of them would not be coming back to England.

Although he had no way of knowing it, Norton's gloomy estimate matched that of Eisenhower's chief for air operations, Sir Trafford Leigh-Mallory. On May 30, Leigh-Mallory, still plagued by visions of slaughtered airborne troops, visited Ike at Portsmouth to make a last, personal appeal for cancellation of the American drop. He thought that the combination of poor landing areas, especially for the gliders, and stiff German resistance would mean casualties of 50 percent among the paratroopers and 70 percent among the glider troops. He was heartsick, Eisenhower would later write, over the impending "futile slaughter" of two fine divisions.[1]

If he was right—and he was the man who got paid to know these things and to render advice—not only would Eisenhower send thousands of American boys to their deaths, but the devastation of those units would mean that the Utah Beach plan, which relied on the paratroopers securing the beach exits, would be in jeopardy. If Utah unraveled, the Allied right flank might falter, putting all of Overlord at risk.

Eisenhower knew that Leigh-Mallory was doing his duty. To protect his subordinate, Ike asked the British general to put his protest in writing, so that, if the dire predictions came true, blame would rest squarely on Eisenhower. Then Ike went off by himself to consider the possibilities. It was his decision, and, as he said later, "professional advice and counsel could do no more."[2]

"It would be difficult to conceive of a more soul-racking problem," Ike later wrote. "If my technical expert was correct, then the planned operation was worse than stubborn folly, because even at the enormous cost predicted we could not gain the principal object of the drop. Moreover, if he was right, it appeared that the attack on Utah Beach was probably hopeless, and this meant that the whole operation suddenly acquired a degree of risk, even foolhardiness, that presaged a gigantic failure, possibly even Allied defeat in Europe."

It was, in part, the domino-like connection of the plan's parts that finally convinced Ike to go forward with the assault. If he canceled the drop, he would have to either cancel the assault on Utah or put the assault force ashore in a place where they could easily be contained by the Germans. If he canceled Utah, the whole plan fell apart. Ike and his principal advisers, as well as Omar Bradley, the commander of U.S. ground forces, had agreed that Utah was essential to the invasion.

Finally, Ike thought, Leigh-Mallory's estimate was just that, an estimate. Eisenhower put his confidence in the airborne commanders and left the plan alone. Ike called Leigh-Mallory with his decision. (Later when it became clear that the airborne drop was a success, Leigh-Mallory called Ike to tell the Supreme Commander how happy he was that he had been wrong, and to apologize for adding to Ike's burden in those last, crushing hours before the assault.)

Ken Russell, a teenage rifleman in F Company of the 505th PIR, was a little amazed to find himself part of this huge drama. Russell had been preparing for this night for a little more than a year, since reporting for basic training early in 1943. The Tennessee farm boy lied about his age when he showed up at the recruiting depot, because he didn't want to be left behind when his buddies went off to war. He was strongly built, with a large head and broad shoulders, which made him look a bit older than he was. He grew up picking cotton just a mile or so north of the Georgia state line, and he used to joke with his new Army buddies that he had picked so much cotton as a child that he wouldn't even buy aspirin because he couldn't stand to pull the little cotton ball out of the bottle.

Initially assigned to the 35th Division, he volunteered for the paratroops because they had more spirit than any other unit he had seen. He joined the 82nd as a replacement in Northern Ireland, and if everything about Ireland seemed strange to the boy from rural Tennessee, he did find that the Irishmen liked to fight just as much as the paratroopers.

They could hold their own, too. The strapping Russell enjoyed mixing it up a bit, though his tendency to be in the wrong place at the wrong time meant that he lost his Private First Class stripes (and the pay raise that went with them) several times. The promotion and demotion were so regular that he never bothered sewing the stripes on his uniform.

Like every one of the nearly 2 million military people in the United Kingdom, Russell could feel the tension building as winter gave way to spring and the expected invasion grew closer. Only a handful of people on the overcrowded island knew the date, but everyone expected summer would be campaign season on the continent.

In May Russell developed a fever after an inoculation and had to be hospitalized. He listened as the doctors and the hospital staff gossiped and speculated about the invasion, and talked about their own training and the vast buildup of medical supplies. Russell became sick with worry that he might, after all, miss the big day. He wasn't getting better fast enough, and he thought it useless to ask his attending physician for a discharge, as others had done the same thing and been turned down. He would have to make it back to his buddies on his own.

Russell had befriended the soldier who was in charge of patients' personal belongings and uniforms they had to surrender when they checked in. Russell asked for his kit, offering no explanation, and the hospital orderly, who had seen a parade of combat soldiers trying to get out of the hospital, turned over the equipment.

Russell had a plan to get back to his outfit. Every day he saw visitors from the various units. It wasn't hard to pick out the paratroopers, with their distinctive uniforms, even from a distance. When there was a good collection of jeeps in the little parking area one day, Russell ditched his hospital gown, put on his uniform, and walked outside, where he found a jeep with 505 markings and a paratrooper waiting at the wheel. He climbed in the back of the jeep and said, "It's about time for us to go, isn't it?"

The driver didn't ask who he was, but merely said, "We have to wait for one more guy."

"OK," Russell said. "I'll just sit back here and wait, then."

If the other troopers who came out were suspicious about their new passenger, they didn't let on; they merely gave him a ride back to Quorn, where the regiment was billeted.

Russell noticed the uproar immediately; the entire regiment seemed to be moving at once, dragging weapons and equipment. Russell hustled over to F Company, where he ran into First Sergeant "Hoss" Pizarro and said, "I'm here, and I'm ready to go."

"Glad to see you," the top kick said. "Go into the tent and pack your stuff, drop it off at the regimental headquarters area."

Russell trotted off and found the rest of the men separating their combat gear from the uniforms they would leave behind in storage. They were moving out, and Russell realized that had he waited even a few hours, he would have been left behind. The young private joined in, happy to be moving, happy to be among his buddies. When he climbed up the tailgate of the truck that would take them to the departure airfield at Cottesmore, he felt exhilaration mixed with fear. No matter what happened, at least he would never have to say that he spent the day of the big invasion listening to BBC radio in his hospital robe.

Like the rest of the troopers in his plane load, in his company, and even on the airfields all around central England, Russell spent June 5 in a state of suspension as wind and rain swept the countryside. After preparing for months, they had been called back at the last moment due to the terrible weather. They had to somehow get some rest and be ready to go as soon as the call came. Almost to a man they suspected that the delay would last just twenty-four hours. For some of the men, those hours would be excruciatingly long. They played endless games of cards, emboldened in their gambling by the same sense of drama that infused everything. They wrote letters, trying to sound upbeat. They obsessively sharpened the knives they counted on for a quick escape from their parachute harness if things went badly. (At the time, the U.S. parachutes did not have a quick-release mechanism.)

For Ken Russell, the seventeen-year-old trooper, June 5 was significant for another reason. Back home, his high school class was set to graduate that evening.

Dutch Schultz spent much of June 5 sharpening his big fighting knife, which had a wicked set of brass knuckles for a handle. Schultz—who would find that his interest in religion spiked before all his battles—also took advantage of the presence of a Catholic priest who visited the departure airfields to hear confessions and say Mass. During the day he saw a trooper named Gerry Colombi, who had come in with him as a replacement, and who had borrowed twenty dollars during a dice game back at Quorn. Colombi didn't have the money, and Schultz said, "Well, what have you got as collateral? You might get killed over there."

Colombi took off his wristwatch and handed it over. Schultz looked at the back and read the engraving; the watch was a high school graduation present from Colombi's parents. Later, when they were close to boarding the aircraft, Schultz saw Colombi again and returned the watch.

"Here's your watch back, Gerry," he said. "You owe me some money and don't you forget to pay me."[3]

Some of the men found relief in the delay, as if they had gotten all of their worrying out of the way and now only had to wait. These soldiers actually felt a great release of tension in that extra twenty-four hours.

Ken Russell found comfort in the presence of men he knew, whose capabilities he respected, whom he had seen perform, at least in field exercises. His jumpmaster was Lieutenant Harold O. Cadish, a young officer from Massachusetts who, like Russell, was going into combat for the first time. The number two man, jumping right behind Cadish, was Cliff Maughn, who already had two combat jumps, as did his squadmate John Steele. Russell thought both of these men, then in their late twenties, were too old to be paratroopers, but they did their share of the work, so Russell kept his opinions to himself.

Among the other privates were Ladislaw Tlapa and H. T. Bryant, a close friend of Russell's from Tyler, Texas, and Charles Blankenship from Swannanoa, North Carolina, a handsome veteran of two combat jumps. Sergeant John Ray, Russell's squad leader, was the noncom in the stick (as the planeload of men was called), the man who got things organized and kept the privates in line. Ray was a Louisiana native, a tall, thin man with a quiet competence they found reassuring. Ray was married, and his wife, Paula, waited for him back home. The couple had no children but expected to have a family when Ray returned from the war.

For Otis Sampson, the mortar platoon sergeant in Easy Company of the 505th, Normandy would be his third combat jump, his third campaign, and by far the biggest battle he had ever been in.

Sampson was one of the most experienced soldiers in the company. He had first served in the Army in the early 1930s, in a horse cavalry unit stationed at Fort Ethan Allen, Vermont. He left the service looking for adventure and had worked his way across much of the West, logging, tending horses, even panning for gold along the Snake River in Idaho. Already thirty years old when he reenlisted after Pearl Harbor, he had the physical constitution of a much younger man. He got a perfect score on the physical fitness test for airborne school, and when the regiment moved to Fort Benning, Sampson—who had been a champion during his first enlistment—went back to the boxing ring. The years of experience as a lumberjack—felling trees with an ax and cutting massive logs with a two-man saw—gave him a devastating punch. He won all his fights, and although he fought at 128 pounds and stood only five foot six, he enjoyed full cooperation and cheerful obedience from his young soldiers, who were too smart to mouth off to Sergeant Sampson.

Sampson knew from experience that, in the days and weeks leading up to the jump, his world would get smaller and smaller, drawing around him like a net. He would concentrate all of his efforts, all of his thoughts, on the mission, shutting out everything else.

The first steps came just before the regiment left the Leicester area, when Sampson paid a last visit to his girlfriend. They spent a quiet day in the spring countryside and in her home, and although the young non-com didn't mention what was about to happen, the invasion was on everyone's mind.

He left her, at last, to ride his bicycle back to the base in the darkness, wondering if it would be the last time he'd see her, the last time he saw these paths he'd come to love. He was subdued, and although he wasn't any more worried about the outcome than in his previous two campaigns, the greater responsibilities he bore as platoon sergeant weighed heavily on him.

On the eve of the invasion, Easy Company was billeted at an airfield in Castlemore. Now Sampson's circle included only the men in his company and the mortar platoon. They spent their time packing and repacking the bundles that held their heavy weapons: mortars, machine guns, Browning Automatic Rifles (BARs). Medical supplies and mines were wrapped in parabundles to be dropped from beneath the aircraft or kicked out the door. Because the parabundles had a way of getting scattered on the drops—and since everything depended on getting men and equipment assembled quickly—the troopers tied the bundles in daisy chains using stout ropes.

With no passes and no distractions, the men had time to attend to their personal affairs. Sergeant Sampson gave haircuts to any soldier who wanted one. Most of the men just wanted their hair cut short, in anticipation of going weeks without bathing. Others wanted a more dramatic effect—or gave in to boredom and peer pressure—and asked for Mohawk cuts, with the sides closely shaved and a narrow strip of hair running down the middle. Some of the men went further, applying the war paint designs they'd seen in Hollywood westerns.

Sampson kept a close eye on one of the men in his squad, Harry Pickels, who had contracted malaria and who was now suffering with the fever's return. Sampson didn't think Pickels would have the strength for the mission, but the soldier spent most of his time on his bunk, willing himself to get better, conserving what strength he had so he would not be left behind.

Finally, Lieutenant James Coyle, one of E Company's platoon leaders, asked Sampson, "What do you intend to do with your boy Pickels?"

Sampson had been putting off making a decision in the hope that Pickels, who had also made the jumps in Sicily and Italy, would spring back.

"I don't know, sir," Sampson said. "But I'll let you know."

Sampson went to the squad tent, where he found Pickels in his usual pose.

"Harry," Sampson said. "We have to talk."

Pickels knew what was coming. "If you're going to tell me you're leaving me back, forget it," Pickels said. "I'm going out that door if I have to crawl on my hands and knees."

Sampson didn't argue. He knew how Pickels felt, and he decided that the squad would do whatever was necessary to help Pickels make the jump.

Outside the vast hangar where Easy Company spent the night of June 4, the rain lashed the parked aircraft. Sampson was glad the jump had been postponed; there was no way the pilots could find the drop zones in the storm.

The troopers guessed that the divisions that were going to hit the beach had already loaded on board their ships. They knew that the longer they delayed, the more chance there was that the Germans would discover the huge concentration of men and equipment now tipping toward the southern coast of England.

Without certain knowledge of what was going on, the soldiers created and were subject to incredible rumors. The one that worried Sampson the most was that the invasion would go on without them, that Eisenhower had decided that they couldn't wait for clear weather for the paratroopers. This possibility was simply too much to bear. He had done what he could to prepare himself and his men, so he crawled into his sleeping bag to get some rest. He knew there'd be little chance for uninterrupted sleep for some time.

Sampson rolled out his bag on a cot that was lost in a sea of cots. Pickels lay nearby, hardly speaking, grateful for the delay and the chance to recover, conserving his strength. All around, men passed the time as best they could, writing letters, sharpening knives, playing cards, reading, or sleeping. Sampson looked up from his cot into the vast space above his head and had a moment to think about how small he was, how small any single one of them was. The circle around him had pulled in as tight as it could go, as his mental rehearsals for the mission gave way to thoughts about his own mortality.

ALL THAT BRAVERY AND DEVOTION TO DUTY COULD DO

At the other end of the vast chain of command, Dwight Eisenhower still had one great question to answer before he turned the operation over to Otis Sampson and the hundreds of thousands of men like him who were poised for the attack.

When?

There was a three-day window, June 5–7, with the right combination of moonlight (for the paratroopers and their pilots) and a low tide at dawn (for the assault troops).

Because late spring weather along the Channel is so fickle, Ike had practiced with his meteorological team in the weeks leading up to the invasion. The team was led by a senior Royal Air Force meteorologist, Group Captain J. M. Stagg, a Scotsman who shouldered a tremendous responsibility: he would tell Eisenhower if the weather prediction was suitable for the invasion or not. Before each practice session, Ike gave the scientists a hypothetical date for the invasion and asked for a picture of the weather conditions. The Supreme Commander wanted more than accuracy. He wanted to observe how the team functioned together, worked out their differences, presented their findings. One of the key things he was looking for: did they have the guts to give bad news to the commander, when they knew all that was riding on their call? Ike learned to trust Stagg's courage, his thorough preparation, and his strict professionalism.

On Friday, June 2, Stagg told Eisenhower and the command group
that the good weather they'd been enjoying was likely to turn bad, although there was no consensus among the scientists. Since the experts
couldn't agree, it fell to Stagg to brief the Supreme Commander and let
him know of their uncertainty.

By Saturday, June 3, Stagg and his group were able to confirm that
the weather on Monday, June 5, would be too rough for the invasion.
The rain and winds would play havoc with the Troop Carrier pilots and
the paratroopers, the soldiers in the landing craft would be tossed
around, and some vessels might founder. The surf along the shore
would be too high for the beach assault.

Ike asked for a briefing at 0415 hours on Sunday, June 4. Neither the
weather nor the forecast had improved. Even though the fleet had already
started moving and many of the assault troops had embarked, Ike ordered
a postponement. Some ships had to be recalled to their home ports, and
a few small craft capsized in the stormy Channel, with loss of life.

Delay was risky because it gave the Germans time to figure out what
was happening and react to it. Eisenhower had great confidence in his
security apparatus, but even with near complete air superiority, even
with the turning of all the German spies in England, the Allies found it
incredible that their enemies would not notice movement in a host that
numbered more than 150,000 assault troops and nearly seven thousand
naval craft of all types.

Besides the risk of discovery, the embarked troops were getting seasick. Ike worried that their effectiveness would be compromised if they
spent too long jammed on the overcrowded ships, with their overflowing latrines and vomit buckets, where many of the men had to wait on
open decks exposed to the weather. Rain-drenched and seasick, they
would get little or no sleep while embarked. Even young men in the
peak of physical preparedness couldn't take much more before their
fighting abilities were compromised.

During the weekend of June 3–4, the pressure on Eisenhower
reached almost unimaginable levels, but he continued to show an optimistic face to the world. He had long ago determined that one of the

principal jobs of the commander was to be optimistic at all times, and he remained upbeat in all of his meetings and especially in his visits with the troops. But his staff saw the toll the pressure put on the old man. Ike chain-smoked four packs of cigarettes a day, drank pots of coffee, suffered from headaches and a sore throat. His staff made every effort to get him outside for some exercise, even if it was just a walk or a horseback ride, to relieve some of the stress.

On June 4 Ike got another unpleasant surprise when Churchill announced his intention to observe the invasion from the HMS *Belfast*. Although Eisenhower had himself considered going ashore late on D-Day (and would go ashore by D+6), the thought of the Prime Minister exposing himself to enemy fire—or being close enough to interfere with the plan—was too much. Eisenhower asked Churchill to reconsider. The PM said that he would sign on as an able seaman, since Ike did not control the muster rolls of individual British ships.

When King George VI learned of Churchill's intentions, he came to the rescue of the American commander. The king sent a message to Churchill saying that while the king would never presume to tell the PM where and how he should serve, his majesty thought it only fitting that as titular head of the empire's armed forces, he, too, should observe the battle from close up, and he looked forward to joining Churchill on the *Belfast*. Churchill relented, and at least one of Ike's problems went away.[1]

At the late evening briefing on Sunday, June 4, Group Captain Stagg told Eisenhower that there would be a window of clearer weather opening up over Normandy late on June 5. While overall the weather would remain poor, visibility would increase and the winds die to a point that made the invasion possible.

Admiral Sir Bertram H. Ramsey pointed out that if the invasion was to proceed on June 6, he needed to give his ships movement orders in the next thirty minutes. Ike polled his commanders, who were hesitant, but all determined that the invasion should proceed. Montgomery was perhaps the most effusive in support of going, but the final decision was Eisenhower's.

The staff officers left the room, leaving the commanders behind.

Eisenhower was quiet, mulling over the most critical decision he'd ever had to make. If the weather turned against them and derailed the invasion, it was quite possible that the Allies could lose the war in the west. At the very least, the fight would drag on for a few years more.

The room was silent. Bedell Smith, Ike's chief of staff, later recalled that the only sounds were the wind and the rain pounding Southwick House while his boss wrestled with the momentous decision.

"I am quite positive we must give the order," Ike said. "I don't like it, but there it is. . . . I don't see how we can do anything else."

With that, the invasion was on—contingent on a final weather brief the next morning. Eisenhower's subordinates rushed from the room to set things in motion.

Just hours later the officers reconvened; it was still possible to postpone the invasion if the weather forecast had changed. Stagg reaffirmed his prediction: there would be a window of acceptable weather. Eisenhower sat in silence for a few moments on a sofa.

"Well, Stagg," he said, smiling, "if this forecast comes off, I promise you we'll have a celebration when the time comes."

Then, after a brief discussion, Ike said, "OK, we'll go."[2]

Sometime during that day, Eisenhower, left alone with his concerns as the vast machine he'd put in motion rolled toward France, pulled out paper and pencil to compose a note he hoped never to use. It was a message to be read in the event the invasion failed.

Ike wrote, "Our landings in the Cherbourg-Havre area have failed to gain a satisfactory foothold and the troops have been withdrawn."

The original draft of the note, saved by Eisenhower's naval aide, shows that Ike crossed out this use of the passive voice, substituting instead a bold claim to personal responsibility. The sentence now ended with "I have withdrawn the troops."

Eisenhower continued in this way, the commander taking responsibility for the actions—and the failure—of the nearly 2 million people involved in the vast operation.

"My decision to attack at this time and place was based upon the best information available. The troops, the air and the navy did all that bravery and devotion to duty could do. If any blame or fault attaches to this attempt it is mine alone."[3]

Eisenhower's reputation and place in history were guaranteed by what happened over the following year on the large stage that was the war in Europe, and in his two terms as president. But this note, with his shouldering of specific, personal accountability, may have been his finest moment as a leader.

About 1900 hours, Ike drove to Greenham Common to visit some of the paratroopers Air Marshal Leigh-Mallory had predicted were going to die by the thousands. Eisenhower and an entourage of officers and photographers walked through the tent city where troops of the 101st Airborne Division had been penned for five days. A buzz went through the camp that Ike was coming.

The men of the 502nd PIR heard a commotion amid the long lines of pyramidal tents, and they came out into the gray overcast to see the Supreme Commander ambling down the muddy street in his dress uniform.

The soldiers did not have all their gear on, but many had already blackened their faces with a combination of burned cork, cocoa, and cooking oil. Some of the jumpmasters wore cardboard signs around their necks showing their aircraft number. The men moved in close; there was very little formal or intimidating about Eisenhower, even with all those stars glittering on his shoulders.

Ike's conversations were typical general officer patter of the "where-you-from-son?" variety. When he asked one group if there was anyone from Kansas, Private Sherman Oyler of Topeka spoke up.

"I'm from Kansas, sir."

Eisenhower asked, "What's your name, son?"

Oyler, who was courageous enough to make a parachute assault behind enemy lines, clammed up at the prospect of addressing the

Supreme Commander. A moment later, his amused buddies said, "Tell him your name, Oyler!"

Eisenhower filled in the gap for the young soldier. "Go get 'em, Kansas," he said.[4]

While a photographer snapped pictures, Eisenhower had a brief conversation with Lieutenant Wallace Strobel of the 502nd PIR, who stood with face blackened and the number 23 on a card around his neck. When Strobel, responding to the general's question, said he was from Michigan, Ike replied that he liked the fishing up there. Strobel, recognizing that perhaps the general was looking to steel his own nerves, assured Ike that they were well trained, well briefed, and ready to go. Other soldiers nearby chimed in to let the old man know that he needn't be concerned, that it was up to them now, and that it was the Germans who should worry now that the 101st was on the job.

Eisenhower, the only one present who knew of Leigh-Mallory's terrible predictions for these men, smiled and chatted, his hands thrust deep in his pockets.

Jim Gavin, remembering how little sleep he got during those first days in Sicily, tried to get some rest on the afternoon of June 5. Everything was packed and ready, and, thanks to the delay, the troops had been in their staging areas for more than twenty-four hours. But visitors kept stopping by to wish him well, and some of the younger officers took comfort in his apparent calm; knowing that Gavin would be there with them made success seem more likely.

Finally, Gavin gave up trying to sleep and found a typewriter. The letter would stay behind in England, and his daughter Barbara and the rest of the family would know all about the invasion by the time it reached the States. Although Gavin had always been optimistic about his own chances of survival, he knew the dangers of this mission better than most, and he was enough of a realist to know that he could not predict what would happen to him. He could, as easily as any private in the division, land on top of an enemy outpost or find himself alone (as he had in Sicily) and running from the antiparatrooper patrols. And even with his boundless confidence in the nearly seven thousand All American troopers he would take into combat, he knew that the invasion itself might fail. For all the Allies' meticulous planning and preparation, finally, the enemy also had a say in what would happen in the next few days.

Gavin found a piece of typing paper and rolled it into the machine. This letter, dated June 5, might become a keepsake in the family. Better it should be readable.

It is now evening, we take off tonight. As well as we can foresee our needs, everything has been provided for. The boys all look fine [and] they are in tiptop shape. This has been quite an experience working with them the past months. I have never seen, heard of or known soldiers like these combat experienced parachutists. For us older professional officers it can be taken for granted that we will do whatever duty requires, for these young lads, just from school, the farm or home, it is quite an undertaking. With few exceptions they are highly idealistic, gallant and courageous to a fault. They will take losses and do anything. Needless to say, it has been a source of considerable gratification to have the privilege of working with them.

There was no hyperbole in what he wrote. Gavin knew the shortcomings of the men he served with, knew that there would be jump refusals and, on the battlefield, preventable mistakes, acts of cruelty and even cowardice. But like so many combat commanders, Gavin was mostly in awe of what the vast majority of the soldiers would do when asked. They had faith in one another and in their leaders. Their willingness was a tremendous gift they offered up in that faith, and Jim Gavin, like so many other leaders preparing for battle, was struck by the immensity of what he had been entrusted with.

Gavin also wrote to the woman Barbara would become, and to the other audiences who might, one day, be curious about his thoughts.

Someday you will no doubt wonder why in the world I got into this business, when there are so many apparently safer ways to go to war. And I expect by the time you are old enough to wonder in an analytical way, the reason will be evident throughout our service. Because, someday most of our Army will be either Airborne or readily capable and trained to be airborne. Nowadays, one reads in some newspapers that bombing will win the war, without the aid of ground forces, and in other papers that the ground forces can accomplish anything that the air corps does. Manifestly, someone is wrong. Because the answer lies in combining the air bombing with the air transporting of troops. During this present phase of our development, the participation of airborne troops in the form of parachutists offers particular hazards, because of the newness of our techniques. But in time, parachuting, or what will take its place, will be no more dangerous than riding a tank is today. Until then, if progress is to be made, risks must be taken by those who believe in what they are endeavoring to accomplish. The presence of danger in present airborne operations isn't the bad thing it is made out to be anyway. It is an essential, in that it exacts of the participants peculiar qualities of courage. These things all contribute to making a soldier what a soldier is supposed to be and what we especially need in an airborne soldier.

Gavin had spent most of the last four years in the forefront of thinking about the use of the Airborne. He had been entrusted, in the past few months, with helping to shape the greatest endeavor yet undertaken by this arm that, incredibly, had been around the U.S. Army for only four years. Now, unlike many theorists, he would put his life on the line in a test of all the plans and designs.

The wheels were in motion, the great machine moving forward. Gavin thought again about the young girl he'd left behind, about the girl whose photos showed her growing so quickly in his absence. He had nothing but his faith to tell him he would even be alive when she read the page in the typewriter before him.

"I will write you as soon as I am able," he typed. He pulled the sheet from the roller and, in his loopy scrawl, signed it, as he always did, "Love, Pappy."

Dennis O'Loughlin, the Montana woodsman who'd joined the 82nd Airborne Division to regain some measure of privacy, had volunteered for duty as a pathfinder, but after undergoing all the training he almost missed the chance to jump. In a fight with another trooper, the belli- cose O'Loughlin had injured his hand badly enough to need a cast. It was obvious to anyone who looked at him that he would not be able to jump, much less operate a weapon, with the cast, so O'Loughlin cut it off, reported for duty, and ignored the pain.

O'Loughlin was only one of scores of soldiers who were determined to make the jump, who left hospital beds or safe, rear-area jobs to join the big fight. Others, perhaps more reluctant, were also returned to their units: soldiers who'd been locked up in the stockade for minor of- fenses such as brawling, AWOL, and petty theft, took their places in the ranks once again.

When the troopers started toward the planes on the evening of June 5, mortar sergeant Otis Sampson took comfort in their sheer numbers. Just from where he stood with the men of E Company, 505th PIR, he could see hundreds of heavily laden men making their way toward the aircraft in slow-moving files. Because it was difficult to walk with so much gear, the troopers left the leg harnesses of the chutes unhitched and waddled to their spots beneath the aircraft wings. They dumped their kit on the ground, went to urinate one more time (it was exceed- ingly difficult for a man in a parachute harness to relieve himself), and began strapping on the accoutrements of war.

Sampson's platoon leader, Lieutenant James Coyle, was trying to fig- ure out what to do with a set of blasting caps. Coyle had removed the caps from the demolition kit in the bundle beneath the plane, fearing

that they'd detonate on impact. He taped the caps, each about the size
of a small pencil, to a wooden block, which he planned to tape to his
boot. But then he worried that the impact might still set them off, this
time taking off his leg or killing him. Sampson didn't have a solution,
but Coyle was already a two-jump, two-campaign veteran, so the
sergeant left the lieutenant to figure it out on his own.

Otis Sampson, who'd fought in Sicily and Italy, believed in firepower.
Like a lot of paratroopers, he wanted his weapons close at hand for immediate use on landing. Sampson wore a Colt .38 revolver snuggled
next to his stomach under his reserve parachute, and had his tommy
gun crosswise on his chest, held in place by a strong leather strap that
wrapped diagonally around his back. There was a twenty-round magazine in the weapon, and more magazines in a carrier around his waist. A
quick slash of his knife would free the weapon; then he'd pull back the
bolt, chamber a round, and be ready to fight.

Sampson had discarded much of his food in favor of more ammunition. He reasoned that he could live a long time without food, but if he
didn't have the ammunition when he needed it, he'd be lost.

Like every other commander and troop leader spread across the vast
staging area that was southern and central England, Captain Roy Creek
had been consumed with all the million details of preparation, of
checking his men and their equipment, ensuring that they knew the
mission of their own unit—E Company of the 507th PIR—adjacent
units, and the entire division. Creek's standard was clear, if not easy to
achieve: every paratrooper in E Company was to know enough about
the entire airborne mission that he could join in the fight at any point
and make a contribution. Although this was Creek's first fight, he had
heard the stories about the Sicily jump, where paratroopers landed as
far as sixty miles from their drop zones.

Creek and his lieutenants and sergeants had spent hours drilling the
men on the mission. On May 29 they'd boarded trucks for the departure airfields, where they'd moved into a fenced-in area and bunked

down in a hangar big enough to accommodate the entire battalion of nearly seven hundred men. Each company commander had been assigned a briefing area, complete with maps and aerial photos, showing in detail the area of operation. Creek used some of the downtime to drill his troops further, and during the extra day they spent waiting (thanks to the June 5 postponement) the troops wandered in and out of the briefing area on their own, to memorize whatever details they could about their target areas.

The slow-moving hours passed, and on the afternoon of June 5, as Creek watched his heavily laden men shuffle into formation, he felt a deep affection for them. Some had been drafted into the Army, but they had all volunteered for the Airborne and the particularly dangerous mission they were about to undertake. They had trained hard for months on end, been shunted around the States and Ireland and England, adjusting and adapting to whatever changes the mission threw at them. They had mastered their deadly new profession, all the details of how to move, shoot, and communicate as a team. They had studied the enemy. When the briefings and talk-throughs were finished, Creek was sure that every man knew the details of his mission better than he had ever known anything before.

They had spent the last few days crammed into a tiny staging area, living on top of one another as each man dealt with the mounting pressure. Finally, when the orders came down, they shouldered their heavy equipment and began to move, not just to the aircraft but to an enemy-held country that they had never visited, where they knew no one. And once there they would take the most amazing risks on behalf of a people whose language they didn't speak, whose culture they did not understand. They accepted the most awful risks—of sudden violent death, of dismemberment and immolation and mutilation—and all they wanted in return was competent leadership. They wanted to know that their leaders would not ask them to suffer or sacrifice needlessly. That if they were asked to die for some tiny hill or unnamed crossroads, that it would be part of a larger plan, something that would shorten the war. Creek stood in awe as he watched them.

He had traveled a long way to join this elite formation. Creek had grown up in Portales, New Mexico, and attended New Mexico State University, where he participated in the Reserve Officers Training Corps (ROTC), as was mandatory at all land-grant schools. He graduated in 1940 with a degree in agriculture and a reserve commission as a second lieutenant in the Army reserve. His first assignment took him to Fort Huachuca, Arizona, and the 25th Infantry Regiment, whose soldiers were all African Americans. As was the norm in that segregated Army, the officers were, like Creek, all white.[5]

Creek spent much of his time coaching the regimental basketball and baseball teams, which wasn't bad duty but was hardly preparing him for combat. He longed for something more exciting and resolved to make his way into a unit that would almost certainly be in the fight. When he had the chance to volunteer for airborne school, he jumped at the chance and afterward was assigned to the brand-new 507th PIR.

As he lugged his heavy equipment toward the tarmac and the aircraft that would drop him behind enemy lines, Creek had to admit that this plan to seek out adventure had worked out very well. He hoped he'd live long enough to talk about it in the past tense.

The men had heard pep talks from Brigadier General Gavin; the 507th commander, Colonel George Millett; and the 2nd Battalion commander, Charles Timmes. It occurred to Creek that this would be the last time he would have his company together before they went into the fight, and that perhaps he should talk to them all one more time. He asked the First Sergeant to interrupt the move toward the planes and have the company pull in tight enough that he could address them all. This was the only part of the invasion he had not prepared for, so when he looked out on all those faces, he simply spoke from the heart.

"We have worked long and hard for this moment," Creek told them. "Collectively and individually, you are the best fighting men in the world. At this time tomorrow, we will be on our first objective and will have made our first contribution toward winning the most awful war the world has ever known."

That was the big picture. But for Easy Company, the war would play out in much more personal terms.

"We won't all be there. Some of us will fall along the way. And as men fall, there will be a doubling of effort from those who stand."

That was it. Anything else he might add about the mission would be extraneous, anything else about their preparation or the enemy unnecessary.

"God bless you," Creek said. "Right face. Forward, march!"[6]

With that, the heavily laden men of Easy Company, a small part of an invasion that would put 156,000 men ashore in France in the next twenty-four hours, shuffled toward the waiting aircraft.

At Spanhoe, where the 505th PIR was loading up, the men were startled by a loud explosion on the runway. They looked up to see one of the C47s engulfed in flames, with troopers stumbling out of the jump door. Most of the men were able to make it out of the aircraft, and the Air Corps ground crews quickly gathered to fight the flames.

Colonel Bill Ekman, commander of the 505th, was nearby and soon had the grim report. At first glance, it appeared that one of the touchy Gammon grenades (plastic explosives tucked into a cloth wrapping, powerful enough to take out a vehicle, but with a touchy fuse) had exploded, starting the fire and setting off sympathetic explosions among the hand grenades, mines, and ammunition the men carried. Three troopers were killed outright, and another seriously wounded man would die that evening in the hospital. Only one man, Corporal Melvin J. Fryer, was unwounded. (Fryer, who jumped with another stick, was killed in action on June 18 near St. Sauveur le Vicomte.) Ekman, who had been mentally preparing himself for the casualties his unit would take in France, was caught off guard. The accident was one tragedy he had not anticipated, and it was not the introduction to combat he had expected.

Ste. Mère Eglise

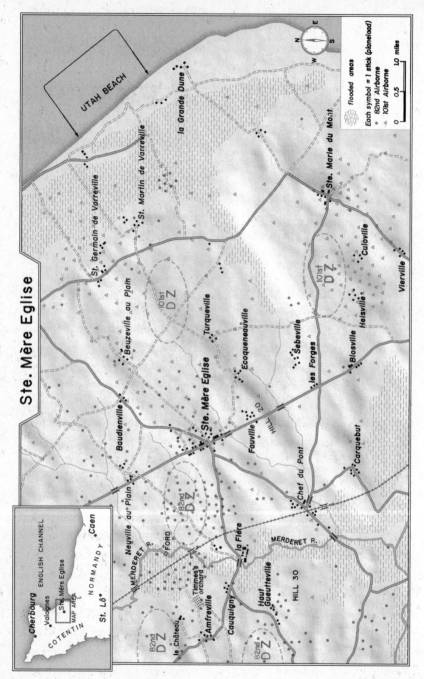

UTAH BEACH

la Grande Dune

St. Germain de Varreville

St. Martin de Varreville

Ste. Marie du Mont

Culoville

Vierville

Heisville

101st
D Z

Beuzeville au Plain

Turqueville

Ecoquenedville

Sebeville

Blosville

101st
D Z

les Forges

Baudienville

Ste. Mère Eglise

Fauville

HILL 20

Carquebut

Chef du Pont

82nd
D Z

Neuville au Plain

FORD

MERDERET R.

la Fière

MERDERET R.

Timmes's
orchard

Amfreville

Cauquigny

Haut
Gueutteville

HILL 30

82nd
D Z

le Château

82nd
D Z

Cherbourg

ENGLISH CHANNEL

Valognes

Ste. Mère Eglise

MAP AREA

NORMANDY

COTENTIN

St. Lô

Caen

N
E
W
S

Each symbol = 1 stick (planeload)
• 82nd Airborne
▲ 101st Airborne

flooded areas

0   0.5   1.0 miles

A FIRE-LIT SKY

Many of the Germans assigned to garrison the little farming town of Ste. Mère Eglise were moved elsewhere during the last weeks in May. Some were sent to the Pas de Calais, where the German high command expected the main Allied attack; some to the nearby countryside to man defensive positions and run antiparatrooper patrols. The townspeople saw them leave, hauling their weapons and equipment on the horse-drawn carts that, thanks to the critical shortage of petrol, had become the mainstay of German transport. The civilian residents of Ste. Mère Eglise believed that the occupiers must be headed to where the real fighting would take place. Perhaps the battle, and its attendant destruction, would miss them and fall on some other unlucky French citizens.

Like so many small towns that would be caught up in military campaigns, Ste. Mère Eglise sat at a critical crossroads, where the highway to Cherbourg intersected the beach road heading toward the Channel. It was this position that caused Ridgway, Gavin, and Bradley's planners to select it as the center of mass for the 82nd Airborne Division.

The town square was centered on a thirteenth-century stone church, in the typical broad-shouldered Norman style of thick walls and small windows, with a stout bell tower rising some seventy feet above the square. On market days, the square was full of farmers trading everything from fruits and vegetables to cattle and sheep. A large shed, used for storing goods for market, sat hard at the northeast corner of the church.[1] The north and west sides of the square were lined with two-

and three-story buildings: storefronts and shops on the first floor and shopkeepers' homes on the upper floors. The south side was dominated by a large home that belonged to the local veterinarian; next to that sat a private home with a tower and crenellated walls. Near the western end of the square was an ancient, ten-foot obelisk, said to date from the Roman occupation; it had been topped in modern times by a small metal cross. Just off the square, on the road leading north to Cherbourg, was the Hotel de Ville, the center of local government, which had been taken over by the Germans and now housed the *Kommandant*, the military governor.

The night of June 5–6 was marked by the familiar sounds of antiaircraft fire, as German batteries responded to Allied raiders. Shortly after 0100 on June 6, the locals were roused from bed by the ringing of the church bell. A fire (probably caused by a spent antiaircraft shell) had overtaken a house on the southeast corner of the square and then spread to the adjacent barn.[2]

The mayor of Ste. Mère Eglise, a strong-willed patriot named Alexandre Renaud, asked the German commander if he could turn out the townspeople for a bucket brigade to help the small fire detachment. The garrison commander agreed, and he called out some of his men to keep an eye on the citizens. It had been German practice to strictly enforce a curfew, in order to keep French civilians off the roads during those dark hours favored by the Resistance. Anyone violating curfew was likely to be shot.

The townspeople and the German guards were in the square, completely focused on the fire, when they heard the deep rumble of Allied aircraft around 0115. The fire-lit sky made it difficult to see anything more than a hundred or so feet in the air, but that didn't keep them from looking up, straining to see.

The harbingers of the huge and long-awaited invasion were, at first, just a couple of oval shapes, just a bit lighter than the surrounding sky, that drifted through the light from the fire. The German soldiers grasped their weapons, while the French civilians pointed and chattered among themselves.

Les parachutistes!

The German noncoms yelled at their men, who hurried toward the south edge of the square, weapons at the ready. Only a few parachutes had passed overhead, but there could be more.

In fact, two sticks of the 506th Parachute Infantry Regiment, of the 101st Airborne Division, had jumped well short of their drop zones and landed south and east of Ste. Mère Eglise. The GIs were still floating down or were on the ground and still tangled in their harnesses when the Germans rushed through the alleys and burst into the gardens and the cemetery just south of the square. They fired as they ran, catching some of the Americans before they could even free their weapons. It was over in a few minutes, and four paratroopers were dead in the darkness at the edge of town. Other troopers managed to make it to the shadows and hedgerows and away from the light. (While this was happening, another dozen or so planes carrying the 2nd Battalion of the 506th PIR also dropped troopers around Ste. Mère Eglise, but these men managed to stay out of the line of fire and move off toward their own objectives.)[3]

The German garrison in Ste. Mère Eglise was now fully alerted. Still, it did not seem likely to these men, used to four years of quiet occupation, that a mere two dozen or so paratroopers could be the precursor of a vast invasion. Perhaps, they thought and hoped, a small force had jumped in to help the partisans. Maybe it was just a raid. Maybe, in the morning, they could resume the quiet occupation duty to which they'd grown accustomed.

Eighteen-year-old pathfinder Bob Murphy was encouraged by the reports Lieutenant Mike Chester called out from his position as jumpmaster in the door of the aircraft.

"We're right on! We're right on!" Chester yelled over the engine noises as the landmarks he'd worked so hard to memorize scrolled beneath the aircraft minutes after they'd crossed the coast. Standing beside Chester, the Air Corps crew chief also watched out the door and gave a silent thumbs-up to the paratroopers lined up and waiting.

Murphy carried lights for marking the drop zone in a big canvas duffel bag, which would hang from the end of a stout line once his parachute opened. The pathfinders were thirty minutes ahead of the main body of troops, meaning they had just a half hour to figure out exactly where they were, find the right drop zone, and set up their lights and Eureka electronic homing equipment to mark the DZs for the following waves. For this reason, the pathfinders had been assigned to and had trained with the best pilots in the 315th Troop Carrier Command. The pilots and pathfinder teams had trained together during their entire time in England. Murphy had confidence in the pilots, in his officers, and in himself and the other troopers, whose training in land navigation rivaled what the officers got. He and the other pathfinders, all of them volunteers, had been segregated from their units for several weeks. Excused from the mundane duties that other soldiers had to perform, such as KP and guard duty, the men could concentrate instead on learning their missions in great detail.

Although he was still a teenager, this was Murphy's second combat jump. He had originally tried to enlist in the Navy at sixteen, using a birth certificate his father helped him forge. The elder Murphy, a World War I veteran, understood his son's eagerness to get into the fight. But a sharp-eyed Navy recruiter picked out the forgery and turned the youngster away. After seeing his brother's best friend come back from Fort Benning with paratrooper wings, Murphy showed up at an Army recruiting station with yet another forged certificate and a determination to get into the paratroops. At the Army depot, a sergeant caught the forgery and called over his lieutenant, who asked Murphy what he wanted to do. The high school student replied that he wanted to be a paratrooper, and what's more, he'd had some military training in high school, which, he was sure, gave him a leg up on most other recruits.

The Lieutenant, who clearly knew the certificate was a fake, decided that Murphy was just the kind of aggressive young man the Airborne needed. He marked the papers "approved" and said, "Robert, you're going into the paratroops."

•   •   •

The pilots carrying the 1st Battalion, 505th PIR, pathfinders not only found the route to the drop zone but also slowed to a good jump speed and the correct altitude, so that Murphy and his comrades came down on target, with none of the equipment losses that so many other troopers experienced because their pilots did not slow down.[4]

Murphy landed fairly easily in an open area and immediately saw a shape moving slowly in the darkness. He could not tell if it was a person, much less an American or a German. In spite of his long months of training with challenges and passwords, he acted on instinct, raising his finger to his lips and saying, "Shhhh."[5]

The other man turned out to be a GI, who kept moving. Safe for the moment from the Germans, Murphy was in a hurry to get out of his parachute and deploy his equipment. He whipped out the razor-sharp knife he carried for exactly this task and sliced through the thick webbing of the parachute harness. In his haste he also managed to cut the straps holding the ammunition pouch for his tommy gun, and so he hurried off to battle with no ammo. (Moving toward a fight without ammunition was bad enough, but Murphy had done the same exact thing in Italy. When he went around asking for ammunition, he had to endure the caustic teasing of his buddies, who accused him of not wanting to carry anything too heavy.)

Chester and his men soon had their portion of the drop zone well marked, and they waited, without being challenged, for the rest of the regiment.

Ken Russell fell asleep on the flight from England and slept while his plane, carrying the 2nd Platoon mortar squad of F Company, made its turns and hit its checkpoints on the long flight from the English Midlands to the Channel and then to the Norman coast. Russell woke up when the German antiaircraft batteries on the Channel islands of Alderney and Guernsey opened up on the massive fleet of aircraft. The fire was ineffective (Allied planners were expecting it and stayed well out of the maximum range of the enemy guns), but it did wake those troopers who, like Russell, were made sleepy by the airsickness pills.

The jumpmaster, Lieutenant Harold O. Cadish, was cheered to see that his aircraft appeared to be on course. For the first few minutes after crossing the coast the countryside below looked peaceful, and Cadish could make out the small roads and geometric shapes of the farmers' fields. Then, shouting to be heard above the roar of the big engines, he gave the first of the jump commands.

"Stand up!"

Russell and his fellow troopers scrambled to their feet. The jumpmasters wanted them up and ready, in case the aircraft was knocked down by antiaircraft fire.

"Hook up!"

Russell grabbed the metal clip at the end of his static line with his left hand, reached for the overhead cable that ran down the center of the aircraft, and snapped the clip in place. The other end of the line wrapped across the top of his packed chute and attached to the top of the parachute itself. When Russell jumped, the static line would play out and pull the chute from its cover before separating.

Russell, making his first combat jump, had been told by the veterans that when the time came, he'd be happy to get out of the airplane. That seemed a little far-fetched to some of the new troopers when they thought about jumping into enemy fire, but now Russell understood. Inside the plane they were helpless, and whatever happened to the aircraft happened to them. Outside, on their own, they felt as if they had a fighting chance.

"Check equipment!"

Russell and the other men patted down their kit, making sure all items were fastened tightly and nothing had worked loose during the long flight. Loose gear might hang up on their chutes and cause a malfunction. Russell made sure his helmet was on snugly, the chin cup in place. His reserve was buckled across his chest, his weapon beneath the belly band that wrapped him tightly. Each man checked the parachute of the man in front, ensuring that the lines weren't tangled. When they finished, the last man in the stick, standing nearest the cockpit of the plane, slapped the man in front of him on the shoulder or backside.

"One, OK!"

The count made its way toward the jumpmaster.

"Two, OK!"

"Three, OK!"

When Lieutenant Cadish got the signal from the number two man, he turned back into the doorway of the plane, his hands on either side, and leaned out to look for the drop zone and see what waited below.

Twenty-five-year-old Wheatley Christensen was in one of the aircraft carrying G Company of the 505th PIR and was about to make his third combat jump. He was one of the original members of the unit, having joined back when the entire company consisted of a single truckload of newly trained paratroopers arriving from jump school.

Christensen had grown up on the eastern shore of Maryland and had been working for the Navy when he was drafted. He volunteered for the paratroopers for the fifty-dollar-a-month jump pay. Now he was a corporal and assistant to the squad leader, Sergeant James Yates. There were eighteen men in his stick, all of them from 1st Squad, 3rd Platoon. Chris, as the men called him, was the "pusher": he was last in the stick and would ensure that everyone in front of him left the aircraft.

The entire stick had already loaded when Chris heard a jeep pull up outside. The Air Corps crew chief had to lower the small ladder again for one more soldier, which surprised everyone. Chris had never seen the man before, and he made his way to the front of the aircraft—and the back of the stick—without explaining himself to anyone. When he got close, Chris could see that the soldier was very young, and that he wore no unit insignia or rank. Chris's platoon leader, Lieutenant Robert Ringwald, came back as the man got behind Chris in the stick.

"This guy is going to jump behind you" was all Ringwald said.

Chris did not ask the lieutenant any questions—something about his tone told him that was all the information he was going to get, anyway.

When they were in the air and Chris had a chance to observe the new addition, he noted that the soldier looked nervous. Chris started up a conversation, and soon the mystery man admitted that this was his first combat jump.

"Who are you?" Christensen asked.

"I'm supposed to go into Ste. Mère Eglise and confiscate the German records," the man told him. "Make sure they don't destroy anything."

Chris knew this meant the man was probably with the Office of Strategic Services, or OSS (the forerunner of the modern Central Intelligence Agency), but he figured that wasn't the kind of question you asked out loud, so he let it go. Whoever the soldier was, he had a unique mission. Chris's job when he hit the ground was to find the guys in his stick, then the hundred-plus men of G Company, then the five-hundred-plus men of 3rd Battalion. This youngster with the unmarked uniform was going out alone.

"Is this jump getting to you?" Chris asked.

"Not the jump, exactly," the man said. "I'm afraid I might freeze in the door."

"Would you feel better if I let you jump ahead of me?" Chris asked, thinking, *If he does tie up the door, I'm in a fix. I'll be separated from my stick in enemy territory.*

Chris made it his mission to calm the soldier down during the flight, to do everything he could to make sure the man left the plane at exactly the second he was supposed to, even if that meant booting him out the door. By the time they crossed the coast, it seemed that the new arrival had calmed down considerably, and Chris thought he was going to be all right.

Shortly after crossing the coast, the 378 aircraft carrying Force A of the 82nd Airborne Division ran into a major obstacle: a huge cloud bank extended across the peninsula for twelve to fifteen miles east to west.[6] Up to this point the pilots had maintained a tight formation, which translated to a tight landing for the paratroopers, who had to consolidate quickly. Now, with visibility suddenly reduced, the pilots became afraid of midair collisions and let the formation drift apart.

Some pilots climbed and were thus able to maintain formation, but they had two thousand feet of elevation when they saw the drop zones, marked with lighted T's set out by the pathfinders. Jump altitude was between four and five hundred feet, but the planes were over the drop zone, and there was nothing to do but hit the green light.

Lieutenant Colonel Ed Krause, the commander of the 3rd Battalion of the 505th, was a jumpmaster in one of the planes that had climbed to nearly two thousand feet. He worried that his men would spend so long in the air that they'd become targets for Germans on the ground, or that the light winds would blow them far off course. But when the green light came on, Krause jumped. Even though he knew they were high, he was still surprised to see another formation of aircraft pass below him.[7]

When the ground fire began, mostly aimed at the planes farther back in the formation, some pilots poured on the air speed in order to clear the area. Experienced jumpers on board could read the sounds of the aircraft engines and knew the pilots were pushing the throttles. The paratroopers knew that a few more miles per hour in airspeed meant a much greater dispersion on the ground. Instead of landing in a line a thousand yards long, the troopers could be spread out over a mile. Instead of taking thirty minutes to roll up the "stick" of jumpers and get into some kind of fighting shape, the paratroopers could spend hours wandering around the countryside, looking for their comrades, their equipment, and their leaders.

Jumpers from these speeding aircraft stepped out into a slipstream that hit them like a hammer, ripping equipment and even weapons from the men. In some cases the sudden shock knocked them unconscious, and many men were stripped of their gear by the slipstream.

Other planes, carrying F Company, 505th PIR, stayed true to course, flying over the correct drop zone but missing the timing of the jump. Instead of landing in Drop Zone O just west and slightly north of town, the F Company troopers got the green light as they were approaching Ste. Mère Eglise. When Ken Russell got to the doorway, the first thing he saw was the beacon of the large fire. He had his first jolt of real fear when he realized that he might land in the burning building.

At 0145 hours, this unlucky stick of F company troopers jumped right over the town square of Ste. Mère Eglise, which was full of star-tled French civilians and the German soldiers who had fired at the 101st Airborne Division troops just thirty minutes earlier.

Russell had an eerie view of the entire scene during the few seconds it took his parachute to descend. Charles Blankenship, the PFC from North Carolina, was drawn toward the fire by the drafts. He screamed once as he plunged into the two-story inferno.

Russell cringed as he looked down from two hundred feet on the heads of the Germans, who were unshouldering their rifles and firing into the air. Ridiculous as it was, he tried to hide behind his reserve parachute, strapped across his belly. His friends Cadish, Tlapa, and Bryant got hung up on telephone poles or on the tall linden and chest-nut trees that lined the square. Shot dead before they could react, they hung there as if crucified.[8] Private Ernest R. Blanchard also got caught in a tree but managed to get a knife out and cut himself loose. He cut off his finger in his haste but dropped to the ground and ran for the shadows. (He was so frightened by the few minutes of terror that he did not even notice the missing finger right away.)

Russell looked down past his feet and saw the church below him. He pulled on his risers, hoping to slip clear of the building, but hit hard on the steep slate roof and began rolling. He was a tangle of equipment and parachute as he rolled, and could not stop himself. Finally, his chute caught the top of the roof, and he came to a stop right at the edge. Russell was vaguely aware of another trooper, John Steele, whose parachute had caught on one corner of the tall steeple. Steele dangled helplessly while the big church bells rang beside him.

Russell was momentarily stunned, but he had a clear view of the church square only twenty feet below him. Sergeant John Ray landed in the square, and just as he hit, a German soldier came around the corner of the church into Russell's view, ran up to the paratrooper, and shot Ray in the stomach at point-blank range. The sergeant fell over, clutching a mortal wound. Now the German turned and looked up to where both Russell and Steele hung helplessly, easy targets unable to fire back. Russell had just a second or two to realize that the German was going to shoot him, when he saw Sergeant Ray, lying on the ground, move. In his dying moment, Ray pulled his pistol from its holster and fired, hitting the German in the back of the head and sending him sprawling into the dust.

Russell grabbed his boot knife and began frantically slashing at the thick parachute harness, one eye on the square below, where German soldiers ran back and forth shooting at the other men in his stick. It seemed impossible that they would miss him and Steele for much longer.

Russell cleared his harness, rolled to the very edge of the roof, and, without hesitating, dropped nearly twenty feet to the ground, his gear clattering around him.

He was now pinned up against the flat wall, with no place to hide while he got his bearings. Afraid that he wouldn't be able to move quickly with all his gear, Russell dropped most of his equipment and, grabbing his rifle and ammunition, ran to the southern edge of the square, where he could see some shrubbery beneath the trees. As he ran, he could hear the zip of bullets going by, hear rounds hitting the stone walls of the church, the ground, the iron fence, and even the obelisk. The square was still lit up, the terrified civilians gone, the Germans running around in confusion.

Russell was determined to get away from the firelight, which made him plainly visible to any alert German. Behind him, John Steele was still hung up on the tower, helpless and playing dead. (Steele had been shot in the foot and would later be cut down and taken prisoner by the Germans. He was freed when the 3rd Battalion took the town.)[9]

Russell cut through an alley between the two large houses on the south side of the square, hugging the shadows, watching for Germans. Just south of the town, he saw muzzle flashes from a heavy automatic weapon. He crept close and soon found, backlit by its own fire, the silhouette of a German antiaircraft gun, a self-propelled flak wagon. He could see the crew working the gun, their eyes on the sky as they fired at Allied aircraft.

Russell did not give much thought to what he did next. He was angry at what he had just witnessed in the town square, the complete massacre of his squad, of his friends.

He dropped to his hands and knees, then to his belly, the sounds of his movement covered by the massive pounding of the big automatic gun. He crept close, holding a large Gammon grenade. When he was within a few yards, and still unseen by the Germans, he unscrewed the cap and fuse, hurled the grenade, and turned to move away quickly. The blast was so powerful, and he had been so close, that the explosion knocked him down. Russell jumped up and ran some distance away, then looked back to see if anyone was following him. There were no Germans in sight; he had killed the entire crew.

As he lay still in the shrubbery and the covering darkness, Russell realized that the gun crew should have had security posted; there should have been sentries to protect the crew from what had just happened to them. The fact that the Germans had made a mistake was small comfort: he hadn't even thought of the possibility of running into guards. He had been so angry that he had thrown the grenade from a point where he came close to blowing himself up.

Ken Russell lay in the darkness south of the town, alone, frightened, and unsure of what to do next. His squad had been massacred; he had no leaders, no buddies anywhere around that he knew of. He was seventeen, and his war was only an hour old.

Russell's squadmate PFC Cliff Maughn landed only a few yards from his buddies, but the distance was crucial: he came down just behind one of the big houses on the south side of the square. Maughn landed in the small kitchen garden of the two-story veterinarian's home, so the German soldiers in the square never saw him.

The veterinarian and his family had retreated to the basement when the firing started. They came upstairs to find the German officer who boarded with them, not in the front of the house where the firing was going on, but in the rear off the center hall, his pistol trained on a man in their garden. The apparition was black-faced and festooned with combat gear, still hooked to his big camouflage parachute, with his hands in the air. An American flag showed prominently on the sleeve of his combat jacket.

At last, the liberation! But for the moment, the German had the drop on the heavily armed American.

Immediately the doctor's young daughter, a girl of about seven, began pleading for the life of the American. The veterinarian spoke to the German, pointing out the obvious: the invasion had begun, and it was only a matter of time before the Americans overwhelmed the garrison. Maughn, who spoke neither French nor German, had no idea what the conversation was about, but sensed that the French civilians, who had already taken a chance by coming out of hiding, were looking out for him.

The doctor persuaded the German officer to turn his pistol over to Maughn. Cliff Maughn came out of the garden alive, with an enemy prisoner.[10]

The veteran Wheatley Christensen knew the pilots were worried just as much about a midair collision as they were about the flak. The aircraft were blacked out, save for tiny wingtip lights, and with the planes bucking, diving, and climbing independently, it was difficult to avoid a collision. All the pilots could do was put some distance between the aircraft.

For the moment, Christensen worried more about falling inside the bucking airplane than he did about getting hit by antiaircraft fire. He held his static line tightly, as did the GIs in front of him. If one man went over, he might knock the legs out from under a half dozen more, sending them to the deck in a tangle of equipment and parachute lines, making it impossible for them to jump.

Outside the door, which was far ahead of him, Chris saw the flares the Germans used to spot their targets. The light silhouetted the men at the front of the stick, Lieutenant Ringwald and Sergeant Yates, who anxiously scanned the ground for landmarks to tell them where they were. The *bang-bang* of exploding shells outside shook the men through their boot soles.

When the green light went on, the stick moved immediately, the men eager to clear the aircraft, which was nothing but a big, slow-moving, low-flying target for antiaircraft gunners. The jumper in front of Chris, the OSS man who had the independent mission, went out as smoothly as the most experienced man.

Chris's first thought when he hit the slipstream was, *We're low*, and indeed it was only a matter of seconds before he hit the ground.

He checked himself quickly. He was unhurt and not under fire. Christensen shucked his parachute, palmed his weapon, and started heading opposite the direction of the aircraft's flight. (The number one man moved in the same direction as the aircraft. Theoretically, they would meet in the middle, with the rest of the jumpers between them.) It was tough going almost from the moment he started walking. This was Chris's first experience with the thick Norman hedgerows that would cause so many problems for the Allies. They were not at all like the hedges they'd grown accustomed to in England, which marked property boundaries but were mostly ornamental. What amazed Chris as he fought his way through one hedgerow after another was that in all those hours poring over sand tables, in all those aerial photos and rehearsals, no one ever mentioned how difficult it would be to move cross-country.

The moonlight played tricks on him, and he saw weird shapes. The fact that there were only one or two ways into and out of the bordered fields worried him; a German waiting in ambush would know exactly where to watch for the next GI to emerge.

As he moved, Christensen could see the reflection, on the bellies of some clouds, of what appeared to be a fire. He thought that perhaps the fire was in Ste. Mère Eglise, the battalion objective. There was a communication cable there that had to be cut, and it was there he hoped to find the rest of G Company and 3rd Battalion. He made a mental note of which direction they'd have to move once he'd found everyone in his stick.

Chris had already picked up more than half of his men when he heard someone calling for him by name. He kept going, struggling to move in a more or less straight line, and found a small knot of men gathered in an orchard. There, on the ground, were Lieutenant Ringwald and Chris's buddy and squad leader, Sergeant Yates. Some of the troopers had helped cut the two out of their harnesses and moved them close together under the cover of some apple trees. The two men were badly injured, Yates with what appeared to be two broken legs, and Ringwald with a broken back. Though they were in excruciating pain, the two leaders kept quiet. No one knew how far away the Germans were.

It was plain to the troopers gathered round, and to Ringwald and Yates, what this meant. There was no way the tiny squad could move the badly injured men. They had no stretchers, for one thing, and even if they did, moving a man with a broken back might paralyze him. No one had to say it out loud, but the healthy men were going to leave the injured behind. Chris and his men did their best to make the two leaders comfortable, making sure they could reach their canteens and their morphine styrettes.

Chris and Yates, who had been together since jump school, including two combat jumps and two campaigns, lied to each other. Yates wished Christensen good luck and told the corporal, now in command of the squad, that the troops coming across Utah Beach in the morning would no doubt find them and take them to a hospital. Yet everyone in the little circle knew that it was at least as likely that the injured GIs would be discovered by Germans. In that case the best the two men could hope for was that their captors would give them medical care before hauling them off as prisoners. The combat veterans knew it was just as likely that a German patrol might shoot them where they lay, rather than dealing with the logistics of hauling around two badly injured men.

Chris delayed for a few minutes, though he knew he should move.

He was now in charge of the squad, but the toughest task he faced was leaving these two very conscious, very alert paratroopers to whatever was going to befall them.

Then Chris heard firing nearby. Some of his men had ambushed and killed a German motorcycle courier. The area was getting hot, and Chris knew they had to leave. He stood up, said his good-byes, and ordered his men to move out into the moonlit darkness.

Gavin's Force A included division artillery troops, whose mission was to establish a communications network for the guns, which were to arrive later on D-Day. One of these communications men was Ed Misencik, a twenty-five-year-old veteran of Sicily and Italy.

Misencik's aircraft flew through some heavy flak, though it wasn't hit. He could see out the door from his position in the stick, and he marveled at how brightly the sky was lit by tracers and flares. As with most paratroopers, his only reaction was that he wanted out of the airplane. His chute opened properly, and Misencik looked down and saw moonlight reflecting on water. He just had time to think, *That looks like water*, before he hit.[11]

Scores of troopers landed in the flooded Merderet plain (at least thirty-six drowned).[12] Misencik was unlucky enough to actually hit the channel of the Merderet River. Instead of collapsing, his chute went into the river, caught the current, and started pulling him along, face-down, overloaded with heavy equipment, and helpless.

Misencik was a big man, six feet and nearly two hundred pounds, but he had over a hundred pounds of equipment strapped to his body. With his reserve chute on his stomach and musette bag hanging on his chest, much of the weight was on his front, which made it impossible for him to roll over in the water.

He tried to pull his knife from the scabbard on his leg, but it wouldn't come loose. For this, his third combat jump, he had taped it in place because in some practice jumps it had popped loose on a hard landing. Misencik desperately grabbed at the risers that connected him to the parachute, but he could not pull them close to him or get control of the chute, and he could not reach down far enough to free his knife. Within seconds, the struggle against the weight dragging him down and the current yanking him along had exhausted him, and Misencik felt himself losing the battle against the water. He was afraid he would not be able to hold his breath long enough to get himself out of this mess.

A second or two of eerie calm passed over him with the clear thought: *This is not how I thought I'd die.*

Just as he was ready to give up and open his mouth, his parachute collapsed and stopped pulling him. The release of pressure was enough so that he could get his face out of the water to draw a breath and then yell for help.

Luckily, Misencik's buddy Sergeant Atwood B. Loper was nearby and heard the struggle. At first he couldn't see anything on the surface of the water, so Loper crouched down and looked across the surface, which was barely lit by a moon that kept ducking behind the clouds. Scanning the water, Loper saw something break the surface. He waded into the channel, which was between four and five feet deep, and pulled the much bigger man toward safety just as Misencik's parachute once again caught the current. Misencik lay on the bank, exhausted but safe for the moment, with a dripping Loper by his side. A lieutenant (Misencik thought it was the chaplain) came up and asked if he could help. Misencik asked the officer to put together his weapon, an M1 he carried broken down in a canvas case.

Misencik wrung the water out of everything as best he could, but there was no time to rest or do much recovering, and soon they were on their way, looking for some sign of Ste. Mère Eglise. After moving carefully through the dark, they came upon a road and soon stumbled across a group of about fifteen paratroopers, with a lieutenant in charge. But the lieutenant had also been badly dropped and could only guess at their actual location. No one knew which way they should go. The officer went out onto the road and peered in both directions, then returned to the small group he had collected.

"Well, men, what do you think?"

When none of the troopers could offer anything more than specula-
tion, the lieutenant pulled out a coin.

"OK then; heads that way," he said, indicating one direction, "tails
that way."

Among the 2nd Battalion troops entering Ste. Mère Eglise that morning
was Lieutenant James Coyle, a platoon leader in E Company. Coyle
reached the town after first light and saw a French civilian come out of
one of the houses to seek out a paratrooper. Coyle spoke only a little
French, but this man's concern was clear to him. The civilian wanted to
know if this was a mere raid—meaning the Americans would leave
again and the Germans would retain control—or if this was the invasion. Coyle wanted very much to tell the man that the nightmare was
over, but the troopers had been ordered not to share information with
anyone they encountered. Without violating his orders, Coyle reassured
the man. "*Nous restons ici,*" he said.

We're staying here.[13]

Colonel Bill Ekman, commander of the 505th PIR, was knocked unconscious by the shock when his parachute opened high above the regiment's drop zone, just west and a bit north of Ste. Mère Eglise. When
he regained consciousness, he was already on the ground, banged up
but in one piece. He also seemed to be alone, except for a cow just a
few feet away. The cow's presence was reassuring—it meant he wasn't
in a minefield—but the animal seemed to be struggling. When Ekman
investigated, he saw that the cow had a broken back. Judging by the
pain in his own legs and back, Ekman guessed that he'd hit the cow on
the way down. He looked around the moonlit fields, trying to get his
bearings. Since there were no other troopers around, he figured he'd
missed the drop zone, so he headed south, in the direction, he believed,
of Ste. Mère Eglise.

The mission finally assigned to the 505th PIR, after the scramble two weeks earlier that changed their objectives, put them in Drop Zone O, a large oval that sat just north of the D15 highway, between the railroad and the N13 highway, which ran on parallel courses north to Cherbourg. From this drop zone, the 1st Battalion, under Major Frederick Kellam, was to head south and west, cross the railroad, and secure the eastern end of the bridge at La Fière. Kellam's battalion was to be a backstop for the 507th PIR, which was supposed to land on the western side of the river and secure that end of the causeway and bridge. The 2nd Battalion, under Lieutenant Colonel Ben Vandervoort, would head north and east, following the N13 as far as the small hamlet of Neuville au Plain, a tiny crossroads just two thousand yards north of Ste. Mère Eglise. Vandervoort's men were to block the counterattacks expected from the north.

Lieutenant Colonel Ed Krause was the most experienced battalion commander in the regiment, having commanded the 3rd Battalion in both Sicily and Italy. Because of this, he was given the main mission: the capture of Ste. Mère Eglise. The town would be the center of the 82nd Airborne Division's foothold in France, and Ridgway and Gavin had already discussed that this would be the place where they would circle the wagons if help from the beach-landing units was long in coming.

But Krause was not a beloved commander. He was loud and abrasive, even abusive to his troops and officers. One incident stuck in the mind of Jack Norton, the 505th PIR Operations Officer, who had been a company commander in then-Major Krause's battalion during training in the States. Norton was at the head of his company on a road march when he saw Krause chewing out another company commander. Krause was enraged about something, and to drive his point home he kicked the officer hard enough to knock the man down. Norton was shocked.

After knocking down the commander, the still livid Krause headed for Norton and began his yelling and histrionics. When he lifted his foot as if to deliver another kick, Norton reached down and grabbed Krause's leg, sending the major sprawling. Norton didn't say anything, and Krause just stomped off.

Gavin had expressed some doubts about Krause's performance on the battlefield, criticizing Krause for not moving aggressively toward the objective on D-Day in Sicily. But when it came time to fight, Krause was at the front, and he was awarded the Distinguished Service Cross, the nation's second-highest award for courage under fire, for fighting German tanks on Sicily's Biazza Ridge.

Combat did not change Krause's ways, and he did not endear himself to Ekman, the new regimental commander. He argued so often with Ben Vandervoort, his counterpart in the 2nd Battalion, that Jack Norton often found himself acting as a peacemaker whenever the senior officers had to work together.

In spite of all these difficulties Krause, promoted to Lieutenant Colonel before Overlord, was still in command of the 3rd Battalion for the Normandy campaign. Just before his men dispersed to board their aircraft in England, Krause called them together and showed them an enormous American flag he had in his kit. It was the very one, he told them, that had flown over Naples when they liberated that city the previous fall. Before the end of D-Day, he promised them, the same flag would fly over Ste. Mère Eglise.

Krause had one of the best landings in the regiment, coming down just a few yards from the lights the pathfinder teams used to mark his drop zone. While rolling up his stick, Krause came across a small field with a distinctive cone shape that he recognized from his study of aerial photos and maps. He checked his theory by heading off to find a patch of woods that, if he was correct, would be close by. He found the woods, which he had picked ahead of time for the location of his command post, or CP. He was about 90 percent sure of his location,[14] and had about forty or fifty of his men with him. Krause set up a defensive perimeter, then sent small patrols to gather the other paratroopers who were wandering around in the dark.

A G Company lieutenant, William F. Mastrangelo, in combat for the first time, took a much more practical approach to figuring out where he was. Mastrangelo landed close to the edge of town and, seeing the buildings, merely walked up to what looked like a house and knocked on the door. A Frenchman, who appeared slightly inebriated (something the paratroopers knew a thing or two about), answered the knock, and the two men managed to communicate. The Frenchman assured the paratrooper officer that this was, indeed, Ste. Mère Eglise. More than that, the helpful civilian said he knew the roads and paths around his hometown, as well as where the German units were garrisoned.

(It is interesting to note that the German garrison, called out to oversee the firefighting and engaged in a small battle with a handful of troopers of the 101st Airborne and an entire stick from F Company, seemed to have retired after that fight. Some may have left town, but at least some of them went back to bed. In what can only be called a stunning failure, there was no organized defense of Ste. Mère Eglise, despite the undeniable evidence that the Allies were launching, at the very least, a raid.)

Mastrangelo may have been a newcomer to combat, but he knew the value of good intelligence, and he asked the Frenchman to help him find the DZ, knowing that the battalion command post would be nearby. The man agreed, and the unlikely pair—the American warrior enjoying a lucky start to his career as a combat soldier, and the festive French civilian—set off for the 505th's drop zone. Wary of being led into an ambush, Mastrangelo had the Frenchman, who was wearing a white coat, lead the way. But the civilian proved as good as his word, and soon they found Krause and confirmed the 3rd Battalion commander's notion that he was exactly where he was supposed to be.

This knowledge also paid off for Major James McGinity, the executive officer of Kellam's 1st Battalion, who showed up at Krause's CP and was able to comfirm that he was in the right drop zone. He still had to find his battalion, but at least he knew where to look.

By 0400 Krause had about 180 men—a little more than a rifle company's worth—but felt that he should not wait until daylight to move on his objective. He organized two provisional companies, under the command of Captain Walter C. DeLong (commander of H Company) and Lieutenant Ivan F. Woods (executive officer of G Company). DeLong led the way, following the helpful Frenchman in the white coat, and closed on the edge of town within thirty minutes.[15]

While Krause quickly gathered his strength, other 3rd Battalion units wandered into Ste. Mère Eglise, looking for a meeting place. Krause had told the men that if they were misdropped, they should join him in town. One stick from G Company, led by Staff Sergeant Ronald C. Snyder, entered the town along the Chef du Pont road while it was still dark. Snyder's men opened fire on a truck full of Germans who were pulling out of town, and arrived in the square just in time to get off a few shots at one of the last antiaircraft batteries to leave for the countryside.[16]

The French guide told Krause that there were just a few antiaircraft units and some service troops billeted in Ste. Mère Eglise. If this proved to be true, it was good news for Krause. The town was the major objective for the regiment and a key to the division's plan, and Krause had been entrusted with the mission. He would strike fast and hard.

His original plan had been to clear the town first, then establish roadblocks at likely avenues of enemy counterattack. But since there was no sign of a strong enemy defense, or even of any movement, he thought he could get the roadblocks in first, to protect his men against the bigger threat. He had trained his men hard, and he knew that they could adapt to a new plan.

Krause broke his unit into small detachments and told them to move through the town as quietly as possible, with no rifle fire. The men were to use mines (each man had been issued a small antitank mine) to block the roads, and set up their automatic weapons to repel counterattacks. Krause waited, and even the quiet was tense as he listened for evidence that the Germans were on the move. He glanced at his watch, and when he figured the roadblocks were in place he led another group, comprised mostly of battalion headquarters troops, into the center of the too-quiet town. Amazingly, the Germans were nowhere in sight, and the helpful Frenchman pointed out the enemy's billets. Krause and his men, it seemed, had achieved complete surprise. They moved rapidly into place, in a well-practiced routine for an assault. They opened fire and rushed the enemy's billets, killing any who resisted and rounding up the stunned survivors. Krause's men took thirty prisoners and killed eleven, and met no serious resistance. By 0500 Krause had his blocking forces in place (though his men would continue to root out snipers all during the morning), and he sent a runner to find the regimental command post with a message for Colonel Ekman: "I am in Ste. Mère Eglise." An hour later, he sent a more definitive message: "I have secured Ste. Mère Eglise."

Ekman had not yet made his way to the command post, but Krause's runner did find the division commander, Major General Matt Ridgway, who was set up in his own command post just west of the town. Now the division commander knew about Ste. Mère Eglise, but Ekman, his subordinate and the man actually responsible for capturing the town, did not. Later, Ekman would make a decision that altered his regiment's mission based on this incomplete picture.

All during those first hours of D-Day, individuals and small groups of paratroopers found their way to Ste. Mère Eglise. Krause and his officers sent them to find their respective units, so that he had as many men as possible under the command of their own noncoms and officers. G Company was sent to cover the Carentan and Gambosville roads (to the south and southwest), while H Company and the battalion Headquarters Company covered the approaches from the north, especially the important N13. By the early morning a little more than half of I Company had been reconstituted, and under Captain Harold H. Swingler they moved to the town center to form the reserve.

Out on the H Company block on the Chef du Pont road, just after first light, Privates Leslie P. Cruise, Lawrence Kilroy, and Richard Vargas were startled to hear a vehicle approaching. When they looked up, they saw a U.S. jeep, barreling down the road toward town, towing a 57 mm gun. The men had been told to expect some of these vehicles and the important guns, which had landed with the first flight of glider reinforcements. But the three paratroopers did not have time to warn the two occupants of the jeep about the mine they'd placed in the road, and before they could do anything the jeep rolled over it, destroying the vehicle and gun and killing the two men. Besides the unnecessary deaths and the destruction of the critical weapon, there was the problem of the roadblock: the three men had no additional mines to reconstitute the block, and so had to cover the approach with their personal weapons until that night.[17] Two other crews made it into town with their antitank guns; Krause put one at the north and one at the south end of the town.

Soon the G Company sector was under a mortar barrage, and the men heard the distinctive sound of flat trajectory artillery fire, meaning that the Germans had a field gun or armored vehicle nearby. Around 1000 hours, the G Company men saw signs of the enemy attack they'd been expecting all morning. A German force of two or three infantry companies, supported by at least two small tanks, could be seen maneuvering toward the southern end of Ste. Mère Eglise. The GIs opened fire with the 57 mm gun. They could not see if their rounds hit the vehicles, but the well-aimed fire discouraged the panzers from getting any closer. The enemy infantry, however, kept coming, using the hedgerows and thick underbrush to hide their advance.

Near the main road into town, PFC Dominick DiTullio manned an outpost and thus was one of the first GIs within range of the advancing Germans. When the enemy got close, DiTullio threw hand grenades, killing the leaders of the first probe and single-handedly driving off the enemy attack.[18] The rest of the enemy company pulled back to covered positions south of town.

The GI defenders knew that their line position was not continuous, that there was no defensive ring around the town. If the Germans were aggressive, eventually they would find the gaps. For a time during those early hours, a combination of rifle and machine gun fire kept the Germans at bay. When Vandervoort's 2nd Battalion moved into Ste. Mère Eglise after first light and took over the defense of the northern edge of town, Krause had more men available to patch his thin line.

Krause wasted no time taking advantage of the failed German assault that had washed up against G Company. He ordered Harold Swingler's I Company to attack Hill 20, the high ground south of town from which the Germans launched the mortar and artillery fire that had supported their morning attack against G Company.

Swingler led his men on a sweep west of the N13, planning to hit the Germans on the flank. But I Company had trouble navigating amid the hedgerows and small fields. They turned too early and came upon the N13 just a bit farther south than the G Company roadblock and still short of the German position.

The German observers on Hill 20 (near Fauville) saw the paratroopers and shifted their fire to hit the Americans, who now had to turn south and make what amounted to a frontal assault on Hill 20. Controlling the company proved very difficult, and the lead elements walked into an ambush set up by German infantrymen who had fallen back from the earlier, failed assault. During this attack Swingler was killed by gunfire, and several other men went down. The American attack, already confused, was momentarily without a leader and soon sputtered to a halt.

The German commander, having pulled back to a position south of Ste. Mère Eglise on the high ground near Fauville, was unsure of what he faced. He mounted no more serious attacks from the south, though the rain of German artillery and mortar fire killed and wounded dozens of men and began the devastation of the town. Twenty-two civilian residents of Ste. Mère Eglise were killed during the fighting, most by indirect fire. Most civilians stayed deep in their cellars. Many of those forced to abandon their homes, either because of damage or because they ran out of water (there was a critical shortage by June 8), gathered by the public well northeast of the church, where there was also a statue of the town's patron, Saint Meer. As the German shells fell, smashing their homes and shops, the civilians prayed to all their saints for deliverance.

OUR SONS

PRESIDENT ROOSEVELT'S D-DAY PRAYER

Almighty God: Our sons, pride of our nation, this day have set upon a mighty endeavor, a struggle to preserve our republic, our religion and our civilization, and to set free a suffering humanity.

Give strength to their arms, stoutness to their hearts, steadfastness to their faith. Their road will be long and hard, for the enemy is strong. He may hurl back our forces. Success may not come with rushing speed, but we shall return again and again and we know that by the grace and righteousness of our cause, our sons will triumph.

They will be sore tried by night and by day, without rest until the victory is won. The darkness will be rent by noise and flame. Men's souls will be shaken with the violences of war. For these men are drawn from the ways of peace. They fight not for the lust of conquest, they fight to end conquest. They fight to liberate. They fight to let justice arise among all thy people. They yearn but for the end of battle, for their return to the haven of home. Some will never return. Embrace these, Father, and receive them, Thy heroic servants into Thy kingdom.

While the troopers of the 82nd Airborne Division tried to find their rally points and objectives, tens of thousands of Allied assault troops were making their first runs at the five invasion beaches that stretched for fifty miles along the coast. At the far eastern end of the invasion area, the British glider troops who were the first to land in France were consolidating their hold on Pegasus Bridge, digging in to await relief from the forces coming over the beach. German troops who survived the naval and aerial bombardment got fleeting glimpses of the massive invasion fleet. The entire Norman coast was erupting into a terrible firestorm.

In Ste. Mère Eglise, those American paratroopers who had never been in battle were also shocked when they saw the bodies of their comrades hanging from the trees and light posts in the otherwise peaceful town square. The combat veterans, who had seen such scenes and worse, merely moved forward cautiously, keeping an eye out for sudden movement that might give away a German sniper.

Lieutenant Colonel Ed Krause, whose men had secured the village in a one-sided fight, picked his way up Rue du Cap de Lain, the road leading from the northwest corner of the square toward Cherbourg. The shops were closed up tightly, though they were not badly damaged (that would change over the next few days). There were no signs of civilians or the enemy. A few hundred yards up the road he came to the Hotel de Ville, the two-and-a-half-story town hall, with its central tower, evenly spaced, large windows, and striped wooden sentry boxes flanking the outside staircase. Until D-Day, the Hotel de Ville had been the offices of the *Kommandanture*, the local German military government. By the time Krause and his tired paratroopers moved up the street, the Germans were gone.

Krause climbed the steps and entered the building, stepping into a grand central hallway. Two staircases led to a landing, where a big window was centered above the flagpole over the front door. Krause pulled out the flag he had shown his men in England: it was huge, a nine-by-twelve-foot, forty-eight-star banner that had flown over Naples when the paratroopers entered that town. Krause fixed the flag to the pole, and Ste. Mère Eglise became the first town liberated by the Allies in Operation Overlord. Though the flag would stay up, the battle to hang on to Ste. Mère Eglise was not over yet.[1]

Just after dawn, Corporal Wheatley Christensen led what was left of his squad into Ste. Mère Eglise. Somewhere in the fields behind him, he'd been forced to leave Lieutenant Ringwald and Sergeant Yates, both badly injured in the jump, to fend for themselves. But he had managed to make his way past the enemy positions south of town to make it to the village; now it was time to get on with the mission.

When Christensen moved up the N13 road from the south and stepped into the town square of Ste. Mère Eglise, the first thing he saw was the bodies of a couple of paratroopers in the trees around the square. The veteran knew this meant things were still unsettled and moving pretty fast, as no one had taken the time to cut the men down.

Christensen had been part of G Company and the 505th since its inception in 1942, and Ed Krause had been the only battalion commander he had known. Like most of the soldiers in 3rd Battalion, Christensen hated Krause for his abusive ways and his love of *chickenshit*, the ridiculous details of Army life that had nothing to do with combat readiness and everything to do with power. Krause was always showing off the fact that he was in command and could order men to do almost anything.

Once in the square, Christensen scanned the area and was happy to set eyes on someone from the 3rd Battalion, even if it was Ed Krause. The corporal had his men wait for him in a covered spot on the road while he went forward to report to the colonel. As soon as Christensen got close, Krause reverted to character, chewing out the corporal because his men weren't moving fast enough, weren't, as Krause put it, "taking this seriously." He swore at them repeatedly, calling them "yellow, stupid bastards."

Christensen was stunned that Krause was still acting this way, even in combat. Finally, however, there was nothing he could say to the colonel; knowing Krause, he realized the best thing to do was to keep his mouth shut. When Krause was finished yelling, he directed Christensen to take his squad back out along the Carentan road to the southern edge of town and set up a roadblock there. Christensen snapped off a sharp salute—unheard of in combat—hoping that some German sniper might spot the pair and identify Krause as an officer and worthy target.

"I was hoping some German would shoot the son of a bitch," Christensen said later.

Twenty-year-old Anthony Antoniou, a bazooka man in B Company of the 505th, spent the morning of D-Day loading resupply aircraft at an airfield in England. He was supposed to be in France with the rest of his company, but things hadn't worked out as planned.

Antoniou's airplane had made the crossing in good order and on time, but things fell apart rapidly when they approached the drop zone. In his three combat jumps, Antoniou had never seen anything like the sky over Normandy. The Germans used parachute flares, which lit up the planes and exposed jumpers to antiaircraft fire as they descended. The machine guns and automatic cannons sent up lighted arcs of tracer fire that looked like a steady stream. The experienced soldiers among them knew that only one in every four or five rounds was a tracer, so there were many more bullets than they could see.

Antoniou and the men in his aircraft wanted desperately to get out, to take their chances outside of the slow-flying target that was the fat C47, with its chunky, unarmored fuselage and ninety-five-foot wingspan. Once they were hooked up, all they could do was wait for the green light. Antoniou knew the waiting would be awful, but that it would eventually end and they would get out.

Then the flak hit them.

Three rounds came through the fuselage, wounding two or three men. The other troops called for the medic, who unhooked his own static line and began tending the wounded men. One of the wounded soldiers had fallen against the release buttons for the parabundles slung under the plane, and those bundles, with their supply of weapons and ammunition, were gone.

Moments later, the plane was hit again, though no one was injured. Finally, as they began to slow for the drop, a bigger explosion lit the aircraft, and everyone went down in a tangle of arms and legs and static lines. Fifteen of the eighteen men in the stick were hurt, some wounded severely, and the deck was soon slick with blood.

Amazingly, Antoniou found that he wasn't hurt. He and the other two unwounded men wanted to jump, and they tried to make their way toward the door. The copilot came back and ordered the uninjured men to stay with the aircraft and take care of the wounded on the flight back to England. Antoniou, determined to jump, kept pushing for the door. Finally, the copilot pulled his .45 from its holster and pointed it at the men to back up his point. By this time the plane was past the drop zone and speeding back toward an emergency landing. That and the loaded pistol finally persuaded Antoniou and the other frustrated paratroopers to stay on board. By the time they were over the Channel, Antoniou was already thinking about how he could get back to his company.

The aircraft made an emergency landing on a field close to London, and when it came to a stop some English civilians at the airfield approached and asked what was going on. Antoniou told them the invasion was on, and they cheered even as they helped remove the wounded from the plane.

Antoniou had a few more surprises when he cleared the aircraft. First was the condition of the plane, which had large chunks of its tail assembly shot off. The troopers were stunned and quite impressed with the skill of the pilot who had brought them back safely. The other surprise had to do with his parachute.

Antoniou unhooked his harness and examined the pack: the shrapnel that had missed him had shredded his main parachute and cut the loop of cloth that connected the static line to the top of the chute. If the copilot had not stopped him from jumping, he would have been splattered on the drop zone.

There wasn't much time to ponder his close call, as an officer ordered the uninjured troopers, who had already been awake for twenty-four hours, to load bundles for the resupply runs that would occupy the jump aircraft for much of D-Day. Finally, the five healthy men persuaded a pilot to take them back and drop them in France.

Antoniou was first in the door for this daylight jump, and he saw a large "SOS" laid out on the ground in white (reserve) parachutes below them. Figuring that this meant there were Americans about, Antoniou kicked two supply bundles out before he jumped. As soon as his chute opened, someone opened fire on him, and he heard bullets tear through his canopy. Fortunately, the pilot had been flying very low, so there was little time for the German gunner to get a good shot at him, and he hit the ground still in one piece.

But the daylight jump had removed any element of surprise, so Germans on the ground were already looking for him before he got clear of his parachute. He quickly pulled out his pistol and chambered a round. Within seconds, Antoniou spotted three Germans moving along the hedgerow toward him. They fired, and two or three bullets zipped by. He had no time to consider the situation or make a decision; he merely reacted. The enemy was too far away for him to hit with his pistol. They had the drop on him, so Antoniou went down and, partially hidden by some undergrowth, played dead.

He was concerned that they might shoot at him again as they approached, but the three were not careful and came on quickly, bunched together, with no one covering him. Antoniou's only plan—his only hope—was to shoot them down before they shot him. He let them get to within twenty feet before he opened fire. He squeezed off three rounds rapidly, and the first two men went down. The third soldier turned and ran, and Antoniou, firing at him, thought he hit the man in the leg. He checked the ones closest to him: they were dead.

Antoniou got his bazooka and three rounds out of the drop bag he carried and put the weapon together. He moved away from the bodies (in case the wounded man who got away sent another patrol) and was considering what to do when seven other paratroopers approached.

The small patrol moved cautiously, unsure as to the direction they should take or how far they might be from friendly troops. Then one man signaled that he heard a vehicle, and everyone's first thought was: *tank*. The men took cover and waited. Instead of a German tank, they were surprised to see a very old truck, which had been commandeered by some paratroopers from the 507th and 508th PIRs of the 82nd Airborne. These men were also lost, and also without an officer or noncom in the group. Still, they knew enough to defer to the soldiers from the 505th, who at least had combat experience.

Private First Class Anthony Antoniou was surprised to find himself the ranking man. Since they had no way of figuring out where they were or in which direction they should move to find friendly units, they decided to hole up somewhere and let the situation develop a bit. Perhaps, they reasoned, an American unit would find them.

The group found a substantial stone farmhouse some distance from a road, which they took over. The cellar of the house was well stocked with apples (one of Normandy's main crops), potatoes, cheese, and jars of fat that the men figured were used for frying food.

They put a defensive ring around the building, dug in what weapons they had, and sent out patrols to scout the area. The patrols were to look for other Americans and to give them early warning of any enemy movement. Antoniou, because he had a bazooka, stayed on the perimeter.

One of the men in the group was an American Indian who went out alone, often at night. When he came back, he showed the others his trophies: ears he'd cut off Germans he'd killed. He kept this up for three successive nights, while the other men dug in around the house and waited for the battle to reach them. On the fourth night, the Indian did not return, and the others speculated that some German finally had gotten the best of him.

It wasn't long before the enemy in the area discovered this little outpost of U.S. paratroopers and began mortaring the house and the surrounding area. The GIs dug their holes deeper and waited for a frontal assault that never came. Either the Germans were too busy with the larger battle, or they had no idea how weak the little outpost was, but they did not try to clear the farmhouse of paratroopers.

The worst part of the shelling was that there was nothing to do but wait it out. Although the GIs were well dug in, there were casualties. The group had no medic, and they soon ran out of their first-aid supplies.

The wounded troopers were in misery. Antoniou moved the five most serious cases into the cellar of the stone farmhouse for some protection from the shelling. One man had a bad stomach wound and knew he was dying; he begged to be shot. His cries were so terrible that Antoniou removed all the weapons from the cellar where the wounded men lay, because he thought someone might go ahead and shoot the dying soldier. The others closed the doors of the house to block out his pleading.[2]

On June 7, a German officer came forward under a white flag and, speaking English, demanded that the paratroopers surrender. Someone shouted at him to "go to hell," and he withdrew. The incoming fire started again shortly after that and kept up intermittently until June 9, when a patrol from the 325th Glider Infantry Regiment found the isolated paratroopers.[3]

Jack Norton, the operations officer of the 505th PIR, was left only semiconscious after a rough landing. He woke to voices speaking French, and though groggy, he had enough of the language to know they were talking about German patrols in the area. He found a civilian who pointed him toward Ste. Mère Eglise. While moving toward the town, he came across Major Ed Zaj, the regimental supply officer, who had a broken leg. Though Norton was dazed, he managed to drag Zaj to the cover of a hedgerow and make him as comfortable as possible. Norton took note of the position and continued on his way. The next trooper he encountered was Bob Gillette, a twenty-three-year-old sergeant in the regimental intelligence section. Gillette, who had landed without injury, led Norton toward the command post, just north and east of Ste. Mère Eglise.

Along the way Norton and Gillette found Colonel Ekman. The two officers looked at their maps, comparing what Gillette knew, what the civilians had told Norton, and what Ekman had observed. Satisfied that they were on the right path, they pressed on for Ste. Mère Eglise. Along the way they compared their jump experiences and speculated on how badly scattered the regiment might be.

Norton told Ekman that his plane had been moving in excess of one hundred miles an hour when the green light came on. The speed worried him because the parachutes were designed to withstand only a ninety-mile-an-hour jump, which meant that some of the troopers might have had their parachutes destroyed by the leap from the aircraft. When Norton hit the slipstream at that speed, he was knocked unconscious. The force stripped him of all his equipment, except for his helmet. He even lost the pistol his father had carried in World War I, which the elder Norton had presented to his son on Jack's last night in the States. (Later he found he still had his harmonica, carried in the small pocket of his jacket where most paratroopers carried a switchblade knife. Norton had played the instrument on the flight over to pass the time and keep himself calm.)

Norton had planned to set up the regimental command post amid some apple orchards just outside and to the east of Ste. Mère Eglise. The area would provide good concealment and was on the side of the town closest to the beach, where they expected reinforcements to reach them. Norton and Gillette had the command post established by 0300 hours, though without wire communications, an effective radio net, or even maps other than what Gillette carried. (The parabundles with this gear had been scattered in the jump.) "Command post," they joked, was something of a glorified name. At this early hour, it was just a node for communications, a place for subordinate units to send their messages.

During those first hours Ekman and Norton ran into Major Fred Kellam, the commander of the 1st Battalion. Kellam reported that his A Company had a good drop and was moving toward the bridge at La Fière. The rest of Kellam's battalion, B and C Companies, were the regimental reserve, and Kellam was working hard to gather up those men.

Company C was not too badly scattered, but they missed the drop zone and landed about two thousand yards north of Ste. Mère Eglise, near the tiny crossroads at Baudenville. One stick was lucky to have made it at all. The plane carrying the mortar squad of C Company's 2nd Platoon was hit by several large-caliber rounds (probably 20 mm anti-aircraft fire) just before the green light came on. When one engine failed, the stopped propeller acted as a drag, pulling the aircraft onto its side and down toward the ground. The troopers inside fell in a tangle of arms and legs, weapons and packs and static lines.

The men in the stick thought they had only seconds to live, but the pilot reacted coolly. First he jettisoned the parabundles, which were on fire. He managed to restart the engine, which ran roughly but gave him some lift. Throughout all of this, he also kept track of their location relative to where the other aircraft in his flight were dropping their troopers, and he wrestled with the struggling airplane to deliver his troopers as close as possible to their drop zone.

Once the pilot got the airplane leveled, the paratroopers disentangled themselves and began yelling at their jumpmaster, Staff Sergeant Herman R. Zeitner, that they wanted out of the airplane. But Zeitner remained calm, or as calm as one could in this situation. Looking out the door, he knew that they didn't have enough altitude to jump safely—there would not be enough height for the parachutes to open.

Zeitner held back the yelling, frightened men until the pilot got them higher; then he jumped, followed by his anxious stick. In spite of all their problems, the squad landed in a good pattern close to the rest of the company.

In other aircraft, pilots were late turning on the green light and so dropped their jumpers east of Ste. Mère Eglise, closer to the invasion beaches. The Germans had concentrated more forces here, in order to counterattack any landing forces. Thus about a dozen men from B Company landed in an area infested with Germans and were captured. Lieutenant James M. Irvin, B Company Commander, and Lieutenant Robert D. Keeler, commander of the 1st Battalion's Headquarters Company, were among those taken prisoner. They managed to escape while being moved toward POW camps, and with the help of the French underground, they made it back to the regiment.

Ben Vandervoort, commander of the 2nd Battalion of the 505th PIR, greeted dawn on June 6 with a broken left leg, which had shattered on landing. Up to that point, he believed, things had been going well. Vandervoort had jumped high—which was dangerous—but the height allowed him to see that much of his battalion was on or near the right drop zone.[4]

After freeing himself from his harness, Vandervoort dragged himself to some cover and was soon found by members of his battalion's S2, the intelligence section. He sent a patrol to find some French civilians to ask about their location. Meanwhile, he watched other aircraft come toward the nearby lighted T that the pathfinders had put on the drop zone. He worried because instead of approaching the marker from the same direction as his plane had (the west), the next waves came at it from all different directions, some from as far as ninety degrees off their planned course. It was as if they had all gotten lost and were now trying to converge on the right drop zone. Vandervoort worried that the follow-on units would be more scattered than his battalion.

Soon the patrol, led by Lieutenant Eugene Doerfler, the intelligence officer, returned with the news that some helpful civilians had confirmed the American paratroopers were in the right place. Now it became a matter of gathering the troopers. Second Battalion's assembly lights—small beacons mounted on telescoping poles—didn't work, but Vandervoort had rigged some flashlights with green covers, and his men used these and green flares instead. By 0410 hours most of the 2nd Battalion had assembled on the correct drop zone. They were now a fighting force, ready to go on to their first mission, the block at Neuville au Plain.

Before they could move, Vandervoort got a message from Matt Ridgway, the division commander, telling him to wait near the drop zone. Ridgway, who had an inkling that the drop had gone badly, wanted to keep at least one intact unit—in this case Vandervoort's 2nd Battalion—close enough to seize Ste. Mère Eglise, which was the division's rallying point.[5] Around 0600, Ridgway got the news from Krause's runner that the town was secure, so Ridgway told Vandervoort to carry on with his mission and move on Neuville au Plain. Unfortunately, the runner did not bother to find Ekman, Krause's immediate superior and the intended recipient of the message, so the commander of the 505th PIR did not have a clear picture of what was happening.

From the perspective of the 505th's regimental command post, it looked to Bill Ekman like some things were going well. He had talked to Kellam and Vandervoort, and both of those men were moving toward their first objectives: Kellam toward La Fière and Vandervoort toward Neuville au Plain. But he had not heard from Krause (whose first message had been delivered right to the division commander, Matt Ridgway, but had skipped the regimental commander). Since Ekman did not know Krause had secured Ste. Mère Eglise, he sent a message to Vandervoort at 0810 hours, telling him to head toward the market town, which was a more important objective than Neuville au Plain.

Vandervoort was having a difficult time moving with his broken leg. He was too big for anyone to carry, but he spotted two misdropped troopers from the 101st who were pulling a collapsible ammunition cart. He asked if they'd give him a lift. One of the sergeants protested that he hadn't come "all the way to France to pull any damn colonel around." Vandervoort persuaded him otherwise and mounted his cart.

The original mission of Vandervoort's 2nd Battalion had been to dig in around the tiny village of Neuville au Plain to block expected German counterattacks from the north along the N13 corridor. Vandervoort knew that his new mission—move to Ste. Mère Eglise and defend that town—didn't make Neuville au Plain any less important; it just meant that he had fewer troops with which to accomplish the same tasks. He figured that a small blocking force on the N13 highway at Neuville could at least provide early warning to the defenders of Ste. Mère Eglise and would complicate the enemy's plan for attack.

Vandervoort picked the 3rd Platoon of D Company, commanded by

Lieutenant Turner Turnbull, for the task. Turnbull was an experienced combat leader with a seasoned platoon, and he wasted no time getting his men moving, with Private Edward Easton as lead scout.

The men hurried north, down the slight incline as the road left the edge of Ste. Mère Eglise. Even though thick vegetation marked the boundaries of the fields and pastures and shielded the roads, the lines of sight opened up as they moved, and the foot soldiers knew they'd soon be visible to any enemy that happened to be watching. They spread out and, wherever possible, stepped off the elevated roadbed and into the shadows alongside. Navigation was not a challenge, since the road ran straight as string from Ste. Mère Eglise.

The men could see for a good distance, and Neuville was easy to spot. There was a stone church right at the crossroads, and a cluster of houses, including a large château just north of the church. All around, the vegetation was thick and green in the wet spring. The fields to the north were mostly open, with a patchwork of walls and lanes visible to the Americans.

Turnbull's men moved through the village to the edge of some slightly elevated ground that gave them a view to the north, east, and west. Although there were hedgerows around them, they had good fields of fire for some six hundred yards in most directions. Just to their left was an orchard that blocked their view, so Turnbull sent an outpost to a group of farm buildings in the orchard. He placed one squad on the left side of the north-south road, behind a low stone wall with a gate that looked north. His other two squads went to the right of the road, also facing north, and dug in along a hedgerow. He put his bazooka team about fifty yards behind this main line, in the shade of some houses and with a clear view north along the road.

Turnbull was decisive and confident, and his men moved quickly, practiced hands at what they were doing. They were, in fact, perhaps one of the best platoons in the division that could have been chosen for his mission: they were mostly intact, after the good landing, and they were combat veterans, operating under a veteran leader whom the men trusted.

While Turnbull was setting his defense, Vandervoort reached Ste. Mère Eglise on his ammunition cart. The men grew silent as they moved into the town square, where a few paratroopers still hung in the trees, killed before they could get free of their chutes.

"Cut them down," Vandervoort ordered.[6]

Vandervoort checked in with Ed Krause, who had overall responsibility for the town. The two quickly decided that Vandervoort would take the northern part and Krause the southern part of the defensive perimeter. Since they didn't have enough paratroopers to form a continuous line, they put roadblocks on the main access roads and observation posts and defensive positions along the most likely avenues for the enemy approach.

Vandervoort got an additional bonus in town: one of the few jeeps that had survived the glider resupply mission that morning—meaning he was mobile again—and two 57 mm antitank guns, along with their crews from the 80th Airborne Antiaircraft Battalion. He put one gun at the northern end of town and checked in with his executive officer, Major James Maness, who had established the battalion command post. Vandervoort decided to run the other gun up to Turnbull at Neuville au Plain.

By the time Vandervoort reached Turnbull with the antitank gun, it was nearly 1300. He dropped the gun near a building on the east side of the highway and directed the crew to set up, with their field of fire to the north along the N13. Turnbull was grateful for the gun, and though things had been quiet so far, every man knew it was only a matter of time before the Germans attacked, most likely from the north. The only questions were: when, how many of them would there be, and would they have tanks? Turnbull had done everything he could to secure the position; when Vandervoort drove up, the lieutenant went to brief him on the defense.

Turnbull had just reached Vandervoort's jeep on the road when a French civilian rode up to them on a bicycle. The GIs were becoming used to seeing civilians, and they had already heard stories of how helpful the civilians could be (even though the Germans had warned that any civilians helping the invaders would be shot). The bicyclist told the officers, in English, that some paratroopers were bringing in a number of German prisoners from the direction of Cherbourg, to the north. Vandervoort and Turnbull went to investigate. From a little rise at the northern edge of the village, they peered through the dense undergrowth and saw a column of troops moving toward them down the middle of the N13. They didn't get much of a clear view, because they weren't very high and because there were trees lining the highway, but what they could see appeared legitimate. Men who appeared to be guards marched beside the column, showing the orange recognition panels the Americans used to signal friendly units. Both Vandervoort and Turnbull knew that there were very likely paratroopers who had landed north of Neuville; perhaps some of these men had bagged some Germans who thought the invasion was a good reason to quit the war.

But as Vandervoort and Turnbull watched, they saw something that didn't quite make sense: there were two tracked vehicles following the little procession. Vandervoort felt a little jolt, as if some alarm just went off in his chest. It seemed unlikely that the vehicles could be American—they'd heard nothing from the units coming across the beach— and it seemed less likely that some paratroopers had captured and were now driving enemy vehicles.

Others in Turnbull's platoon also noticed the advancing column and—good combat veterans that they were—also became suspicious. The assistant platoon leader, Lieutenant Isaac Michelman, on the left side of the road, moved a squad forward into an orchard to flank the advancing troops. Michelman and Private Joseph C. Hudy climbed to the loft of a barn for a better view, leaving Sergeant Bob Niland in charge of four men and a machine gun at ground level. All eyes were on the advancing column as it moved south along the highway, appearing and disappearing behind the trees. The men checked their weapons and their ammunition, calculated the range and angles of fire.

Vandervoort told Turnbull to have his machine gun fire a burst in the direction of the advancing troops, but off to the side a safe distance. The battalion commander wanted to watch the reaction. If they were

American paratroopers, they'd take cover and begin yelling and cursing. (By this point the Frenchman who had brought the news had disappeared—another suspicious development.)

When the machine gun on Turnbull's right fired, the troops in the column dived for the roadside ditches and began firing back. They had not been disarmed; it was a German column trying to get into the American position using a ruse. Suddenly Turnbull's platoon-sized outpost was in a pitched, close-in firefight.

Some of the Germans who had spotted Michelman's move forward opened fire on that outpost, and a round went through the wall of the barn and drilled the lieutenant through the cheeks of both buttocks. Down on the ground below the barn where Michelman was hit, Sergeant Niland caught fleeting glimpses of enemy soldiers moving to flank his little squad. He ordered his machine gunner to open fire, but because of the folds in the ground the gunner, Private Horace Brown, had no targets at first. Private Stanley Kotlarz, covering the squad's left, spotted some German infantrymen moving to outflank them, but the enemy was out of range of his tommy gun. Michelman came down from his post in the barn and did a quick analysis: a larger German force was pressing him from the front and now from his exposed left flank. They used the cover well, getting closer to his thin line with every passing minute. Any advantage he had gained by moving forward earlier was quickly being lost because of the enemy's aggressive reaction. Michelman ordered a withdrawal back to their original position by the stone wall, and he moved out with his men, using his carbine as a crutch and hobbling along as fast as he could go.

The vehicles that made Vandervoort suspicious in the first place turned out to be self-propelled guns. They fired smoke canisters in front of them to mask their movements and pushed for the American position. When the lead vehicle got within five hundred yards, they opened fire, knocking out Turnbull's bazooka team with one of the first shots. Another round was a near miss on the 57 mm gun and sent the crew scrambling for cover in nearby buildings. Vandervoort yelled at the men to return to the gun. They overcame their fear by going into action, pumping rounds back at the enemy. After the inauspicious start, the crew settled down, and within a few minutes they had destroyed both German vehicles.

Turnbull and Vandervoort knew what would happen next: this would be a battle between foot soldiers, with the larger German force moving to outflank the outnumbered Americans. The German commander could easily determine that the paratroopers were centered on the road; all he had to do was push his men right and left to find the end of the American line. With only about thirty paratroopers deployed, the line wasn't long.

Vandervoort and Turnbull ducked incoming fire and watched from the edge of the village. They got momentary glimpses of German infantry, just out of range, moving east and west to find the flanks of the tiny American position. It wouldn't be long—a half hour perhaps—before the attackers overwhelmed the GIs. Vandervoort told Turnbull to hold on, and he set off in his jeep toward Ste. Mère Eglise to get help.

Within minutes the German assault intensified, with the attackers now dropping mortar rounds on the American roadblock. The little crossroads was full of flying shrapnel, which kept the GIs from moving about and adjusting their defensive position to meet the new threats. The paratroopers were pinned in place by the accurate fire, while the enemy, mostly out of sight, pressed closer.

To the right of Turnbull's position was a wood that ran to the east side of Neuville and provided the enemy an excellent, concealed approach. Turnbull worried that if the Germans got in among the buildings, not only would he not be able to flush them out, they would cut off his route back to Ste. Mère Eglise. With steady pressure from that side and amid falling mortar rounds, Turnbull reoriented his tiny platoon to face east, where the Germans were using the wood to get close. Meanwhile, another detachment of German infantry began to encircle Turnbull's left. The paratroopers managed to put accurate, killing fire on any Germans who exposed themselves, but the GIs worried more about the ones they couldn't see.

When Vandervoort got back to Ste. Mère Eglise, he collared Captain Clyde Russell of E Company, whose 1st Platoon was the battalion's only reserve. The situation at Neuville was desperate, he explained. Turnbull was being pressed by at least an infantry company of 180 to 200 men and may already have been overrun. The E Company paratroopers responded immediately, and soon Lieutenants Theodore Peterson and James Coyle were leading the reserve platoon north. Peterson, unsure of the exact positions of his fellow paratroopers at Neuville, took his platoon off to the left, advancing along the west side of the N13, taking advantage of the cover offered by hedgerows and trees. If the Germans had overrun Turnbull and were now heading south, he'd collide head-on with them but would have a fighting chance among the hedgerows. The men moved as fast as they could, keeping watch for a German ambush. Every field, every hedgerow, every stand of trees was a danger zone, but still they pushed forward.

Before Peterson arrived at Neuville au Plain, Turnbull's situation deteriorated to a dangerous degree. The Germans reached some buildings at the edge of the village on Turnbull's right rear and were using the woods on the east side of the little town to pull even closer. Up to this point the German mortar fire had been the cause of most casualties. Now at least one enemy sniper shot at them from somewhere in the town. The aggressive enemy unit also managed to put a machine gun team into the barn where Michelman had been wounded (and from which he had been forced), and the gun poured heavy direct fire into the paratroopers.

Private Clifford Keenan went looking for the sniper in the village but was shot to death. Corporal Joseph Treml, who was with Keenan, saw that the Germans had not yet completely closed the noose around Neuville. He reported back to Turnbull that there was still a way out of the tightening trap.

By this point Turnbull had twenty-three troopers who could still move on their own, but he didn't have the manpower to carry out his eleven wounded. He did not want to leave the men, so he decided to fight in place until he was overrun.

The platoon medic, Corporal James I. Kelly, told the lieutenant he would stay behind with the wounded, take care of them, and surrender to the Germans. Then Sergeant Robert Niland, along with Private Julius Sebastian, a BAR man, and Corporal Raymond Smithson said that they'd form a rear guard so the rest of the platoon could get out; they'd stay behind and take their chances.

Turnbull now had another option: he could save part of his force by leaving the wounded and the rear guard behind, or he could stay put and ensure that everyone was captured or killed. It was an excruciating decision, even for an experienced combat leader. As Turnbull considered his choices, the E Company platoon sent to his aid made a noisy arrival somewhere off to his left rear. The distraction gave him his best chance to escape. He ordered the uninjured men to move south toward Ste. Mère Eglise while the volunteer rear guard—three men—turned to fight off the enemy approaching from the north, west, and east.

It was nearing 1600 hours when Peterson and his E Company relief platoon closed in on Turnbull's location, and his timing was good. His platoon, moving fast and ready for a fight, ran into the side of a German advance that was headed east toward the N13 corridor and Turnbull's left flank. Peterson, coming from the south, hit the side of the German advance and quickly overwhelmed the surprised enemy, knocking out a machine gun that had been brought forward to support the attack.

Sergeant Otis Sampson, E Company's talented mortar platoon sergeant, had also come with Peterson and wasted no time in getting the tube set up. Sampson and Harry Pickels—who had made the jump in spite of his malaria—set their tube in a grassy area from which they could see the Germans moving. Sampson watched as the Germans ran across an open road one at a time, under direct fire from the E Company riflemen. Sampson timed the interval and dropped a round into the tube just when he thought another enemy would break cover. The round exploded on the road right next to the German infantryman. Sampson then kept watch with his tommy gun while he brought some of the new members of his squad up to work the mortar under fire. He wanted his men to get as much experience as they could as quickly as possible.

The attack by the E Company platoon relieved the pressure on the left of Turnbull's position, and the rear guard squared off against the enemy probes still pushing from the north and west. Turnbull used the brief window of opportunity to pull the remainder of his men out. Once they were clear of Neuville, Turnbull linked up with the E Company platoon, and the two units began a cautious withdrawal south toward Ste. Mère Eglise.[7]

Forty-three men of D Company had gone to Neuville au Plain that morning; sixteen came out with Turnbull.

Sergeant Otis Sampson pulled his E Company mortar squad out and walked beside Turnbull on the way back toward Ste. Mère Eglise. Sampson was surprised at how calm Turnbull seemed after the hours of intense, close-quarters fighting and the loss of so many of his men. The young officer was sad, but he remained in complete control of himself and what was left of his platoon. Behind them, Sampson heard the Germans yelling, trying to draw the paratroopers into giving away their positions. It reminded the sergeant of an unfinished ball game, with one side taunting the other.[8]

By their all-day stand at Neuville au Plain, the men of Turnbull's platoon kept the Germans from launching simultaneous attacks on both the north and south ends of Ste. Mère Eglise at a time when the defenders were stretched thin. Their stand allowed their comrades to organize a stable defense of the town, which was a critical base for the entire division. The volunteers who covered the platoon's withdrawal— Niland, Sebastian, Kelley, and Smithson—enabled the bulk of their unit to escape and join the defense of Ste. Mère Eglise, where every rifle was needed.[9]

When Roy Creek, the nonswimming commander of E Company, 507th PIR, waded into the Merderet floodplain early on D-Day, it was full daylight and the Germans who had been harassing the paratroopers opened fire again. The men spread out, fifteen to twenty yards apart, holding rifles and ammunition high out of the water and moving as rapidly as they could. Still, it was slow going, and the only thing that made the move possible was that the Germans weren't on the banks in strength, and they lacked the long-range weapons that could have massacred the paratroopers out in the open. Creek could see water spouts from the incoming rounds and hear the crack and zip of a near miss, and periodically one of the troopers was hit and went under, but the group kept pushing forward toward the eastern bank and the promise of dry ground.

For Creek, the biggest threat came from the water itself. If he stepped into a hole or found a channel in the water, there was a good chance he might not come up again. But there was nothing to do except move forward.

As Gavin's aide, Hugo Olsen, had promised, the 150-odd men hit the raised Cherbourg railroad after crossing a thousand yards of deep water and tall grass. The embankment was over six feet high and offered dry, firm footing, which Creek was grateful for. The men crawling to the top were exposed but soon discovered that the Germans behind them couldn't reach that far with their small arms. They helped the wounded onto dry ground, reorganized, and were soon moving south toward the bridge at La Fière. Roy Creek led a group bringing up the rear, watching for Germans who might discover them on the railroad embankment. In his position, he could not see much of what was going on up at the front of the column, where decisions were being made by Gavin.

About a half mile north of La Fière, the group ran into some troopers from the 1st Battalion of the 505th. They told Gavin that their commander, Major Frederick Kellam, was already moving against the east end of La Fière. Gavin had great confidence in the 505th PIR, which was the only combat veteran regiment among the three that had jumped with him. Gavin had been frustrated by the slow response of the 507 men he'd spent the night with on the western bank near where he'd landed, but he sized up the 505 men as being "in great shape." With some faith now that La Fière Bridge would soon be under Kellam's control, Gavin turned his attention to Chef du Pont, the next bridge and causeway to the south.

Gavin's party included two senior officers from the 507th, Lieutenant Colonel Edwin Ostberg and Lieutenant Colonel Arthur Maloney, and they had molded the collection of men from their regiment into two pickup forces. Gavin stuck with the Ostberg group, following the railroad, while he told Art Maloney to head east and then south, to hit the same town from a slightly different approach. The two forces moved south on parallel routes toward the causeway and bridge near Chef du Pont, which was a bit smaller than Ste. Mère Eglise.

Gavin didn't know what was in front of him, if he'd run into concentrations of U.S. paratroopers or a stout German defense, or even if an aggressive enemy might be waiting to ambush them. The lines of sight along the railroad and narrow lanes were limited by the thick undergrowth and the trees in full flower. Roy Creek, responsible for security in the rear of the moving formation, knew that his right flank was safe, because the Germans couldn't hit him from the flooded Merderet plain; but his left was exposed. Safety came from moving quickly and being prepared to respond to whatever they ran into.

During the whole of this movement Creek was on the lookout for firepower: the stray bundles that might contain mortars, BARs, machine guns, and ammunition. He had the wounded and injured troopers, who no longer needed their weapons, give up their tommy guns, hand grenades, and Gammon grenades to the uninjured.

About two thousand yards south of the La Fière–Ste. Mère Eglise road, the northernmost buildings of Chef du Pont clung to ground that was only slightly higher than the flooded marsh to the right. The troopers on point signaled that they could see the town, and they scanned the area, being careful not to expose themselves to any waiting snipers.

Suddenly, the paratroopers heard movement from the direction of the town, but it wasn't the sounds of men on foot, or even of armored vehicles. It sounded like a train. The scouts passed the word back, and as they watched, a train pulled out of the Chef du Pont station, moving slowly and heading north along the track the Americans had been following. German troops aboard the train opened fire as soon as they saw the first GIs in their path. With no time to set explosives and no heavy weapons, the paratroopers could do little to stop the train except sharp-shoot at the individual enemy soldiers they saw. The firing grew in intensity, the train slowed down, and the Germans began leaping off and scattering into the nearby buildings.

Gavin's men cleared the train, and the general was surprised to find that it consisted of a half dozen or so boxcars filled with empty bottles. (Chef du Pont had and still has a large dairy.) In the middle of the train was a car with an antiaircraft battery—also abandoned. The men liberated some Normandy cheese, but there were no Germans anywhere around, so Gavin's band pushed into the village, turning right at the main intersection, heading back toward the Merderet. The lead elements came under fire again, but there did not seem to be a large enemy presence. After scouting the area around the causeway and the bridge, Gavin left Ostberg in command of about seventy-five men and headed back for the La Fière–Ste. Mère Eglise area, which was the center of the division's area of operations.

A French civilian came out to tell Ostberg that the Germans were not in Chef du Pont, at least not in any strength. Ostberg figured that any Germans in and around the town were disorganized and on the run, and he didn't want to give them time to consolidate and dig in.

Now was the time for speed. Ostberg, leading from the front of a group that was smaller than a rifle company, pushed into the town proper. Now the troopers had to pay attention not only to what was in front of them but to what was above them, on the rooftops and in upper-story windows (favorite haunts of the very effective German snipers). In addition, the side alleys and narrow roads offered the enemy opportunities for ambush.

Ostberg planned to turn to the southwest, toward the bridge and causeway, but he wanted to make sure he didn't have any German units behind him, so he sent a squad to the northeast corner of town to clear the area. He drove the troops hard, because speed and surprise were his chief advantages. His lead squad came under fire as they closed in on the bridge, and so had to clear the buildings: entering each one, working their way to the top floor or rooftop, keeping track of which rooms had been cleared. It was slow, tedious work and would have been extremely dangerous but for the fact that most Germans had pulled out. Ostberg held the town and the tiny railroad station by ten in the morning.

The paratroopers worked their way along the road leading southwest toward the causeway, past the creamery on the south side of the road. Here the little plateau that sat above the flood narrowed; from above, it looked like a funnel, with its narrow end on the bridge and causeway, its flared top back near the creamery.

Like the bridge at La Fière, the stone arch over the Merderet at Chef du Pont was no more than thirty yards long and lifted the roadway just high enough over the water for very small boats—rowboats and flat barges—to pass beneath it. And just as at La Fière, the deliberate flooding by the Germans made the bridge and causeway (longer here than at La Fière) the only way across the flat plain.

Ostberg's men had pushed about forty Germans out of the town, and the enemy had moved onto the causeway, taking their automatic weapons and dropping into foxholes they'd dug earlier. Because it blocked the view to the west, the little rise of the bridge gave some cover to the Germans who had made it across.

For the German defenders, this was a do-or-die position. There could be no maneuver or reinforcement, as anything moving above ground would be easily seen from the American positions at the eastern end of the bridge. It was, Creek thought, a bad plan for the Germans, but it did deny the GIs the use of the causeway, for the moment, at least.

But if the Germans couldn't move, neither could the Americans advance; the defenders had a clear view of any GI approaching. Ostberg, a battalion commander in the 507th, had been prepared to fight for the western end of La Fière; now he was at the head of a small, ad hoc force from nearly every company in his regiment, battling for the eastern end of a completely different bridge.

The road was achingly open, and once the advancing paratroopers passed the last houses on the road, there was very little cover. Roy Creek immediately saw that the creamery, a two-story stone building with an enclosed courtyard and windows looking out in all directions, offered an important vantage point. A man up there could spot any Germans approaching from the exposed, southeast flank.

With a well-trained mortar squad and a supply of ammunition, the paratroopers could have pummeled the Germans or at least made them keep their heads down during an assault. If they had use of just one of the tanks that was supposed to be coming ashore at that very hour, they could simply drive up and down the causeway demanding surrender. But the GIs had none of those things. They had a single mortar and no ammunition, a couple of light machine guns and BARs, and an urgent need to get to the other side of the causeway before more Germans arrived.

Ostberg's men moved forward, crawling and rushing on the narrow strip of dry ground just above the water's edge, moving close to the first German foxholes on the east side of the bridge. The lead paratroopers knew that the enemy was only a few feet away, but, pressed to the ground, they could see nothing but sky and a few feet of grass in front of them. The Germans were in no better position, hunkered down in their foxholes, peering over the edge, trying to see the GIs sneaking up on them, waiting for a hand grenade or a rifle shot or a rush and spray of automatic weapons fire. Over a few minutes that seemed like hours to the men involved in the deadly game, the tension built.

A German soldier, unable to stand the pressure and unwilling to wait for death to come to him, stood up abruptly in his hole, shouting, "Kamerad!" But the sudden move proved too much for a nearby GI, who was just as frightened. The startled paratrooper fired, knocking the German back into the hole. Seconds later another German, who may or may not have known what had just happened, also stood up, and was shot down.[10]

Now the Germans trapped on the east side of the bridge knew that there was no retreat, no surrender, nothing to do but fight. Ostberg's men were forced to crawl close enough to throw hand grenades or use rifle fire, but they picked off the positions steadily, moving toward the bridge. The Germans on the far side of the little span kept a keen eye, and any paratrooper careless enough to expose himself was shot.[11]

Ostberg and Creek saw that the slow, hole-by-hole approach would take them only to the eastern end of the bridge. There was no way to maneuver through the marsh on the sides, no way to get at the enemy on the far side of the bridge except by crossing it, and crossing it quickly.

Ostberg, thinking perhaps that he had better move while he still had some momentum, while the Germans on the causeway were still used to falling back, gave a few quick commands, then broke cover at a dead run, heading for the bridge.

Ostberg and Second Lieutenant Elliott Wagoner of A Company were in the lead, followed by a handful of troopers. Other men on the east side placed aimed fire on what they could see of the German positions on the causeway. The charging troopers fired as they ran, trying to make the Germans keep their heads down. But once the Americans were out in the open, they were easy targets for the Germans on the west side of the bridge.

Four or five paratroopers went down hard, the two officers among them. Roy Creek saw Ostberg fall off the roadway and land half submerged in the water near a guardhouse on the near side of the bridge. The colonel was still moving, but Creek couldn't tell which of the other men might still be alive.

Creek yelled for the GIs on the eastern end to put more suppressive fire on the enemy, and he quickly organized a second assault. Creek and Sergeant Glen LaPine ran forward, dodging, bent over, under fire. The first troopers they reached were dead, as was Wagoner. Creek slid off the embankment and into the water (the fourth time this nonswimmer was in the water in just ten hours since he landed in France). With fire going in both directions over his head, he grabbed Ostberg, who was still alive. Unsure how badly Ostberg was wounded, Creek and LaPine tried not to do any more damage. As gently as possible under the circumstances, they pulled and tugged the colonel so that his head, at least, was clear of the water. They could not move him back under fire, so they made him comfortable and made sure he wouldn't slip in and drown if he passed out.

• • •

Just as Ostberg's attack failed, Lieutenant Colonel Art Maloney arrived in the area with seventy-five men, the other half of the scratch force that had come down from La Fière. It was clear to Maloney, as it was to Creek, that there would be no major attack (or, for the Germans, a withdrawal) along the causeway, without supporting fire in the form of mortars, artillery, or large-caliber direct fire weapons.

Maloney and Creek moved into a position from which they could see the bridge and most of the causeway. Ostberg's men had cleared the Germans from the eastern side of the bridge, killing about twenty-four in the process and taking some half dozen friendly casualties. In the meantime, they thought they could see Germans on the far bank of the floodplain moving heavier weapons into place to fire at the Americans.

Maloney and his men had been with Creek only a short time when a runner came from the vicinity of La Fière with orders for Maloney to return to that area with most of his men. By midafternoon the regimental exec and his small force were gone, leaving Creek to hold whatever he had gained, and to try to keep the Germans from retaking the bridge, the village of Chef du Pont, and one of the critical avenues for a counterattack against Utah Beach. Creek had thirty-four troopers with him.

STE. MÈRE EGLISE

Wheatley Christensen, the trooper who saluted Lieutenant Colonel Ed Krause in the town square in the hope that a sniper was watching, took his men back out of the town square to the south to join the defensive line. In daylight Christensen had a good look at the town; because of all the time spent poring over aerial photos and sand tables back in England, the whole setting seemed familiar, like someplace he had visited.

He now had twenty men with him, his entire stick—minus the two injured men they'd left—plus four men from the 1st Battalion of the 505th, who would rejoin their own unit as soon as Christensen could figure out where everyone was. The squad moved back down the narrow road, between the houses and shops that lined the N13, to the last two houses on the southern edge of town, where Christensen made a quick survey of the area.

Just beyond the town the land begins a slow rise, reaching a ridge line less than a thousand yards south of the southernmost buildings. Krause had told Christensen to stick to the southern edge of the village, because if he moved any farther, he'd have to go all the way to the top of that ridge in order to be able to see what might be approaching on the N13. There were almost no lines of sight and lots of ways a determined enemy could get close without being seen. Christensen opted for the security of the last stone houses on the edge of Ste. Mère Eglise.

While Christensen was looking around, his troopers occupied some defensive trenches dug by the Germans. The ready-made trenches seemed a godsend for men who'd been awake for more than twenty-four hours and didn't want to dig in. But Christensen didn't like the layout of the trenches, which kept his men bunched too closely together. Also, the Germans had dug their trenches in straight lines; if the enemy got a machine gun at one end of the trench, it would be an easy matter to spray the entire length. (This fire from the flank is called *enfilading fire*.) So Christensen had the men get out, and he positioned them where they'd have the best roadblock and the best chance of surviving an assault. Then he told them to dig.

Things had quieted down. There were no signs of any French civilians, no incoming fire. When the exhausted men finally settled into the freshly turned earth of their new foxholes, they started to drift off to sleep. Christensen moved from position to position to keep the men awake. First light was a good time for a German counterattack, and the veteran corporal knew that enemy doctrine called for strong counterattacks at the earliest possible time.

The Germans were good with their mortars, and Christensen made his men dig deep. When the fire started coming in, Christensen saw that the Germans shelled their own recently abandoned trenches first. They had expected the GIs would do the easy thing and take over the ready-made trench line. The Germans were close enough to put direct fire on the GIs, and any movement above ground drew fire. Christensen and his men kept low and watched for an enemy advance.

They didn't have to wait long.

Christensen had positioned a machine gun at the top of a draw that led south from the edge of town. As he expected, the enemy tried to use the protection of the draw to advance, but his gunner took them under fire right away and beat back the first attack.

The Germans pressing the north end of Ste. Mère Eglise continued to drop mortar and artillery fire on the town and by late afternoon were moving into the vacuum left by the withdrawal of Turnbull's platoon. Paratroopers manning the roadblocks reported enemy movement to the front: foot soldiers and what looked like more armored vehicles.

Lieutenant Colonel Ben Vandervoort, who had responsibility for the northern half of the town's defense, sent for the U.S. Navy Shore Fire Control Party that had jumped in with the troopers and was now located with the 2nd Battalion. The Navy lieutenant in charge was eager to engage the armored vehicles and infantry bearing down on the roadblocks. After some initial difficulty, he was able to establish radio contact with the USS *Nevada*, which was providing offshore fire support for Utah Beach. The *Nevada* had survived the attack on Pearl Harbor and, after refitting, had fought in the Pacific before steaming to Europe to support the invasion. Now, after some quick back-and-forth with the Navy lieutenant-turned-paratrooper, the ship was ready to put some of her fourteen-inch shells on the advancing Germans.

The first salvo came in about 2145 hours, right on target, with the huge explosions straddling the road that was the German axis of advance. The geysers and lingering smoke reminded Major James Maness, executive officer of the 2nd Battalion, of a West Texas dust storm. It took more than a quarter of an hour for the smoke and dust to clear sufficiently for the Navy lieutenant to see the target and call in another salvo. By the end of the second barrage the German advance was completely broken up, the survivors fleeing north.

While Vandervoort's men fought to hang on to the northern edge of Ste. Mère Eglise, Colonel Edson Raff struggled to reach the southern end of town with a heavy task force he had brought over the beach. Raff, who had previously commanded the independent 509th Battalion (which had jumped as part of Operation Torch, the invasion of North Africa) and battled the Germans in the desert, had a critical D-Day mission: get to Ste. Mère Eglise and bring firepower to the paratroopers. Raff's task force had twenty-one Sherman tanks, two armored cars, and ninety glidermen from the 325th Glider Infantry Regiment of the 82nd.[1]

The force came ashore at Utah Beach in one of the follow-on waves behind the 4th Division. The tankers quickly removed the canvas waterproofing kits (skirts designed to keep the engine compartment from flooding when the tanks went into the shallow water from their landing craft) from their vehicles and set out to find an open road to Ste. Mère Eglise, which was a little more than six miles in straight-line distance from the beach. Once ashore, Raff had received word that the paratroopers held Ste. Mère Eglise, but there was no two-way communication; thus Ridgway, waiting for help to arrive, did not know if Raff was ashore or if he was closing on the town.[2]

At first Raff made good progress, with the glider troops riding on the hulls of the tanks and the reconnaissance unit leading the way. But by the afternoon of D-Day, Raff found himself stuck behind slow-moving elements of the 8th Infantry Regiment (4th Division), which had difficulty overcoming German resistance.

By 1700 hours Raff was within sight of Hill 20, the low ridge just south of Ste. Mère Eglise, from which the Germans had launched their early attacks on the town. Raff's lead tankers had been warned that the Germans held the ridge and some dug-in positions around the tiny crossroads of Fauville. This was a big problem. The area just south of Hill 20, between Fauville and Les Forges, was to be the landing zone for the next big wave of reinforcements, 175 gliders scheduled to begin arriving at 2100 hours.[3] The incoming gliders would land practically at the feet of the Germans on Hill 20 and would make easy targets for the defenders.[4]

Raff sent a scout car and tank forward to determine enemy strength. Shortly afterward, he heard two large explosions, and the lieutenant in charge of the reconnaissance came back on foot. The shaken young officer reported that the Germans had ambushed them. The first incoming shell had hit the staff car, and though it failed to explode, it pushed the car backward into the tank, which threw a tread. The GIs bailed out of the vehicles in a hurry.

Raff made a quick decision: he had to clear Hill 20 in order to protect the vulnerable gliders, which were due in a matter of hours. But getting his force organized in the compartmented fields proved difficult, and the Americans ate up precious time just getting in position to attack. The German defenders, alerted by the earlier probe, used the time well. When the U.S. armored vehicles pushed forward, a well-placed antitank ambush destroyed several of the Shermans. Now there were casualties and burning vehicles spread across the small battlefield, and for this expenditure the Americans had advanced only a few hundred yards.

While Raff organized his attack, a group of paratroopers who'd wound up with his force due to a misdrop went on their own offensive. Lieutenant Roper R. Peddicord, an Indiana native and platoon leader in Easy Company of the 505th, had landed with his men near Les Forges. They sorted themselves out from some misdropped 101st Airborne Division troopers and eventually linked up with Raff's force to catch a ride to Ste. Mère Eglise.

After seeing the results of the antitank ambush, Peddicord decided his footsoldiers could root the enemy out of the defensive positions. Peddicord and his men dismounted from the tanks and set off for the crest of Hill 20, using the cover and concealment offered by the thick vegetation and shady lanes. The aggressive platoon leader and his men caught some of the German defenders off guard, grenading several positions and even liberating a few captured paratroopers.

They were playing a deadly game of cat and mouse in the shadowy lanes and small fields, advancing, listening, trying to see the enemy without giving away their own position. But after the first assaults the Germans knew the Americans were on the move, and they prepared their own ambush. Peddicord, leading from the front, walked into a kill zone. A machine gun opened up, killing him instantly and nearly hitting Private Harry Anderson, who was behind the young officer. The remnants of Peddicord's platoon pulled back and rejoined Raff's force.

As the sun rolled westward and the hands on his watch inched toward 2100, Edson Raff still did not have control of Hill 20, and the gliders scheduled to come in were in danger of landing right on top of German positions.

Ridgway had not heard from Raff and was unaware of Raff's efforts to break through to Ste. Mère Eglise, but the division commander did know that the Germans were on Hill 20 with enough strength to disrupt the glider landings south of town. Division headquarters tried to redirect the glider force toward the original drop zones of the 505th PIR, north and slightly west of Ste. Mère Eglise. Ridgway ordered the pathfinders of the 505 to drag the lights, signal panels and even the electronic Eureka system out to mark this alternate landing zone area, but he remained concerned that the glider pilots would not react in time to the signals, or might—if they were suspicious—ignore the new markings. In addition, the area north of Ste. Mère Eglise did not belong entirely to the Americans; there were plenty of Germans in the area who could attack the glider troopers before they had a chance to regroup on the ground.

Some of the glider pilots saw the new markers and headed for the landing zone north of town, where they met heavy small arms and automatic weapons fire. The pilots tried to force the aircraft down as quickly as possible, but the fields here were too small. Vandervoort's 2nd Battalion paratroopers watched helplessly as gliders smashed into hedgerows and trees.

Otis Sampson saw one of the gliders approach a landing field near his position that was filled with Rommel's asparagus. The pilot, seeing the posts at the last minute, slipped sideways to cut his speed, then straightened out and plowed through the stakes. Sampson watched, fascinated, until he realized that the big aircraft was coming right at him. Sampson dived over an embankment and balled up on the ground, listening as the glider crashed into the trees and broke up with a sickening sound.

Once the danger was past, Sampson clambered up the bank to see if he could help. The glider had come to rest with its tail up in the air at a forty-five-degree angle. Sampson moved toward it, then heard a noise and saw the side of the fuselage give way as the men inside kicked their way out. The men cleared the big target as quickly as possible and made their way to cover.

Sampson yelled at them, "You're in friendly territory," but the glider troops were too intent on getting to a position they could fight from to listen to him. Moments later, Sampson found the pilot, who had been badly injured but lucky enough to land near the 2nd Battalion aid station.

Just before the gliders came in, an E Company trooper named Ed Carpus left his foxhole for a nearby ditch in order to move his bowels. A glider landed on top of him, pinning him in the ditch and injuring him badly enough to require medical evacuation.

Lieutenant James Coyle, who had tried to reassure the French civilian that the paratroopers were staying in France, took cover behind a tree as another glider plowed into his command post. Coyle flattened himself out and wasn't hurt, but wound up crawling the length of the wing to get out from under the wreckage.

Otis Sampson waited until some of the firing died down before he tried to get a jeep out of the glider nearest him. His first idea was to blow the tail off the Horsa using the explosive charge rigged in the fuselage for that purpose, but Sampson couldn't figure out how to do it. Instead he backed off and threw a Gammon grenade at the tail, which all but disappeared in the explosion, leaving the jeep intact and in plain view. After the dust settled, Ben Popilsky, a soldier in Sampson's squad, came around the wreckage of the glider. Popilsky was on the other side of the wreck when Sampson threw the grenade and was convinced that the Germans were trying to blow him up.

The men of D and E Companies wasted no time in recovering the important equipment and supplies on board the gliders, and helping the wounded and injured glidermen. They secured only a fraction of the food, ammunition, 57 mm guns, jeeps, and medical supplies the glider reinforcements brought in, but every scrap was important.

● ● ●

Colonel Edson Raff watched the gliders come down on Hill 20, their original landing zone, which he had been unable to clear. Just as they did on the north side of Ste. Mère Eglise, the Germans opened up with heavy concentrations of small arms fire against the gliders, whose plywood (Horsa) and canvas (Waco) sides offered no protection and only served to keep the troops trapped inside when they landed.

Raff saw a glider land beside one of the burning tanks that had been hit in the earlier ambush; the glidermen jumped clear before the aircraft also caught fire. Another landed on top of the German positions, and while the amazed men of Raff's force watched, the uninjured crew removed their jeep, collected their equipment, and drove away from the still-firing Germans—as calmly as if they were on a field exercise in England—down the road to the American position south of the landing zone. Meanwhile, a stream of wounded and injured made their way slowly toward Raff's lines, held up by their buddies, shepherded by their officers and noncoms. Raff sent out his own troops (some of them glider infantry from the 325th Glider Infantry Regiment) to help their comrades.

Wheatley Christensen, who had forced his squad to abandon the German trenches, was in a foxhole near the southern end of town when the gliders started coming in. There was no advance warning, just a sudden rush of wind nearby and a huge dark shape going right overhead, startling the men in their foxholes. Christensen heard one of the aircraft break apart, its wings torn off, its fuselage battered by the hedgerows and trees. One GI—he turned out to be the pilot—made his way to the paratroopers' line. Christensen pulled the frightened airman into his own foxhole and told him to stay low. The pilot stayed there the entire night. Every once in a while, he asked Christensen what was going on, but he never raised his head above ground level.

As sunlight faded on June 6, Raff pulled his men into a defensible position, out of range of the German guns on Hill 20, and well south of his planned linkup with the troops in Ste. Mère Eglise. His men had run into stiff resistance and cleverly dug-in defenders, and had witnessed the dizzying number of ways gliders could kill their own occupants. Raff did not send word to Ridgway that he was close,[5] even though a determined patrol, or even a few men on foot, could have gotten around the German defenses and found their way to Ste. Mère Eglise.

Raff had received a message, while he was still on the beach, that had originated at Ridgway's headquarters, so he assumed that there was two-way communication and that Ridgway would have heard that Raff's force was on the way. He later said it was "inconceivable" to him that Ridgway did not have contact with the landing force. In any case, as D-Day drew to a close, Ridgway still did not know that his critical relief force was nearby.

Private First Class Ed Ryan, a twenty-two-year-old from Hyde Park, New York, was still soaked to the skin when he landed in Normandy. He and his comrades in the 319th Glider Field Artillery (75 mm pack howitzers) spent their last nights in England in the open at their airfield in a pouring rain, all their equipment packed up, all their tents put away. The men were wet through by the time they were ordered to the flight line to board the aircraft.

Ryan and his comrades, forward observers and communications men, got another surprise at the airfield: they were going in on a British-made Horsa glider, rather than one of the smaller American-made Wacos, even though they had never trained on the Horsa. Instead of a meticulously planned load with proper tie-downs and distribution, Ryan and twenty-three other GIs, plus the two British pilots, crammed into the big wooden box. In the center of the aircraft was a jeep trailer full of radios and communications gear. The rough ride soon had the men airsick, and Ryan noticed that the floorboards ran green—they'd had spinach with their supper that afternoon.

There were no windows inside the glider, but Ryan was close enough to the pilots to see the airspeed indicator. He was alarmed that it still read over a hundred miles an hour as the big aircraft made its final approach. As the dark rim of the earth came up toward them, the men braced themselves for landing by locking arms.

The crash was tremendous, everything spinning around and around. Ryan heard what sounded like a wing tearing off. Then the glider flipped onto its side and went sliding across the ground. When it finally came to a halt, Ryan was standing upright on the bulkhead that had been opposite his seat. Both pilots had been killed, crushed in the flimsy nose of the aircraft, but Ryan was alive and relatively unhurt. He and a few others who could move punched a hole in the fuselage, on what was now the top of the wooden craft. When they got out, they mustered only eleven able-bodied men. The tail of the Horsa had come off in the crash, so Ryan and the other survivors pulled the jeep trailer free of the wreckage.

One of the men in the group was Lieutenant Radcliffe S. Simpson, a 1942 graduate of West Point whose father was a general officer. Simpson took a look around and figured that they had landed southwest of their objective, Ste. Mère Eglise. He divided the men into teams: one would pull the trailer and its critical equipment while the other kept watch; then they'd switch. When they moved out, Simpson took the lead.

As they moved down a sunken road, Ryan looked up to see a coal-bucket helmet silhouetted against the sky. He said nothing. After they had gone a bit farther, someone asked if anyone else had seen the German walk by. Ryan said he had. Another voice in the darkness said, "I would have shot him." Still another GI said, "That's why we didn't tell you."[6]

Lieutenant Simpson was still out front, acting as the scout so they didn't blunder into an ambush. He saw what looked like an intersection, and called a halt while he went forward to check things out. Ryan and the others waited in the darkness, breathing heavily and adjusting their equipment.

Suddenly the night was split by flashes of small arms fire in the intersection, and Simpson went down.

Unsure of the enemy strength in front of them, the troops abandoned the trailer and set out cross-country to find Ste. Mère Eglise.

Ryan had seen nearly half of his buddies killed in the crash, only to emerge and find that theirs was the only glider in the area. He had no idea where they were, but the lieutenant's decisiveness made him feel better. After Simpson was killed, the men were left to move through the dangerous countryside, hoping to find the rally point but afraid they'd find another ambush.

The suddenness of the transition from a training environment to the battlefield was disorienting for many of the men. Private Clarence Hughart of C Company, 507th PIR, anticipated the change on the drive from their tents to the airplanes on June 5. The men around him were quiet, each lost in his own thoughts, and with none of the horseplay and grab-ass that attended nearly everything they did together. Hughart thought about the journey he was on: he was going to a place where men he'd never met would try to kill him, and where he was expected to kill them first.

Hughart saw no one around him when he landed, and had the sensation that he was completely alone in a very dark and too-quiet field. Seconds later, a squad of German soldiers approached, and Hughart stood to fire at the first one that came into sight. But his leg collapsed under him, and the Germans simply surrounded him, pointing their weapons at his head. He expected his life to end in this dark field.

But instead of shooting, the Germans grabbed him and took away his weapon, his watch, and his billfold. They all seemed to speak at once, but Hughart understood nothing until someone asked in English, "Are you an American?"

They gestured for him to stand, but Hughart's leg would not support his weight. He lay back down on the ground, and soon one of the Germans appeared with a slender tree branch, which he fashioned into a splint to brace the American's shattered leg. Then Hughart's captors carried him across the field and laid him in the bed of a truck. By this time other patrols had collected some parachutes, and Hughart's handlers tried to make him comfortable on the silk chutes.

The GI was in tremendous pain, but not so distracted that he forgot to be amazed. His captors—these men he had come to kill—could simply have shot him where they found him and been done with it. His body might not have been found for weeks. Yet here they were trying to take care of him.

At a company command post, a medical orderly looked at him and determined Hughart had a broken femur. He spent several days on a bed of straw right near the command post and was eventually evacuated to a German military hospital in Cherbourg. He was freed when the Allies captured that port city, and told anyone who would listen that, in spite of his grave injury, he'd been one of the lucky ones.

LA FIÈRE BRIDGE

Company A of the 505th PIR had an excellent drop, one of the best in the 82nd Airborne Division. The commanding officer, Lieutenant John Dolan, was a Boston native, like the teenage pathfinder Bob Murphy. Dolan had a year of law school under his belt, with plans to return to his studies after the war. Originally assigned to I Company as a platoon leader, he'd been moved up to command A Company when the original company commander was wounded in Italy. Dolan was a tough, nononsense Irish American (the soldiers called him "Red Dog" because of his hair color) who trained his men hard. He impressed the A Company soldiers immediately with his competence, and with the fact that he respected their experience.

Dolan and his lieutenants gathered on the drop zone to plan their first move, while around them the noncoms and soldiers recovered weapons from the parabundles. The 60 mm mortars and light machine guns in those bundles would be the mainstay of their firepower until relief reached them from the beach.

The tight drop was a good start, and pathfinder Bob Murphy, who'd been on the ground waiting for the rest of the company, saw that the men were in good spirits as they worked. Murphy had seen this before among the paratroopers: they'd reached the drop zone, landed safely and were still alive, and each man felt a little sense of elation at making it to this point.

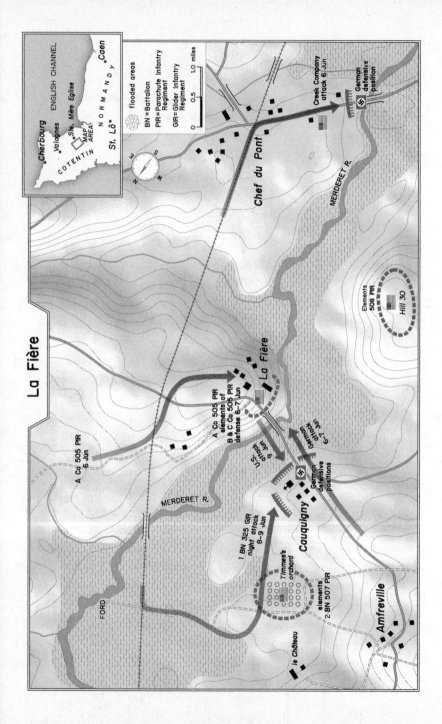

La Fière

Inset map (top right):

ENGLISH CHANNEL

Cherbourg

Valognes

Ste. Mère Eglise

MAP AREA

COTENTIN

NORMANDY

St. Lô

Caen

Legend:

flooded areas

BN = Battalion
PIR = Parachute Infantry Regiment
GIR = Glider Infantry Regiment

0   0.5   1.0 miles

Map labels:

A Co 505 PIR 6 Jun

MERDERET R.

Chef du Pont

Creek Company attack 6 Jun

German defensive position

Elements 506 PIR

HIll 30

La Fière

A Co 505 PIR elements of B & C Co 505 PIR defense 6–7 Jun

U.S. attack 9 Jun

German attack 6–7 Jun

German defensive positions

Cauquigny

1 BN 325 GIR night attack 8–9 Jun

Timmes's orchard

elements 2 BN 507 PIR

le Château

FORD

Amfreville

A friend of Murphy's, Corporal Darrell Franks, approached the pathfinder on the ground. Franks, a native of Asheville, North Carolina, was looking for their squad leader, Sergeant Bill Owens. Franks, who shared the sense of relief on making it to the ground in one piece, managed a bit of humor: "Hey, Murphy, you seen any of those Vou-lay vous cooshares tonight?"

Within thirty minutes of landing, Dolan had determined exactly where he was and where his objective lay, and before dawn he had accounted for nearly 90 percent of his men.[1] Dolan kept one of his company's pathfinders, a German-American named PFC Charles Burghduff, with him as an interpreter. First Platoon, under Lieutenant William Oakley, took the lead, followed by Dolan's headquarters element, 3rd Platoon (which had two lieutenants), and 2nd Platoon in the rear under G. W. Presnell.

Every man knew the mission: get to the bridge at La Fière as quickly as possible, without becoming engaged anywhere along the way. The soldiers were so well disciplined that when a German motorcyclist passed them in the darkness, headed east toward Ste. Mère Eglise, the paratroopers did not open fire. They were intent on getting to their objective.

The Merderet River is not much more than a creek where it makes a series of picturesque turns through the flats west of Ste. Mère Eglise. The little stone bridge just west of a sizable farm called Le Manoir La Fière[2] is a graceful, low arch only twenty yards from end to end. A farmer using a flat-bottomed boat to move goods toward the Douve River would have to duck almost to the floorboards to fit under the bridge.

But La Fière loomed large in the minds of Allied airborne planners who studied the maps of the lower Cotentin Peninsula in the months leading up to D-Day, and was particularly important to Matt Ridgway, Jim Gavin, and the men of the 82nd Airborne Division.

There were three main avenues German forces could use to smash through the lightly armed paratroopers in a counterattack on the Utah landing beaches. One came through Ste. Mère Eglise from the north, along the N13 (where Turnbull's men made their stand on the afternoon of D-Day). A second was across the Chef du Pont causeway and bridge, which lay to the southwest of the town. The third and most direct counterattack route was the road from the St. Sauveur le Vicomte area—where the Germans were known to be in strength—across the bridge at La Fière and through Ste. Mère Eglise. Ridgway had to hold these three doors closed to the counterattacks, and had to control them so the vast VII Corps, coming ashore at Utah, could make its break across the neck of the peninsula.

As with the rest of the Merderet Valley, the area around La Fière flooded when the Germans closed the locks near the mouth of the Douve River, creating a shallow lake nearly a thousand yards across on the valley floor. Any force trying to cross the Merderet near Le Manoir La Fière would be channeled onto the narrow, six-hundred-yard-long causeway that carried the road above the surrounding flood.[3]

The division battle plan designated one parachute regiment to seize each of the two key bridges. The 507th PIR was to drop west of the La Fière causeway, establish a base near the tiny crossroads at Cauquigny, and hold the critical avenue until relieved. The 508th PIR was to do the same thing with the Chef du Pont causeway. The mission of the 1st Battalion of the 505th PIR was to grab the eastern end of La Fière as a backup to the 507th.

Before A Company left the DZ, Dolan was joined by Major Jim McGinity, the executive officer of the 1st Battalion. McGinity had spent his first hours on the ground determining where he was (on target) and looking for his boss, 1st Battalion Commander Fred Kellam. He had no luck finding Kellam or the combat engineers of B Company, 307th Airborne Engineers, who were to accompany the battalion and remove any explosive charges the Germans might have put on the bridge at La Fière. When he couldn't find the engineers, McGinity joined A Company and told Dolan they would move without the engineers.[4]

What Dolan did not know as he headed toward his objective in the growing light of D-Day was that the bad drops of both the 507th and 508th negated the original plan. Instead of backing up a friendly regiment of nearly two thousand men across the river, Dolan and his 150 or so men would be the front line on this critical avenue.

The main road runs east from the bridge, rising about sixty feet over two hundred yards before making a sharp turn to the northeast and Ste. Mère Eglise, about two miles away. The soldiers came to refer to this as the upper road. Just east of the bridge, a "lower road" breaks off to the north, parallel to and just a few feet above the river, heading northeast and eventually connecting with the N13 highway at Neuville au Plain. The buildings that comprise the manor are clustered on the south side of the road immediately to the east of the bridge. The high ground between the two roads dominates both the causeway and bridge, as does the manor.

Le Manoir La Fière is a collection of centuries-old stone buildings. The manor house itself is eighty feet wide across the front, and another twenty feet deep. On the back of the house, facing east and away from the bridge, is an enormous three-story tower enclosing an interior staircase. Below that is a cellar that serves as a storeroom for farming equipment, with doors at ground level. A cluster of barns and smaller buildings huddles around the manor, and much of the estate is enclosed in a stout stone wall. From the tower, and from the rooms on the upper floors, an observer has long views of the rolling fields to the east. The complex is not an ideal defensive position, as there are numerous covered and concealed routes an attacker could use to get close.

A large berm circles the manor on the east side, a reminder that this piece of ground was significant to warriors in other ages as well. The berm, twenty feet high in places, was built centuries earlier, probably as a means of defending a river-crossing site.[5]

The Germans recognized the significance of the causeway at La Fière, but they did not have the resources to defend every foot of ground in Normandy. They dug defensive positions, facing the flood, on the western end of the causeway near Cauquigny, but these were empty when the paratroopers landed early on June 6. And it took until the last hours of June 5 for the Germans to do anything about securing the manor and the eastern end of the bridge.

Just before midnight (about two hours before the first pathfinders jumped into France), some German soldiers appeared at Le Manoir and woke its owner, Monsieur Louis Leroux, to tell him they were taking up positions on his property. In the four years of German occupation, this had never happened before. Leroux thought the sudden change meant something big was about to happen, so he woke his family and sent his wife and children to the cellar for protection. Meanwhile the Germans, part of an engineer unit, picked out some defensive positions around the grounds, then tried to get some sleep.

Whether because of poor communication or uncertainty about their mission, the engineers failed to bring explosives for blowing the bridge if that became necessary.[6]

While "Red Dog" Dolan and the men of A Company, 505th PIR, were celebrating an on-target drop, Lieutenant Colonel Charles Timmes, commander of the 2nd Battalion of the 507th PIR, was struggling in the flooded Merderet. Timmes's parachute stayed inflated just above the surface of the water, dragging the helpless paratrooper and threatening to drown him. Finally, after covering a few hundred yards, much of it under water, Timmes hit a bank and was able to free himself.[7]

Timmes gathered ten men, most from his own stick, but had no idea where the rest of his battalion might be, and had no radio with which to contact Colonel "Zip" Millett, his regimental commander. Unlike many of the troopers who started out in the marsh, Timmes was able to figure out where he was pretty quickly.

Timmes saw the silhouette of a railroad bed on the other side of the flood and guessed that he was west of the Merderet and east of Amfreville, which was his objective. Around 0400, two gliders landed close to his position, and he collected ten more men. With stragglers making their way out of the flood, he now had about thirty troopers. But the gliders drew fire from some nearby Germans, so Timmes hurried his preparations to get his tiny force out of the area.

By dawn Timmes could hear firing to his west, near Amfreville, and he put his men in movement order—flankers out, scouts to the front—and set off through the orchards and fields for the little hamlet. Along the way he met Lieutenant Louis Levy, who had also gathered some thirty men. Now numbering around sixty, the Timmes force moved as if expecting enemy contact, but they were still caught off guard and ambushed by a German machine gun team. Four men were killed in the initial burst of fire, and as Timmes pulled back, he saw the Germans getting ready to pursue. Fearful of getting surrounded in open ground, Timmes hustled away from Amfreville, toward an apple orchard near where he had crawled out of the water. He used the flooded marsh to protect his back, and by 0930 he had formed a defensive perimeter (near the spot where Jim Gavin had landed hours earlier).

Timmes sent Lieutenant Levy on a combat patrol to Cauquigny, a crossroads hamlet at the western end of the La Fière causeway. Since securing Cauquigny was another of the 507th PIR objectives, Timmes hoped Levy would find some of the regiment there. He told Levy to take ten men, move to the area near the church, and dig in so that his weapons covered the approaches in both directions. Levy left almost immediately, moving cautiously so that he didn't run into any more ambushes in the thousand or so yards he had to cover.

On the way to his objective, Levy came across Lieutenant Joseph Kormylo of D Company, 507th PIR. Kormylo had twenty troopers from various units in the 507th, as well as a .30-caliber machine gun and crew. Levy sent the bulk of this force to reinforce Timmes in the orchard but kept the machine gun. Kormylo wanted to accompany Levy to Cauquigny, and Levy agreed.

The Americans moved carefully through the farm fields and orchards, staying clear of the few roads and quiet farmhouses. Levy was pleased to find that the enemy had not occupied Cauquigny, though the Germans had prepared foxholes along the edge of the flooded area, facing east toward the La Fière end of the causeway. Levy and Kormylo checked out the old stone church, its roof crushed by a bomb, its walls punctured. A tiny graveyard spread out on the east side, not more than a few dozen simple headstones surrounded by a low fence. The rest of Cauquigny consisted of only a few houses, set close to the dirt road.

This tiny crossroads, only a few feet above the flood, was one of the principal objectives of the entire 82nd Airborne Division. The VII Corps, in its push to break out of the lodgment area, needed the La Fière Bridge, the causeway, and Cauquigny. When Levy arrived with his ad hoc force, the area was quiet and up for grabs. After setting his machine guns and his men, Levy allowed his patrol to break out some rations and eat lunch. It wasn't long before a French farmer appeared, offering the men milk and cider. The entire scene was deceptively peaceful, which might have contributed to oversights by two officers: Timmes did not come to have a firsthand look at the important bridgehead, and Levy did not push a patrol across to make contact with the 1st Battalion of the 505th PIR. The loose hold they had on Cauquigny would be tested before the end of the day.

Dolan's A Company encountered no trouble as it moved toward its objective at La Fière. When they were about three hundred yards east of the manor house, the company scouts came across a narrow lane that broke off the main road and headed east. Lines of sight were short: the thick hedges and trees bordering the fields made it difficult to see more than a few hundred yards. Dolan's company was just shy of this crossroads when they took some sniper fire from the thick brush ahead of them. There would be no sidestepping the Germans now. They were in front of him, and his job was to push them out of the way. Dolan sent word back to his trail platoon, under Lieutenant G. W. Presnell, to move up and around the right side of the company, to attack the manor from the north.[8]

Presnell led his men almost as far as the river and then turned toward the manor and bridge from the north, hoping to flank any Germans at the crossing. Presnell got to within a few hundred yards of the bridge, where he could just see the tops of the stone buildings that made up Le Manoir La Fière, when a German solider, dug in near the road, opened up on his lead scout from close range.

The GI, instead of returning fire, calmly unscrewed the cap on a Gammon grenade and tossed it at the German, killing him. Presnell himself moved down to the low ground by the river and got close enough to the bridge to see that there were no demolition charges on it. He moved gingerly, since the explosion of the Gammon grenade had alerted the Germans that they were under attack. The defenders opened fire on the advancing paratroopers, and Sergeant Ralph W. Barr died in the initial hail of bullets. Presnell also heard a machine gun firing from somewhere in the manor, though it did not seem to be aimed at his men. He could not move to his right, because the river ran along this flank. Moving left would put him right back in the path that the rest of the company was using, which might expose his men to friendly fire. The enemy blocked the route straight ahead, where they had killed Barr, so Presnell pulled his men back.

Meanwhile Dolan, now down to two platoons, continued to press toward the bridge from the east. His axis of advance was the main road running toward the bridge from Ste. Mère Eglise. The road was lined with hedges, trees, and undergrowth, making it difficult to see what was ahead. Dolan paused a few hundred yards short of the manor house, where he could see the top of the tower and the flat plain of the flooded Merderet Valley. Just ahead of him was a relatively open field, about one hundred yards deep and seventy-five yards wide, which gave good fields of fire to any German defending the manor. *This would be the place to defend*, Dolan thought; the problem was that the Germans had chosen the place for this fight. They would know the stone walls, the covered lanes, and the hedgerows, which gave them an advantage. But Dolan could choose the point of attack, and the combat veterans of A Company were in the habit of capturing their objectives.

Dolan called his 3rd Platoon leader, Lieutenant Donald G. Coxon, and the two men looked out from the concealment offered by the hedgerows. Just in front of them, the land dipped down toward a deep ditch. Anyone who went forward from here could be seen from the upper floors of the manor house, which was just a few hundred yards away. There was an eerie quiet after the earlier firing, and a maddening lack of knowledge about where the Germans were.

Coxon had only to look through the green brush to see that the next move—across the mostly open field—was dangerous. It was entirely possible that some German would be watching his every move, was in fact watching even as he peered through the grasses and vines that choked the ditches and lined the hedgerows. But this is what it all came down to: all the talk of aggressiveness, of taking the fight to the enemy, of rooting the Nazis out of France, even all the high-minded rhetoric about liberation and victory. It came down to a few young men willing to move from some protected spot and step into what might be a killing field.

Dolan told Coxon to bring up his platoon scouts, and Coxon replied, "Well, sir, if I have to send someone out into that I'll go myself."[9]

Coxon took two scouts and led the way himself, crawling forward along the hedgerow toward the distant manor and the bridge that lay beyond it. The three men had gone about a hundred yards when a machine gun opened up. Coxon was hit, one scout was killed instantly, and the other, Private First Class Robert Ferguson, was mortally wounded. The A Company men immediately returned fire. Though they could not pinpoint the enemy gun, they hoped that spraying the manor with small arms fire would force the German gunner to keep his head down. Coxon tried moving back to his men, who were not far way, but was immediately struck again, this time a gruesome stomach wound.

The call went back along the line for a medic, and Sergeant Fred Morgan, a twenty-two-year-old from Edgartown, Massachusetts, moved forward, one hand on his helmet, the other holding his first-aid bag.

Morgan was a veteran of the campaigns in Sicily and Italy, and he had seen many of the awful things high-velocity weapons could do to a human body. The medics enjoyed a tremendous reputation among the paratroopers they cared for. When a man was wounded and the call went out for a medic, a medic came up. It didn't matter that the wounded man was under fire, or that shells were falling, or that the medic himself might become a casualty. When they were needed, they responded, and for this the infantrymen loved them.

Coxon was hit badly, and Morgan saw immediately that the young officer was going to die. Even if he could be moved, there was no way to evacuate him, no field hospital to receive him. There would be no support until the paratroopers linked up with the units coming across the beach. As he would do many times in the coming campaign, Morgan did what he could to make the dying man comfortable. Coxon quickly bled to death.

The 3rd Platoon now came under the command of Second Lieutenant Robert McLaughlin, a big Montana native with a wide-open smile. This was McLaughlin's first combat action, and his first task was to step forward and take the place of a predecessor who had just been killed leading his men from the front.

McLaughlin tried another route along the edge of the field where Coxon was hit. The soldiers advanced in short rushes, each man moving on his own from one covered spot to the next. Corporal Frank Busa, who operated the platoon radio, saw an opening and ran forward in a crouch, bent forward as if in a driving rain. There was another burst of fire, and Busa went down.

McLaughlin was only a few yards away, and he moved quickly to drag Busa out of the line of fire, but was hit himself and crumpled to the ground.

Now Dolan, also watching from nearby, moved to his lieutenant as the paratroopers tried to suppress the enemy fire. Dolan reached McLaughlin and found the lieutenant's midsection a bloody mess: at least one round had hit him in the leg and traveled through his lower stomach, coming out his back and probably shattering his pelvis. Nearby, Busa was clearly dead.

Dolan moved to drag McLaughlin back to cover, but the young officer was in terrible pain, and he begged Dolan not to move him. Dolan's only recourse was to overcome the German defenders and clear the area so McLaughlin could get whatever medical attention the medics could render.

With five of his men killed in a short time, and with his company no closer to the manor house, Dolan decided to take the point himself. He and Major McGinity led the remnants of 3rd Platoon on a swing to the left, toward the south, where they would try to circle around the defenders. Dolan suspected that the Germans were not firing from the buildings themselves but had moved into the thick brush and hedgerows east of the manor.

McGinity was in the lead, keeping his left shoulder tight to a thick hedgerow. Dolan was three or four paces behind him and to McGinity's right. By not hugging the hedgerow, Dolan thought he might be able to see into the opening the Germans were firing through.

But the defenders were waiting for them again and opened up with at least two machine pistols at very close range. McGinity was hit multiple times and died instantly. Dolan spotted some leaves fluttering and thought that opening might be the source of the fire; he squeezed the trigger on his tommy gun, sending a stream of .45-caliber slugs into the hedgerow. As he fired, he also dived for a foxhole—apparently dug by the Germans as part of their defense—that was just to his left. He kept shooting, though he was only guessing where the enemy might be. The lead men in 3rd Platoon—just behind him—were also under fire, and Dolan wanted to give them some covering fire so they could react. As far as Dolan could tell from his hole, the paratroopers were under fire from two directions: from the hedgerow and from some other weapons that seemed to be farther away, though he didn't think the fire was coming from the manor house.

Dolan was stuck in the foxhole, and he told his 3rd Platoon noncoms to hold fast. He could hear machine gun fire at other points around the manor house and buildings, but he did not know who was engaged.

Meanwhile, Presnell and his platoon were still trying to get at the Germans from the north side. Presnell and Private Harold J. Paul crawled along the riverside toward the bridge, but the Germans spotted them and one of them drilled Presnell's canteen with a rifle round.[10] Others in Presnell's platoon pushed ahead but were also turned back after two more men were killed by accurate German fire.

• • •

A soldier studying a map of the La Fière area might conclude that an infantry assault, while not easy, would be a fairly straightforward affair. Any defenders holed up in the thick stone buildings had the advantage of a formidable position but gave up the ability to maneuver. The troops inside the manor house had their backs to the river and flooded plain, and the only route of escape—once the paratroopers had moved in from the east—was across the painfully exposed causeway. And even the stoutest fortress can be cracked eventually.

But the farmland east of Le Manoir la Fière was a quilt of small fields, part pasture and part orchard, cut by ditches overgrown with vines and trees. Here the A Company men also encountered the thick hedgerows that would turn the campaign in Normandy into a bloody, close-range slugfest. Soldiers in one pasture might remain completely unaware of what was happening in an adjacent field, and intense firefights were heard only as confusing sounds. Even identifying the sounds of firing as coming from an enemy or American weapon—a critical skill for a combat soldier—was difficult in the deadly compartments.

While the men of Dolan's A Company were trying the German position from two different directions (Presnell along the low river road and Dolan from the east), another group joined the attack.

Captain Ben Schwartzwalder, the commander of G Company, 507th PIR, landed east of the flooded Merderet plain and rapidly assembled about forty men, roughly one-third of his company. Schwartzwalder, who had captained the West Virginia University football squad in 1933, was tough, action-oriented, and used to being in charge. He had volunteered for the paratroopers in 1941, after leaving a job coaching high school football in Ohio, where he won two state championships coaching boys not much younger than the paratroopers of G Company.[11]

Schwartzwalder quickly determined that he and his men were on the wrong side of the Merderet (his objective was the western end of the bridgehead) and that they would lose precious time trying to wade across the flooded plain. Better to move quickly to one of the crossings he knew of, and link up with the rest of his regiment on the far side. So far things hadn't worked out according to the detailed plan laid out in England, so he took charge, giving his men a simple instruction, "We're moving out."

Schwartzwalder and one of his platoon leaders, First Lieutenant John W. Marr, followed the railroad south to where it intersected with the Ste. Mère Eglise road, which they followed toward the bridge at La Fière. Marr and four scouts were the lead element of G Company and were about 150 yards out in front of the main body. Marr led them around to the south side of the manor house and had closed to within 200 or 300 hundred yards from the manor when firing broke out all around them. The lieutenant, surprised that they hadn't all been killed, ordered his men to pull back, and they regrouped in the shelter of a hedgerow to look for another approach.

A stone wall that was part of the manor complex seemed to offer some cover. But when the men moved toward it, a machine gun opened fire on them. The patient German defenders had let the Americans get within ten yards before opening up, and so caught Tech Sergeant Gaspar A. Escobar and Corporal Harold M. Lawton in the open near a cattle fence. The two men went down with leg wounds.[12]

Now the fight was at close range, with the Germans no farther than the other side of the hedgerows. The defenders fired machine pistols and machine guns through the vegetation, and the paratroopers answered with rifles and grenades. Escobar, bleeding badly from his leg wounds, used his tommy gun to fire in the general direction of the enemy. Suddenly, a German soldier stood to throw a potato masher grenade at the GIs, and the wounded Corporal Lawton shot him with his carbine. After a few minutes of this back-and-forth, Marr and his men thought they had a bead on where the defenders were located. Lawton, losing blood from his wounds, and Private Marion Parletto tossed fragmentation grenades at the German position, destroying the menacing machine gun and killing the three-man crew.[13]

With Lawton bleeding badly and with fire still coming in from concealed defenders, Marr decided that he'd done enough with his small contingent. He told the men they were pulling back, picked up Lawton, and carried him through several hedgerows to where the medics could work on him. Marr then found Schwartzwalder to brief him on the situation.

It was around this time that yet another group of paratroopers arrived on the increasingly crowded scene at La Fière.

Lieutenant Colonel Roy Lindquist, the commander of the 508th PIR, had also landed east of the river and found his way along the railroad bed to the Ste. Mère Eglise road. Lindquist and his collection of men from the 507th and 508th were, like Schwartzwalder, looking for the quickest way to get to where they were supposed to be: the west side of the Merderet.

Lieutenant John H. Wisner, the intelligence officer of the 2nd Battalion of the 507th PIR, was in the lead element of the Lindquist group when they came under fire. One of Wisner's soldiers was wounded in this initial burst, and the group slowed down to try to determine exactly where the Germans were.

By this time, probably before eight in the morning, the number of paratroopers converging on La Fière was growing, though the Germans still had the advantage. They were in a veritable fortress, with stone walls more than a foot thick, while the Americans did not have a clear understanding of what they were facing. But the German defenders surely felt the noose tightening around them.

Presnell's A Company platoon was near the river road north of Le Manoir, while Dolan and the rest of A Company crouched due east of the complex. Schwartzwalder's group and the men who'd arrived with Lindquist were threatening from the southeast.

Company C of the 505th PIR was also on the march toward La Fière. Captain Anthony M. Stefanich's men did not have the great drop that A Company had; they had landed some two miles from the DZ near the village of Baudenville (north of Ste. Mère Eglise). Yet Captain Stef, as the men called him, wasted no time in assembling his men and getting them moving to the battalion objective at La Fière. They were near Neuville au Plain when it became light enough to see, and happened to be close to a road when a German communications truck drove by. The C Company men set up a hasty ambush, destroying the truck, killing some of the enemy soldiers, and capturing two.[14]

About an hour later, C Company closed in on La Fière. The first group Stefanich encountered was Presnell's platoon. Presnell told Stefanich about the machine gun, and the C Company commander took two men with a Browning Automatic Rifle and moved to upper Ste. Mère Eglise road, using a hedgerow for cover. When they hit the road, they turned toward the manor and moved forward until German machine gun fire drove them back, wounding one of the C Company men. Stefanich pulled the man back and tried to stop the bleeding, but the wound was severe and the captain hurried back to his company to get a medic.

Major Fred Kellam was also in the area of the bridge early on the morning of D-Day, traveling with just his operations officer, Captain Dale Roydson, and his runner, Private First Class Francis Buck. While the situation was developing at the manor, Kellam sent Buck to retrace their steps from the drop zone and send any 1st Battalion men he found to La Fière. Along the way to the DZ, Buck ran into Lieutenant Colonel Ekman, the commander of the 505th PIR, who was wandering alone after a rough landing and confusing night. Buck led the colonel to meet with Kellam.

When Gavin, who had also moved along the railroad to check on the situation at the bridge, learned that both Lindquist and Kellam were in the area, he figured that between them they should be able to take La Fière.[15]

Three enterprising lieutenants from the 307th Airborne Engineers also arrived in the bridge area with part of an engineer platoon and a 57 mm antitank gun they had salvaged from a glider. Lieutenants John L. Connolly, Adrian J. Finlayson, and Robert E. Klein knew the gun, which came in on the 0400 glider mission, would be an important part of the defense once La Fière was secure. Connolly, the senior officer, took command of the engineers and some infantrymen from B Company of the 505th and reported to Dolan, who held them in reserve.

All during the morning hours of D-Day, the uncoordinated attacks by the paratroopers pushing toward Le Manoir la Fière continued.

Lindquist was not in communication with Dolan, but he could hear the firing and assumed that Dolan's men were attacking along an axis north of the main road. Lindquist then sent his own force moving toward the manor on the south side of the road.

Captain Anthony Stefanich maneuvered his C Company toward La Fière and a spot from which he could join the fight. He was at the front of the company, looking for the best route of advance, when a German sniper fired at him. Stefanich jumped into a roadside ditch, but not before one of the sniper's rounds hit a smoke grenade fixed to the suspenders on his chest. The grenade burst into flame, and Stefanich rolled around in the ditch trying to put out the fire that threatened to engulf him. One of his platoon leaders, Lieutenant Gerald Johnson, saw that Stefanich was in trouble. Johnson pulled the pin on his own smoke grenade and tossed it into the road. When the cloud of smoke had grown to the point where he thought it hid him from the sniper, Johnson dashed across the road and dived into the ditch, where he put out the flames. The platoon leader then slung his company commander over his shoulder and carried him to the rear, where the medics could get a look at him.

By 1000 hours, Dolan's A Company had lost ten killed and twenty-one wounded. He was not in contact with Lindquist or Schwartzwalder, nor had he achieved any significant break in the German defense. The center had proved too tough to crack, and Presnell was still bogged down alongside the river. A frustrated Dolan decided to try again with his reserve platoon. He also sent a runner out to tell Lindquist about the casualties, including the 1st Battalion executive officer, Major McGinity. Lindquist relayed this information to Major General Matt Ridgway, who came up to see what was going on. Ridgway told Lindquist to take command of the bridge area and capture the objective.

Dolan could hear firing on the east and south side of the manor complex, and so knew the Germans were being engaged by someone else. He sent Lieutenant William Oakley, leading 3rd Platoon of A Company, to press the north side of the manor to see if he could get at the defenders from there.

Sergeant Oscar L. Queen, walking point for Oakley's platoon, got all the way to the manor's courtyard before he was knocked down by the explosion of a grenade that had been tossed from an upper floor. Queen was fired on by a sniper, whom he spotted in a tree. Lying on the ground, still dazed from the near miss of the grenade, Queen returned fire and killed the sniper. Captain Dale Roydson, the 1st Battalion operations officer, who had accompanied Oakley's patrol, was close behind Queen and emptied his pistol at a German who appeared briefly at an upper-floor window to throw another grenade.

Oakley moved a machine gun up and had the gunner fire into the windows and doors of the manor buildings, especially the big house itself (where the Leroux family was still holed up in the basement).

Meanwhile, Schwartzwalder was ready to try again from the east side. He pressed the attack, taking some casualties but finally getting to the stone-walled shed that ran along the southern edge of the courtyard. His mixed group of 507 and 508 men also fired into the manor house windows and doors.

For the German defenders, time had run out. The Americans had killed or captured all the outposts that had been protecting the manor, and were now in the courtyard. It was only a matter of minutes before they were in the building, and even though the defenders could exact a heavy price in room-to-room fighting, there would be no surrendering once the fight was joined at such close quarters. If the Americans had to fight their way inside, the German defenders would all die.

One batch of Germans, nearly twenty men, surrendered to Oakley's platoon on the west side of the property, closest to the bridge. Seeing this, the A Company men thought the battle was over, and Dolan began walking around what he now thought of as a safe area. He gave instructions for Oakley's platoon to dig in on the north side of the road, and for 3rd Platoon, which had lost two lieutenants, to stay on the south side. He put Presnell's platoon in reserve some four hundred yards to the rear, to keep watch for any German force trying to break out of the Ste. Mère Eglise area and escape across the bridge.

While he was moving about, Dolan found Colonel Ekman, the 505th Commander, who'd been escorted to the area by Buck, the 1st Battalion runner. Dolan and Ekman stood together in the open, casually looking over the area, until a German fired on them from the upper floors of the manor house. The two officers ducked for cover.

Schwartzwalder's patrol of 507 and 508 men, who were less than a hundred yards away on the opposite side of the property, saw this firing and engaged the ten or twelve Germans still shooting from the upper windows of the manor house. After a few minutes of this exchange, one of the defenders waved a white flag from a second-floor window. One of Schwartzwalder's lieutenants told a sergeant to go up and tell the prisoners to come out *"Haende hoch"*—hands up. The sergeant pointed out that it was a better idea to have all the Germans come out of the building first, before any of the troopers exposed themselves. At that moment, a young paratrooper went forward to accept the surrender and was shot dead, apparently by a German who did not know that his comrades on the upper floor had already surrendered.

Another trooper rushed into the ground floor of the house, a storeroom that opened on the back corner, and fired through the floorboards to kill any Germans still resisting inside the house.[16]

The several hours of on-again, off-again fighting around Le Manoir la Fière had done nothing to dull Ben Schwartzwalder's drive to get across the Merderet to his original objective at Amfreville. Late in the morning, after the prisoners had been cleared from the manor and A Company of the 505th had begun digging in on the eastern end of the causeway, Schwartzwalder pushed across.

The flat, flooded plain on either side of the raised roadway was mostly open ground, but there were quite a few trees clinging to the sides of the road as it came down off the bridge and snaked westward. There were stretches of road where advancing troops were completely concealed and other places where anyone moving along the roadway was exposed to long-range fire from the riverbanks.

The paratroopers had learned from a captured German noncom that there were rifle positions all along the causeway, and Schwartzwalder—in order to be safe—had to assume that these would be occupied by Germans who had fled the manor. Once again, Lieutenant Marr got the nod to lead the move, and the men spread out and hustled over the curved stone bridge at the eastern end of the causeway. Private First Class Johnnie Ward had the point, with Private James Mattingly about a hundred yards back. No sooner had Mattingly crossed the bridge when a German popped out of a foxhole just a few yards away and fired at him. The shots cracked by him, and Mattingly, thoroughly startled, emptied his rifle at what he could now see was a machine gun position. When the metal clip flew from his weapon, indicating it was empty, Mattingly dropped to the ground and hurled a grenade at the machine gun nest.[17] When the smoke and dust settled, he had several wounded prisoners and an empty rifle. Rather than pause to reload, he bluffed, gesturing for the prisoners to move back across the bridge toward the manor house and covering them with the useless weapon.[18]

Other Germans on the east end of the causeway, perhaps disheartened because of the loss of the strong defensive position that the manor offered, surrendered to Marr's men. Marr led his patrol west along the causeway, where they spotted some GIs. They broke out an orange signal panel (the prearranged signal to identify friendly troops) and were answered by orange smoke from near the Cauquigny crossroads.

Schwartzwalder moved across the causeway and found Lieutenant Louis Levy of the 507th, who'd been sent to Cauquigny by Lieutenant Colonel Timmes, commander of the 2nd Battalion of the 507th PIR. From Levy, Schwartzwalder learned that Timmes (who was not Schwartzwalder's battalion commander but at least was in the same regiment) had dug in and was holding a position about a mile north of the crossing, near a low hill marked Hill 30 on the Allied maps. He also learned that Timmes had been repulsed in his first attempt to take Amfreville, which was also Schwartzwalder's objective.

Schwartzwalder had to make a decision on what to do next. He reasoned that La Fière was in hand: the 505th PIR held the eastern end. And while Levy's group at Cauquigny church was small, the enemy had shown little interest in the causeway. Timmes's small group had not been able to take Amfreville (a principal objective on the western side of the river), but perhaps the addition of the Schwartzwalder group would tip the balance and allow them to capture the town. Schwartzwalder left Cauquigny to join Timmes.[19]

Levy, who had been unmolested in Cauquigny all morning, finally crossed to the eastern end to learn what was going on there. He made contact with Dolan's A Company, but neither unit could establish radio or wire communications across the causeway. Levy also learned that Dolan didn't have the manpower to reinforce his outpost at Cauquigny. For the morning, the two American positions—one at either end of La Fière—remained separate and unable to reinforce each other in the likely event of a German attack.

Ridgway had given overall command of the La Fière area to Colonel Roy Lindquist, whose badly scattered 508th PIR was assembling in small groups. Lindquist made his command post in the stout buildings of Le Manoir la Fière after it had been cleared of Germans and vacated by the Leroux family, who left to find a safer place to hide.

Lindquist made a quick run across the causeway to check on the troopers at Cauquigny. When he saw how thinly that area was held, he gathered a crew of misdropped artillerymen and headquarters men from various units, designated them a provisional B Company, and sent them off across the causeway to lend a hand.

Meanwhile Dolan and his A Company dug their positions on the low hill that overlooked the bridge and causeway. Sergeant William D. Owens, a squad leader, ordered his men to place their antitank mines in a string across the road where an advancing German tank could see them but could not drive around. The GIs pushed a disabled German ammunition truck, which had been parked in the manor yard, to the bridge to add to the roadblock. Owens's plan was to force any approaching tanks to slow down enough so that the A Company bazooka teams, now going into position on the north and south sides of the roads, would have a better target.

By midmorning Major Fred Kellam had control of his battalion's A Company, under Dolan; C Company, now under Lieutenant Jack Tallerday (since Stefanich was wounded); and a smattering of troops from B Company, who were in reserve. Still, he was eager to police up the rest of his missing troopers. Thinking that some 505 men might have been caught up in Schwartzwalder's move west, or that some had been stranded on the west side of the river, he sent his resourceful runner, Francis Buck, west along the causeway to look.

Kellam had recognized a self-reliant streak in Buck, a twenty-four-year-old midwesterner who was a machine gunner in the battalion's Headquarters Company. When it came time for Kellam to find a runner who could be trusted to operate on his own and think on his feet, he asked Buck.

Buck was born in Iowa and raised in Kansas during the lean years of the Depression. One of thirteen children, he left home at the age of fourteen to ease the burden on his parents. He made his way to northern Kansas, where he found work tending cattle and harvesting wheat for a dollar a day plus room and board. He was working on the West Coast when the war came, and joined the paratroopers because, as he told the recruiter, he believed they were the "damndest outfit in the Army."

In his D-Day jump, Buck landed nearly two miles from his drop zone, but managed to find Kellam and Captain Dale Roydson, the operations officer, almost immediately, though the three men did not know where they were. When they came to a farmhouse, Roydson knocked on the door to see what he could learn. In another of the many examples of courage shown by French civilians that night, a man from this house (who would have been shot by the Germans if he had been discovered aiding the invaders) led the Americans to a point close to the bridge at La Fière. Kellam, Roydson, and Buck joined A Company shortly after the fight got under way.

When Colonel Lindquist sent the provisional B Company, made up of stragglers from the 508th, across the causeway, Buck fell in at the rear of the column. By this point he had been awake for some thirty hours, had already made a strenuous combat jump, and had moved alone for miles through the night and enemy terrain (including the round-trip escorting Colonel Ekman).

Buck reached Cauquigny without seeing anyone familiar, though he did find a discarded machine gun tripod that he thought would be useful. When he reached the little hamlet, he was a bit alarmed to see that the defensive position on the west side was even smaller than what the 505th had established on the east end of the causeway.

Then Buck heard tanks approaching.

A veteran of campaigns in both Sicily and Italy, Buck had seen what tanks could do against the lightly armed paratroopers. There was no way the tiny defense mounted by Levy was going to stop a determined push; Buck's next thought was that he had to warn Kellam and his buddies on the east side of the causeway. Still carrying the tripod and with the rest of his equipment banging awkwardly against his chest and back and legs, he began running east along the roadway.

A redheaded officer he did not recognize challenged him, "Where do you think you're going?"

Buck didn't even break stride.

"I heard tanks, Major," he said. "And I know where they're going. I'm going back to warn Major Kellam."

Back along the causeway he ran, and as he approached the stone bridge he could see men from A and Headquarters Companies digging in beside the road and on the slight rise just above the bridge.

"Dig deep boys," he called to them. "There's tanks coming this way."

The soldiers picked up the pace of their work and kept one eye on the long causeway.

Buck found Kellam and warned him about the tanks. The major sent runners to pass the word to Dolan, Tallerday, the acting C Company commander, and the B Company contingent under Lieutenant Connolly of the engineers. He also checked on the 57m antitank gun, the biggest weapon in the American position. The crew had moved the gun to a spot just on the south side of the upper road and set it back amid

some brush. It was some three hundred yards behind the manor house
with a direct line of fire over the bridge and down the causeway.

The men of Kellam's battalion, the 1st of the 505th PIR, were as prepared as they could be. They crouched in their holes, scanned the
causeway and the far shore, and did what soldiers do: they waited.

Levy had approximately ten men with him in Cauquigny, as the reinforcements who had arrived earlier left with Schwartzwalder, and the
provisional B Company was just arriving when the Germans attacked.
Levy's men were dug in an arc along a hedge that ran around the
churchyard facing west. He put his lone machine gun inside the church
wall where it could sweep the road. The riflemen were in individual positions, spaced some fifteen yards apart, with the lieutenants (Levy and
Kormylo and two others who had stayed rather than go with
Schwartzwalder) interspersed with the riflemen.

Levy didn't want to completely cede the initiative to the Germans, so
he took Kormylo and a private (whose name has been lost) forward into
a sunken lane that bordered the church property and ran perpendicular
to the Amfreville road. If the Germans advanced on that road, he reasoned, he might be able to hit them in the flank. Levy found a firing position beside a hedgerow and told the other two men to go forward. If
things got too hot for them to stay, Kormylo and the private were to pull
out first, and Levy would cover their retreat back to the church.

Kormylo and the soldier now occupied the forwardmost position, and
they didn't have long to wait for the Germans. The turrets of two small
Renault tanks came into view, and then Kormylo spied, in glimpses
through the undergrowth, some German infantrymen in the lead of the
tanks. (In this standard tactic, the foot soldiers' job is to uncover any antitank ambushes.)

Kormylo and the private opened fire, dropping some of the German
infantrymen, but also drawing return fire from the rest of the disciplined troops. The two GIs moved back at a run, yelling at Levy, who
was covering them, that they were pulling out.

The Germans brought a machine gun team forward to a position from which they could fire on the churchyard and the Americans. Kormylo saw the gun crew move forward, and saw Levy lob a hand grenade over the hedgerow at the enemy. Levy then pushed through the hedgerow into the roadway itself, to finish off the stunned German machine gunners with his rifle. The private who'd been with Kormylo rejoined him, and the two men got into position to cover Levy's retreat.

There was more firing, most of it not visible to Kormylo, who tried to strike a balance between being able to see and keeping himself hidden. Levy reached them moments later, helmetless, his jacket torn, his shoulder bleeding, but laughing in some sort of hysterical release.

The German foot soldiers were aggressive and pushed toward the churchyard; within minutes they were separated only by a hedgerow from the GIs defending themselves in a short-range firefight. The opposing sides threw grenades over the hedges. Kormylo saw the helmet of a German trying to push through a hole in a hedgerow, and he fired his carbine at point-blank range into the top of the man's head.

Kormylo then saw Levy and the nameless private still holding out, firing at the enemy and throwing grenades at the advancing Germans. Kormylo yelled at the two men to get out. Levy made it as far as Kormylo's position, but the private was killed.[20]

Meanwhile Private Orlin Stewart held his original position near the churchyard as the fight drew nearer. He had been part of a bazooka team that had bolstered Levy's defense earlier in the day, but the bazooka had been sent back to Timmes, leaving Stewart with a BAR and a supply of Gammon grenades. He watched the German tanks come closer, and was surprised when one of them was hit and disabled. (Stewart did not know of any other antitank positions or weapons at Cauquigny.)

He moved forward, headed toward the road, using a roadside ditch as cover and watching the remaining two tanks. Stewart looked up to see two other GIs, one of them a First Sergeant, also in the ditch and moving into position. The First Sergeant was loaded down with Gammon grenades, and he greeted Stewart cheerfully. When the tanks were within a few yards, the noncom and private rose and started hurling the grenades at the tanks. They were doing such a great job that Stewart gave them his own grenades, then got into position to cover the tanks with his BAR.

The two Renaults, rocked by multiple explosions from the powerful grenades, rattled to a halt, with flames licking from their engine compartments. When the crews tried to clear the wrecks, the GIs opened fire and tossed more grenades, killing every man who moved.

Moments later another tank appeared in the roadway, with a large group of German infantry running behind. The three paratroopers, out of grenades and seriously outnumbered, used the cover of the ditch to move back toward the causeway and Lieutenant Levy. The battered survivors of Levy's group collected their weapons and, abandoning Cauquigny, headed north toward the Timmes group.

Meanwhile the ad hoc collection that Lindquist had designated B Company arrived on the western end of the causeway at exactly the wrong time. The advancing Germans used tank fire and machine guns to cut off any retreat back along the causeway. The GIs who had already made it to the west side turned south down a narrow lane to escape the oncoming tanks but were pinned up against the flood. Some of the men tried to make their way individually back across the flooded Merderet, but the thick grass and deep water slowed them down to the point where they made easy targets for the Germans now pulling up in Cauquigny.

Across the wide floodplain, the men of A Company of the 505th watched the carnage: the tiny figures wading into the marsh, the distant crackle of gunfire coming in fits across the water, the fleeing men disappearing one by one. Because their own weapons could not reach all the way across the floodplain, they could do nothing more than watch.

Levy, Kormylo, Stewart, and a few others made it to the orchard where Timmes and Schwartzwalder were dug in amid the apple trees along the bank of the flooded Merderet. It was to be their last move for several days.

The Germans in Cauquigny knew they had to recross the Merderet to get at the invasion beaches, but a direct assault across the La Fière causeway would be costly. They planned instead to use a submerged ford that crossed the river about a mile north. But Timmes, who had about 140 paratroopers with him by the afternoon of D-Day, was blocking the way (although he didn't know about the ford) by his mere presence. Timmes had gathered some mortars and bazookas, as well as a handful of light machine guns, which he used to create a strong defensive position.

Levy gave Timmes the bad news about the loss of Cauquigny, and Timmes set out to make his perimeter ready for an attack. The battalion commander ordered vigorous patrolling, both to keep the Germans at bay and to put feelers out to make contact with the help he knew was bound to come.

During the afternoon of D-Day, the Germans began shelling the American perimeter, but the paratroopers dug in deeper. For the next forty-eight hours, Timmes and company would hold on to this position, with no resupply or relief, with wounded men dying for lack of medical care. One quarter of his men would be wounded or killed, with another one quarter walking wounded. For all the damage the Germans inflicted, they could not force Timmes to move and so could not reach the ford. It was thus by accident—Timmes happened to pick a spot for his defense that blocked access to the ford—that the stubborn American defense denied the Germans a critical avenue of advance across the Merderet.

Thus far, D-Day for Francis Buck had meant walking or running for miles, back and forth to the drop zone, back and forth across the causeway, around La Fière looking for stray troopers from the 505th who could help stabilize the defense. Now a sweating, winded Buck joined his boss, Major Kellam, and the operations officer, Captain Roydson, in one of the gullies that crisscrossed the hill overlooking the causeway. Behind them and to their left, the snout of the 57 mm antitank gun peeked from behind some foliage where the road made a sharp turn. On either side, men of 1st Battalion peered from their fighting positions, readied their ammunition and grenades, and waited for targets to appear. Company A had the front, with parts of B and C Companies backing them up. Behind them, the stragglers from the 507th and 508th, some of whom had barely survived a retreat from the west side under fire, were moved back to where the north-south railroad line cut the Ste. Mère Eglise road. This position, some six hundred yards to the rear, was to be a final backstop in the event the Germans got across the bridge. But every GI could see that the best place to stop a German advance was right at the small stone bridge. It was a natural choke point, where any enemy advance would have a frontage of only one tank.

From his position in the hillside gully, Buck looked down the length of the causeway and ducked under the intermittent mortar fire. To Buck, the seconds rolled by like hours as he watched the empty road.

Dwight Eisenhower speaks to paratroopers of the 101st Airborne Division hours before D-Day. Ike's air adviser predicted that the U.S. Airborne forces would suffer thousands of casualties. Although the Supreme Commander's jovial conversations with the troops were tinged with this worry, outwardly he was the picture of confidence and optimism. *Courtesy of the National Archives and Records Administration*

PIR Pathfinders of the 505th load on the afternoon of June 5, 1944. Eighteen-year-old Bob Murphy is standing, third from right, with cap. *Courtesy of Bob Murphy*

Infantry soldiers of the 325th GIR loading British-made Horsa gliders for Normandy. These wooden aircraft, dubbed "Flying Coffins" by the troops, often broke apart on impact. *Courtesy of the 82nd Airborne Division Museum via Phil Nordyke*

Demolition troopers of the Regimental Headquarters, 507th PIR.
Courtesy of Martin K. A. Morgan and Dominique François

Horse-drawn German supply wagons leave Ste. Mère Eglise in the
weeks before the invasion. Civilian residents hoped it meant the battle
would be elsewhere. *Courtesy of the office of the mayor, Ste. Mère Eglise,
France; and ICL Graphics, Valognes, France*

Ste. Mère Eglise before the battle, looking down the road toward the Channel beaches. The road to the left leads to the Hotel de Ville (city hall), where Ed Krause raised the American flag on D-Day. *Courtesy of the office of the mayor, Ste. Mère Eglise, France; and ICL Graphics, Valognes, France*

The same intersection after the battle. *Courtesy of the office of the mayor, Ste. Mère Eglise, France; and ICL Graphics, Valognes, France*

Destroyed panzers on the eastern end of La Fière causeway. The narrow frontage (the flooded area was just beyond the trees on either side) made any attack across the causeway extremely risky. These light tanks were captured from the French early in the war. *Courtesy of Martin K. A. Morgan, via the National Archives and Records Administration*

Private First Class Charles N. DeGlopper, Company C, 325th Glider Infantry Regiment, posthumously awarded the Medal of Honor. "DeGlopper yelled for his comrades to pull back, then stood up and stepped from the ditch onto the road and into the open." *Courtesy of the 82nd Airborne Division in World War II Web site (http://www.ww2-airborne.us/units/325/325_trp.html)*

Roy Creek. "'We had done some things badly,' Creek would say later. 'But overall, with a hodgepodge of troops from several units who had never trained together as a unit, [who] didn't even know one another and were engaged in their first combat, we had done okay. We captured our bridge and held it.'"As the minute hand on his watch passed twelve, Roy Creek marked the end of his first day in combat, and thought that it was going to be a long way to Berlin. *Courtesy of Roy Creek*

Matt Ridgway (*left*) and James Gavin pictured in winter 1944–1945, when Ridgway commanded the XVIII Airborne Corps and Gavin commanded the 82nd Airborne Division. *Courtesy of Barbara Gavin Fauntleroy*

Ken Russell. "Russell cringed as he looked down from two hundred feet on the heads of the Germans, who were shouldering their rifles and firing into the air. Ridiculous as it was, he tried to hide behind his reserve parachute, strapped across his belly." *Courtesy of Ken Russell*

Waverly Wray, Company D, 505th PIR. "Wray's reconnaissance had become a one-man combat patrol, and though he didn't know it yet, he had decapitated the 1st Battalion of the 1058th Panzer-grenadier Regiment by killing most of the unit's leadership." *Courtesy of Bob Fielder, 505th PIR*

Marcus Heim. "Heim and Peterson did not dive back into their hole. They did not run or flinch. They were connected to each other by a flimsy metal tube, by a sense of mission: they had to destroy the tank before it killed them." *Courtesy of the 82nd Airborne Division in World War II Web site (www.ww2-airborne.us)*

Robert McLaughlin, Company A, 505th PIR. "This was McLaughlin's first combat action, and his first task was to step forward and take the place of a predecessor who had just been killed leading his men from the front." *Courtesy of Bob Fielder, 505th PIR*

James McGinity, Executive Officer, 1st Battalion, 505 PIR. "McGinity was in the lead, keeping his left shoulder tight to a thick hedgerow. . . . But the defenders were waiting for them again, and opened up with at least two machine pistols at very close range." *Courtesy of Bob Fielder, 505th PIR*

Wheatley Christensen. "Christensen delayed for a few minutes, though he knew he should move. He was now in charge of the squad, but the toughest task he faced was leaving these two very conscious, very alert paratroopers to whatever was going to befall them." *Courtesy of Wheatley Christensen*

John Dolan. "He had just one antitank gun, a handful of light mortars, and not much ammunition for either. He would conduct this fight with what he had on hand." *Courtesy of Bob Fielder, 505th PIR*

Dutch Schultz. "Like a lot of soldiers in the lead-up to the invasion, Schultz thought more and more about religion. . . . He figured that if he did live, he'd probably start sinning again, but that didn't stop him from going to Mass every day as the invasion approached." *Courtesy of Arthur Schultz*

Ben Vandervoort, Commander, 2nd Battalion, 505th PIR. "Vandervoort and Turnbull ducked incoming fire and watched from the edge of the village. They got momentary glimpses of German infantry, just out of range, moving east and west to find the flanks of the tiny American position. It wouldn't be long— a half hour perhaps—before the attackers overwhelmed the GIs." *Courtesy of Bob Fielder, 505th PIR*

Donald Coxon. "Dolan told Coxon to bring up his platoon scouts, and Coxon replied, 'Well, sir, if I have to send someone out into that, I'll go myself.'" *Courtesy of Bob Fielder, 505th PIR*

Ed Misencik, standing on the left. Sergeant Loper (*seated*) saved Misencik from drowning in the first hour of the invasion. *Courtesy of Rick Misencik*

Fred Morgan. "Fred Morgan had learned in his first campaigns that the trick was to focus on the task at hand—stop the bleeding, check the airway, treat for shock—to keep from being overwhelmed by the carnage. Now that he was a sergeant, it was also his job to set a calm example for the junior aid men, who would need shoring up before the day was out." *Courtesy of Fred Morgan*

James Gavin as a major general and commander of the 82nd Airborne Division around VE Day. *Courtesy Barbara Gavin Fauntleroy*

Jack Norton, operations officer of the 505th PIR in Normandy, at the sixtieth-anniversary commemoration in Ste. Mère Eglise, June 2004. This would be his last visit to France. *Courtesy of John Norton*

Ed Krause, commander, 3rd Battalion, 505th PIR. Krause's troops captured Ste. Mère Eglise, the first town in France liberated in the invasion. *Courtesy of the office of the mayor, Ste. Mère Eglise, France; and ICL Graphics, Valognes, France*

American medics established a large aid station on the northern end of Ste. Mère Eglise in what is now a home for the elderly. German medical personnel (*in cloth hats*) also helped take care of the wounded of both sides. *Courtesy of the office of the mayor, Ste. Mère Eglise, France; and ICL Graphics, Valognes, France*

A GI helps civilian refugees return to Ste. Mère Eglise after the fighting had moved on. *Courtesy of the office of the mayor, Ste. Mère Eglise, France; and ICL Graphics, Valognes, France*

An American parachutist, killed before he could free himself from his harness, hangs in the square in Ste. Mère Eglise. *Courtesy of the office of the mayor, Ste. Mère Eglise, France; and ICL Graphics, Valognes, France*

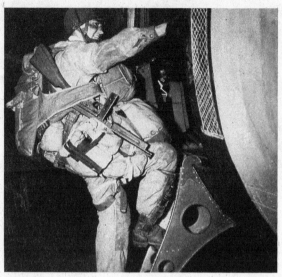

A combat-loaded soldier boards his plane on June 5 in England.
Courtesy of Martin K. A. Morgan, via the National Archives and Records Administration

Aerial view of La Fière, looking west, with Manoir la Fière in the foreground. The band of fields that runs across the middle of the photo was flooded on D-Day, which channeled all movement onto the narrow causeway. *Courtesy of Martin K. A. Morgan*

GIs pass a knocked-out U.S. Sherman tank. *Courtesy of the 82nd Airborne Division Museum, via Phil Nordyke*

The crash of this Horsa glider killed these troopers before they could get into action. *Courtesy of the 82nd Airborne Division Museum, via Phil Nordyke*

Gliders in Norman fields. The tight confines of these fields, which were bordered by massive hedgerows, made landing a tricky business. *Courtesy of Martin K. A. Morgan, via the National Archives and Records Administration*

A mortar team of the 325th GIR in action in Normandy. Note the field telephone that connects the crew with the forward observers and fire direction center. Unlike the paratroopers, the glidermen wore standard GI footwear with canvas leggings. *Courtesy of the 82nd Airborne Division Museum, via Phil Nordyke*

Cauquigny Church, July 9. Private James Schaffner of the 325th GIR poses on the east side of the church. By this time, the fighting had moved westward, toward Le Motey. *Courtesy of the 82nd Airborne Division Museum, via Phil Nordyke*

Captain Robert Rae (*pointing*) and 507th troopers prepare for a training jump in 1943. "'At that instant I'm going to wave at you,' Gavin told Rae. 'I want you to jump up with all your men yelling their heads off and go right through them [the glider troops] and take them with you.'" *Courtesy of Martin K. A. Morgan and Albert "Bud" Parker*

French priests say Mass over the graves of Allied soldiers in one of the three temporary cemeteries established in Ste. Mère Eglise. *Courtesy of the office of the mayor, Ste. Mère Eglise, France; and ICL Graphics, Valognes, France*

A C47 daylight training flight over England in 1944. At night the planes flew with lights blacked out. The tight formations made midair collisions a major concern for pilots. *Courtesy of Martin K. A. Morgan and Bill Rentz*

Lieutenant Colonel Arthur Maloney, executive officer of the 507th PIR. "The men turned pale when it became clear what Maloney was asking for: they were to make the same assault—in reverse—that had slaughtered so many Germans on June 6 and June 7." *Courtesy of Martin K. A. Morgan, and Dennis and Barbara Maloney*

UNDER FIRE

Less than two hundred yards from where Buck, Kellam, and Roydson watched the road, a twenty-year-old soldier from upstate New York also waited to see what would happen next.

June 6 was Marcus Heim's first day in combat, and it had started off with a near disaster. Heim landed just a few yards from a road, and before he could get his rifle out of its canvas carrier and assembled, he heard a motorcycle approaching. He lay still, rifle in parts in his hands, and watched as two German soldiers passed close by him. They did not look around.

Things got better after that, as Heim was able to locate the other men in his stick. Heim was the loader on a bazooka team and so was used to moving with his partner, a Swedish immigrant named Leonold Peterson. The two men found each other and the equipment bundles that held A Company's bazookas and rockets, then set off with the company for the bridge over the Merderet.

The bazookas were A Company's principal antitank weapons and, along with the lone 57 mm gun recovered by the engineers, gave the paratroopers at La Fière their only chance of stopping any German armor. But the rockets were not powerful enough to do much damage to a tank by hitting its front (where the armor was thickest). The bazooka team's best chance was to strike the less heavily armored sides or even the rear of the enemy vehicle. In practice this meant the bazooka teams had to let the enemy tanks get close, or even wait until the armor had passed. This tactic was hazardous because the Germans almost always sent infantrymen alongside the tanks to protect the vehicles from bazooka teams lying in wait. Finally, the bazooka itself was not a particularly reliable weapon. In training, many of the teams took to wearing their gas masks, to protect them from the hot gases shooting from the rear of the rockets. The weapon was reliably accurate only inside a range of about one hundred yards—while the machine gun on a tank could hit the bazooka team from hundreds of yards away. The rocket launcher itself was cumbersome, the ammunition heavy, and its effectiveness against armor chancy.

Gavin, in an attempt to give his bazooka teams some recognition for the dangers they faced, had small embroidered patches made for the men's uniforms after the campaign in Italy. The badges were completely unauthorized and against Army regulations, and the men wore them proudly.[1]

After his company had secured the manor house, Lieutenant John Dolan of A Company surveyed the area around the bridge to see how he could best hold it; it was obvious to him where the bazookas would have to go. One bazooka team would dig in north of the bridge at the very edge of the Merderet, well forward of friendly lines and looking up at any German tanks attempting to cross the bridge.

On the south side of the bridge, the river makes a sharp ninety-degree hook to the west. Thus there was a point of land on the friendly side of the river that gave his bazooka team a clean flank shot against a tank. But it also put the men far forward of the A Company line, twenty feet below the road surface, and made them a fairly easy target for an enemy on the bridge or on the nearby roadway.

Heim and Peterson took up a position on the south side, pushing forward to the edge of the Merderet so that they were looking at the bridge from the side. There was a concrete telephone pole on this point of land, and the two bazooka men dug a position just behind its base. The nearby causeway was lined with brush and small trees, so that there were few clear lines of sight. Peterson, the gunner and a combat veteran, pointed out that they would have to leave their foxhole in order to get any kind of shot.

The other A Company bazooka team, Private First Class John Bolderson and Private Gordon Pryne, dug in on the north side of the bridge, close to the river channel. Dolan positioned a few riflemen by the water's edge to help protect the teams, and placed a light machine gun not far behind them in the yard of the manor house. Looking back over his shoulder and up the hill, Heim could also see the snout of the 57 mm antitank gun poking from its concealed position alongside the upper road. Up on the roadway itself were the antitank mines laid in a visible line some fifty or sixty feet from the bridge on the west side, and the disabled German truck the men had pushed, dragged, and sweated from the manor house yard. All the obstacles were in plain sight so that any advancing tanks would slow down and make easier targets for the bazooka teams and the crew of the 57 mm gun.

This was a critical spot, not just for A Company and the men of the 505th, but for the entire 82nd Airborne Division and the VII Corps, which was even then streaming across Utah Beach, unloading men and equipment and the vast weight of weapons needed to hold the lodgment area and make the push across the Cherbourg Peninsula. It fell to the 1st Battalion of the 505th PIR to protect Utah Beach, and by extension the entire invasion, from German counterattack.

Marcus Heim knew some of this as he prepared his little supply of rockets in the hastily dug foxhole, making sure they were free of dirt and ready to load. Even from the perspective of this one foxhole the young man could feel that he and his buddies had their backs up against the wall. Their job was to shut this door to the beaches in the face of the Germans, but hold it open for the Americans who would eventually come up the road from the east. Down at the water's edge, the four men of A Company's bazooka teams watched the causeway, checked and rechecked their temperamental weapons, and waited.

The incoming fire picked up sharply in the afternoon, which everyone recognized as the signal that the Germans were about to launch a direct assault.[2]

For Fred Morgan and the medics, who had established an open-air aid station about five hundred yards to the rear of the bridge, the incoming fire signaled that their work was about to pick up.

Captain Gordon Stenhouse, the 1st Battalion surgeon, and the senior medics had worked hard in the months leading up to D-Day to prepare the new men for what it would be like to function under fire, to evacuate the wounded, to treat them as best they could with limited supplies and capabilities. In civilian practice, Stenhouse was an obstetrician, but he was also a veteran of the campaigns in Sicily and Italy and had won the respect of the company aid men, like Fred Morgan, for his calm. Stenhouse knew what the medics could do, and he let them do it without looking over their shoulder, and without trying to do the sergeants' work of running the aid station. The arrangement benefited the wounded, as the doctor could then spend more time with the most serious cases.

The mortar and artillery pounding the eastern banks of the Merderet made all movements difficult and dangerous, but the medics weren't about to cower in their foxholes. Morgan and the other company aid men crawled and crab-walked through the roadside ditches to move back and forth to the A Company line. There were one or two litters around—they'd been dropped in the equipment bundles—but they weren't very useful under fire. Instead, the medics dragged the wounded men toward the rear. Every yard was a struggle, with equipment and uniforms getting caught on brambles and branches, with badly injured men trying to propel themselves so they wouldn't be dead weight, with the constant threat of enemy fire. Once they were behind the top of the hill that overlooked Le Manoir la Fière, the medics carried the wounded to the aid station.

The flow of casualties picked up as soon as the Germans began firing. Because A Company was so shorthanded and needed every man on the line, only the most seriously wounded men came back to the aid station. There were a number of serious head wounds (a man in a foxhole is most likely to be hit in the head), and the medics did what they could to make these men comfortable; they were not likely to survive with the limited care the aid station offered.

The airborne medics worked under two major handicaps: the relative lack of supplies (they had only what they could carry or wrap in a parabundle) and their inability to evacuate the seriously wounded to a waiting field hospital. Some paratroopers died of wounds that would not have killed a soldier in one of the beach landing units, if only because that man could be moved to a field hospital (or one of the fifteen hospital ships lying offshore). Such knowledge was a terrible burden for the medics. Fred Morgan had learned in his first campaigns that the trick was to focus on the task at hand—stop the bleeding, check the airway, treat for shock—to keep from being overwhelmed by the carnage. Now that he was a sergeant, it was also his job to set a calm example for the junior aid men, who would need shoring up before the day was out.

Morgan was moving through the roadside ditch, trailed by his assistant, Private John Clancy, when a shell landed close enough to bury the sergeant in a shower of dirt. When he recovered from the hammerblow, Clancy saw Morgan's feet sticking out from the overturned earth. He was not moving. Clancy made his way to the aid station and reported that Morgan was dead.

Morgan was momentarily stunned but came to a moment later to find that he could barely breathe, that there was dirt in his mouth and nose and pressing in on him all around. He pushed, dug, and clawed for a frantic minute or two to fight his way clear of a hasty grave. He didn't see Clancy around, so he went back to the aid station and surprised the men there, who had written him off as yet another casualty.

PFC Thomas A. Breisch, a clerk in the 1st Battalion's Headquarters Company, wrestled a workable jeep from a crashed glider and drove it to the aid station. In spite of the incoming fire, in spite of the fact that the Germans could clearly see the upper road, Breisch drove the jeep back and forth between the aid station and a spot just behind the manor to evacuate the most seriously wounded. All day long, he raced the open vehicle as fast as the bumpy road would allow, shifting with one hand and spinning the steering wheel with the other as he bounced along. By the end of D-Day, Breisch had evacuated eighteen men with his salvaged jeep.[3]

•   •   •

The A Company men caught their first glimpses of the enemy advance through breaks in the undergrowth. The German move east along the causeway was led by two light tanks, separated by fifteen to twenty yards, with panzergrenadiers (infantrymen assigned to tank units) on foot on either side of the road. A third tank rolled another fifty yards back, with another group of foot soldiers bringing up the rear.[4] As the Germans closed on the bridge, the artillery and mortar fire lifted, and the paratroopers scrambled to their firing positions, rifle ammunition and grenades handy.

The machine gunners from A Company opened fire as soon as the German infantry was in range, forcing the enemy to go to ground on the narrow causeway, where there was little cover. Dolan was concerned about the ammunition supply. Because he had no way to predict when he would get more, he instructed his men to conserve ammunition and choose their targets carefully. Meanwhile, the tanks pressed on, oblivious to the machine gun fire.

The lead tank stopped within a few yards of the mines and the disabled truck on the west end of the bridge. The tank commander, to the surprise of the GIs watching him, popped open his hatch and stuck his head out to get a better look at the obstacle. It was his last move, as he was almost immediately killed by fire from one of the light machine guns positioned near the manor. Then the riflemen joined in, adding to the hail that kept the Germans pinned down on the causeway.

Amid all this fire—much of it passing just a few feet overhead—Leonold Peterson and his loader, Marcus Heim, scrambled out of their foxhole and moved a few yards closer to the edge of the Merderet for a better shot at the two tanks no more than fifty yards away. Peterson leaned against the concrete telephone pole to steady his aim, and the two men, hoping for a clean shot through the tree branches, waited for several agonizing seconds as the tanks inched forward.

The paratroopers' lone 57 mm gun, back on the hill behind the manor house, also opened fire. Return fire from one of the tanks punched through the gun's front shield, killing one GI, wounding another, and driving off the rest of the gun crew.

Heim saw the first tank, now without a commander, stagger as it was hit, although he couldn't tell if it was fire from the 57 mm gun or the other bazooka team. He jammed the rockets into the back of the tube as fast as he could manage, and Peterson squeezed off one round after another at close range.

Heim watched over Peterson's shoulder as the small turret on the lead tank turned toward them—it would be nearly a point-blank shot for the enemy. The tank's gun cracked, and the telephone pole beside them toppled over; the two GIs scrambled out of the way to avoid being crushed.

But Marcus Heim and Leonold Peterson did not dive back into their hole. They did not run or flinch. They were connected to each other by a flimsy metal tube, by a sense of mission: they had to destroy the tank before it killed them. Heim's world had collapsed to a small, violent stage: Peterson's back, the smoking end of the tube, the sleek, pointed rounds with their long fins, the small but dangerous tank and its chattering machine guns, the slugs thumping into the ground at their feet, the crushing noise.

As the bazooka teams plinked away at their targets, the A Company riflemen poured heavy fire on the German panzergrenadiers, to keep them from shooting the bazooka men. For Bob Murphy and the paratroopers on the hillside who took a second to look, the sight of those teams—firing as fast as they could load and from a completely exposed position, standing practically toe-to-toe with the enemy tanks—was one they would never forget. Murphy thought that the teams operated as coolly as if they were on the firing range back at Fort Bragg.

The lead tank now burned on the roadway, and the second tank came up to push it out of the way. Heim and Peterson adjusted their position, stepping to the side and moving a few yards closer to the target. They were now less than fifty yards from the dangerous machine, and completely exposed. At any second, any one of the panzergrenadiers on the causeway might rake them with automatic weapons fire. Still, Peterson managed to hit the vulnerable turret ring, where the turret is connected to the body of the tank. This seemed to do some damage.

"I got him! I got him!" Peterson yelled in his strong Swedish accent, all the while calmly working his weapon.

Another rocket knocked a tread loose, leaving the tank unable to maneuver on the narrow roadway. It was dangerous as long as its crew was safe inside and able to use the guns, but the bazooka teams kept pumping rounds at it until it, too, was on fire.

Peterson and Heim were now almost out of rockets, and the third tank, some fifty yards back, was still moving and dangerous. Peterson turned to Heim and told him to cross the elevated roadway, find the other team, and see if they could spare some rockets.

Heim ran from the water's edge in a loop to the base of the bridge and a spot where he could climb onto the roadway. He was partially shielded from the Germans by the smoke and the hulks of the burning tanks. Running as fast as he could, he could hear the crossfire rounds from both the Germans and Americans snapping hotly through the air all around him. His mind was blank, empty of everything except the need to reach the far side . . . and *run, run, run.*

He made it across the road the first time, but when he got to the opposite side, there was no sign of Bolderson or Pryne. There was one dead GI, probably one of the riflemen sent out to protect the team. There was also Bolderson's bazooka, which had been smashed by small arms fire. The other team, with no rocket launcher, had apparently pulled back. But Heim found some of their extra rockets, grabbed them up, and ran back for another go at crossing the fire-swept road. Much to his surprise, he made it again—unscathed.

Heim dropped in behind Peterson, and the team put the new rockets to good use, firing at the third tank, which was now trying to reach the bridge through a maze of burning wreckage. The paratroopers on the hillside kept up their fire, and the relentless bazooka team kept sending rockets downrange until the third tank was also disabled. The tank and crew were still dangerous, at least until Private Joseph C. Fitt of

C Company ran into the fire on the roadway, leaped onto the tank's deck, and dropped a grenade into its hatch.[5]

With their last tank out of action, the German infantrymen began to withdraw, chased by small arms fire from the paratroopers positioned around the manor and on the hill overlooking the bridge. The indirect fire picked up again to cover the retreat of those Germans who were still alive.

When the last panzergrenadiers were finally gone, Heim and Peterson retreated to their foxhole. On the hill behind them, they could see the wrecked antitank gun and a few troopers, but they felt isolated, too far out in front of their own line. A noncom from A Company came forward to help reconstitute the position. Many of the infantrymen positioned beside the bazooka teams had been killed or wounded, but, miraculously, not one of the four bazooka men had been hit. Bolderson and Pryne had withdrawn when their weapon was destroyed, but they would get another and return, because the Germans were sure to counterattack.

Francis Buck, the runner for the 1st Battalion commander, Major Fred Kellam, watched the initial German advance from a ditch south of the manor house, and saw Joseph Fitt make his one-man assault on a wounded but still dangerous tank. Buck, Kellam, and the 1st Battalion operations officer, Captain Roydson, stayed in their sheltered spot as the Germans covered their withdrawal with mortar and artillery fire.

Kellam was concerned about the amount of bazooka ammo the A Company teams had used, so when there seemed to be a lull in the shelling, he turned to Buck and Roydson and said, "I saw some bundles this morning that might have some more bazooka ammo. We need it. Let's go get 'em."

The three men backed up from the edge of the flooded plain, crossed behind the manor yard, and headed north across the Ste. Mère Eglise road, passing close by the small aid station where the medics were tending the wounded. They moved northeast, on a line generally parallel to the Merderet, toward the collection of houses that was also called La Fière (Le Bosc on modern maps) some five hundred yards north of the bridge. Kellam was very consciously retracing the path that had brought them to La Fière that morning. When they had gone a few hundred yards, Kellam turned to his runner and said, "Buck, this is where they got Eddie Lambros." Kellam indicated a body lying a short distance away. The rumpled uniform belonged to a GI.

Private Eddie Lambros, a New Yorker, was another of Kellam's runners and had been a friend of Buck's in Headquarters Company.

"Can I pay my respects?" Buck asked.

"Sure," Kellam said.

Buck took three or four steps off to the left, toward Lambros's unburied body, while the two officers continued straight ahead.

At that moment, a German mortar or artillery round landed nearby, knocking Buck to the ground. He was stunned and unaware of how much time passed before he struggled to his feet. His leg hurt badly, and his head rang with the aftershock. Buck turned to see Kellam and Roydson lying motionless on the ground nearby. Other GIs—alerted by the incoming fire—soon appeared to help him back toward the aid station he had passed just minutes before. While there, Buck learned that Kellam was dead and Roydson badly wounded. John Dolan and Lieutenant Brock Weir carried Roydson to the aid station, where the captain died of his wounds.

Ridgway's officers, his combat commanders, were falling quickly. In the 505th, Kellam was dead (as were the next two most senior officers in the 1st Battalion), Vandervoort had a broken leg, and Krause had been wounded and taken himself to the aid station in Ste. Mère Eglise. The 507th Regimental Commander, Zip Millett, was captured near Amfreville. Battalion commander Charles Timmes was pinned against the west bank of the Merderet above Cauquigny; battalion commander Ed Ostberg was severely wounded at Chef du Pont, and battalion commander Ed Kuhn had been badly injured on the jump. Although Ridgway wasn't in contact with the 508th PIR battalion commanders, they were scarcely in better shape: Herbert Batcheller (who had commanded the 505th PIR after Gavin) was killed in action on D-Day, and Thomas J. B. Shanley was isolated on the west side of the Merderet opposite Chef du Pont.[6] In the vast majority of these cases, the next most senior leaders stepped up and took over the missions with very little loss of momentum. Sergeants took the place of lieutenants, who were being killed by the handful; platoon leaders became company commanders, staff officers took command positions. It was a great testimony to the aggressive and duty-bound culture of the division that, in spite of these losses, the paratroopers closed ranks and continued the mission.

At the 1st Battalion aid station behind Le Manoir la Fière, Francis Buck tried to shake off the effects of the devastation he had seen. When he examined his bloody knee, he found a small entry wound on the back side, about the size of his thumb. But the shrapnel had done some damage inside. This soldier who had walked miles during the first hours of D-Day was unable to walk another step. He asked for a shot of morphine, which a medic gave him, and that helped with the pain.

The wounded were being collected in a shallow depression just a few hundred yards behind the A Company line, well within earshot of the small arms fire. Buck, floating on morphine, lost track of time, but at one point he became aware of a firefight close by. Looking around the littered aid station, he saw a pile of weapons and decided that if the fighting got closer, he would help himself to one to protect himself. He intended to go out fighting, if it came to that.[7]

When Dolan saw that 1st Battalion Commander Major Fred Kellam was dead, he sent a runner to find the regimental command post back in Ste. Mère Eglise. The messenger found Lieutenant Colonel Mark Alexander, the capable regimental Executive Officer, who immediately headed toward the 1st Battalion area to assess the situation.

Alexander, who had been an outstanding battalion commander during the Sicilian and Italian campaigns, had a simple rule for handling emergencies: the leader must move to the trouble spot and see firsthand what is going on. It was nearly two miles to the bridge from the regimental command post on the east side of Ste. Mère Eglise, and Alexander hustled the whole way, following the road running southeast from town. The Americans did not yet control the area, and there were German patrols moving in the gap between Ste. Mère Eglise and La Fière, so the executive officer stayed on the lookout and tried not to make himself an easy target in the open areas.

Alexander found things well in hand at the bridge. Dolan had reorganized his defense after the first German attack, moving up what reinforcements he had and placing the men from the other 1st Battalion companies in a small reserve some distance back from the bridge, but still overlooking the area. Dolan was now the ranking 1st Battalion officer present (Kellam, McGinity, and Roydson were dead, Stefanich of C Company was wounded, much of B Company, including its officers, were still missing), and Alexander put him in charge of the 1st Battalion's effort at the bridge. Alexander made a few minor suggestions for the defense, then headed back to the regimental command post.

Along the way Alexander ran into Gavin, who was moving toward La Fière. Gavin had heard an erroneous report that the 1st Battalion had lost the bridge, so he was glad to see Alexander and get some reliable information from this trusted and experienced combat leader commander.[8]

Although Dolan and his men had done well, Gavin knew the Germans had not given up. The bridge was too important to leave its defense in the hands of a lieutenant, however competent. Gavin told Alexander to go back to La Fière and take command of the 1st Battalion elements there.

Alexander asked what Gavin had in mind for the bridgehead.

"Do you want me on this side of the bridge, the other side of the river, or both sides?" he asked the assistant division commander.[9]

Gavin told Alexander to stay on the east side of river, where A Company's defense was anchored at Le Manoir la Fière, and hold on there. Alexander reached the bridge area at the same time that the Germans renewed their shelling. The colonel jumped into a hole with an A Company medic, Private Kelly Byars, who was moving about and taking care of the wounded. Byars and Alexander spent thirty minutes crammed tightly into a hole barely big enough for one man.

Alexander knew Byars from the early days of the regiment, when the young medic participated in the first-ever regimental-sized jump at Camden, South Carolina. During that jump, a transport plane lost power in one of its engines. Losing altitude, it plowed through some helpless jumpers who were suspended below their chutes. The plane's working propeller shredded Byars's chute all the way down to the static lines. Fortunately, Byars had enough altitude and presence of mind to deploy his reserve parachute. He landed close to Alexander and Gavin, who were absolutely transfixed by the terrible tragedy they were witnessing. Private Byars walked up to Colonel Gavin, threw the reserve chute on the ground at the commander's feet, and said, "You can shove this chute up your ass. I'm through with parachuting."

Gavin, all but speechless, could only answer, "OK."

A few weeks later Byars was jumping again, and D-Day found him risking his life to drag wounded men to safety.[10]

Not far behind where Alexander and Byars huddled together under fire, two junior officers from the 1st Battalion's Headquarters Company were also digging in near the Ste. Mère Eglise road.

Twenty-four-year-old Lieutenant Dean McCandless was the battalion communications officer, and one of his jobs was to establish a battalion command post so that subordinate units would know where to send messages. The radios had been lost in the jump, so McCandless had no idea of how the larger invasion was going. He and Lieutenant George Golden, the battalion adjutant, had picked a spot just off the road and a few hundred yards back, and they dug as German shells landed around them.

By this point, McCandless knew that both his battalion commander and executive officer were dead, as was Roydson, the battalion operations officer. The toll for these first few hours of battle had been high, and as McCandless dug, he thought about the men he'd worked for.

McGinity had been quiet, athletic, serious about soldiering, and, McCandless thought, destined for greater responsibilities. Roydson was from Montana and loved to talk about horses and riding. But McCandless was especially struck by Kellam's death. The battalion commander took his responsibilities very seriously, but he also liked to have fun, and could frequently be heard, back in England, singing songs. Kellam had a son born in October 1943, after he left for North Africa; the officer had seen his boy only in photographs.

From their command post, which was a glorified name for a couple of shallow holes, McCandless and Golden kept runners moving all morning, trying to locate lost men, keeping the link open to the 3rd Battalion and the regimental command post, trying to find the important equipment bundles. But with the incoming fire picking up and seemingly becoming more accurate, McCandless worried that some German artillery spotter had seen the runners coming and going and figured out that this spot was a command post. The two lieutenants talked about moving to another place. The problem was that company runners would have a hard time finding them, which would make communications, already difficult, even more troublesome.

As the two junior officers dug, ducked incoming fire, and discussed their options, they saw a GI headed their way, walking upright with his rifle slung on his shoulder. This was exactly the kind of movement, out in the open, that had probably given away their position to the Germans in the first place.

"You'd better get down or you'll get your ass shot off," Golden yelled at the GI, but the soldier just kept walking toward them. When he got close, McCandless was surprised to see their visitor was Jim Gavin.

The Assistant Division Commander asked what was going on, and McCandless gave him a rundown of the not-very-encouraging picture, mentioning that they were thinking of moving the command post. Gavin sensed that the lieutenants were a bit rattled, more by the casualties among their leaders than by the incoming fire.

Gavin reassured them that the 1st Battalion was in pretty good shape: it had achieved its objective and was now holding the critical piece of ground. Gavin was sure things would turn out just fine, and that the two officers should simply stay put and run their post from where they were.

"Besides," he said, grinning at them, "there's no place to go."

Gavin's gallows humor relieved a bit of the tension everyone was feeling, and the lieutenants resumed their digging.

Down at Chef du Pont, Captain Roy Creek set about reorganizing the thirty-four men who'd been left to guard the bridge and causeway. Amazingly, not a single man there was from his company. He recognized a few of the noncoms from the regiment, but he had not worked with any of these men before, and generally they did not know one another. Because they were paratroopers, who had volunteered for hazardous duty and trained hard to be part of an elite outfit, he trusted they would do their duty; he was determined to do his.

Creek moved around the area, skittering from position to position, counting his men and forming them into squads, getting some sort of span of control. He put in charge men who'd impressed him over the last twelve hours, including Sergeant LaPine and First Sergeant Hicks of A Company. Charles Ames, one of his own lieutenants who had jumped with the pathfinders, came walking up the road from the village of Chef du Pont, giving Creek another junior leader to rely on.

Because he had no radio or wire communications, Creek chose several runners to carry messages. He established a command post in the courtyard of the creamery and put a team on the upper floor to keep an eye on the wider area.

Creek was moving around the area, checking to make sure they could withstand an enemy assault, when the Germans on the far bank, who had been peppering the area with machine gun fire, opened up with something bigger. Creek guessed from the sound that it was an 88, a deadly accurate and versatile cannon that could be used as an antiaircraft gun, an antitank gun, or, in this case, an antipersonnel gun.

Creek was moving around and exposed when the heavy shelling began. He made a dash for the small building he had seen earlier, a sentry house near the east end of the bridge. He ducked inside and stumbled on a gruesome sight: the still-burning body of an enemy soldier who had been hit with a white phosphorous grenade tossed inside during the earlier attack. Creek knew the body belonged to a German only because of the shape of the helmet.

Since the sentry box was designed to hold only one man standing, there was no room for him. Besides that, the smoke and stench and the fact that the box was probably an aiming point for the enemy gun crew made it a bad place to be. Creek, figuring he'd rather take his chances out in the open, ran back outside. He sprinted for the slightly lower ground on the south side of the roadbed, the side away from the enemy gunners.

After his close brush under artillery fire, Creek got some disturbing news from his observation post in the creamery. A line of German infantry was visible moving near the south side of Chef du Pont, about three hundred yards behind him. Creek and his tiny force now faced envelopment.

He quickly moved some of his limited firepower to face this new threat. Although it seemed unlikely that the Germans west of the bridge would charge his men, he couldn't completely rule it out, and he made mental notes about how he would fight off simultaneous attacks from both sides. The troopers had been awake for the past thirty-six hours, had made a combat jump into enemy territory, had crossed a wide marsh under fire (some of them more than once), and had engaged in a deadly close-quarters fight with a determined enemy. The artillery fire from the far bank quickly caused fourteen casualties, further depleting his tiny force. Now he was asking these men—men he did not know and who did not know him—to do even more, and they responded without hesitation.

While he tried to create an all-around defense with twenty men, and while he waited to see what might develop behind him, Creek thought about his situation. He knew there were paratroopers in and around Ste. Mère Eglise, and although he didn't know the situation at La Fière, he guessed there was probably fighting going on there. If the Germans gave up on La Fière, they might concentrate their forces to roll across Chef du Pont, crushing Creek's small band. He could expect no help from the Ste. Mère Eglise area, so he and his men would do whatever they could.

By early evening Creek figured that the enemy squad his men had seen moving near Chef du Pont had been headed somewhere else, though he didn't withdraw his rear guard. About that time Captain Hugo Olson, Gavin's aide, showed up with a message from the general. Olson explained the situation: Gavin's Force A had a tenuous hold on the eastern end of La Fière. When reinforcements from the 325th Glider Infantry Regiment were in place on D+1, Gavin and Ridgway intended to cross at La Fière and push for the western side of the Merderet. In the meantime, it was imperative that they hang on to the footholds they had on the bridges. Gavin's message to Creek: hold at all costs.

If the situation hadn't been so serious, Creek might have appreciated the humor. First, it was doubtful he could hold on to something he didn't really have in the first place. He looked around at his twenty unwounded, exhausted, undersupplied, and lightly armed GIs and thought, *Well, it can't cost too much; there aren't enough of us.*

Creek asked Olson to carry back the message that he needed reinforcements. Then Olson disappeared again, back to his dangerous mission of moving around a countryside crawling with trigger-happy German and American patrols.

It was the evening of D-Day, with several hours of daylight still left, when a large flight of C47s cut across the Cotentin Peninsula. Parabundles with yellow markings landed inside their position; the yellow meant mortar ammunition. Since he had a mortar but no ammo, Creek sent a team scurrying after the bundle, and they came back with a supply of mortar rounds. Things were looking up. Creek and his men could now put indirect fire on the German foxholes on the far side of the bridge. The mortars, which fired at a high angle (thus, indirect fire), were the perfect weapon for hitting dug-in troops.

Within thirty minutes of this gift from the sky, Creek pointed out to the mortar crew where he thought the German fire was coming from on the far bank, and the GIs immediately opened fire with the mortar. Since the Germans were concealed and probably dug in, there was no way to tell if the GIs hit their target, but the incoming fire decreased and Creek's troops at least felt they were striking back.

Shortly after the parabundle dropped on them, Creek received almost a platoon's worth of reinforcements, sent back by Gavin and Captain Olson. He reorganized his position once again, selecting a small assault team and a fire support team for another go at the bridge and the west side of the causeway. He found a tiny spit of dry ground that jutted out into the flood just north of the bridge, and he put a machine gun team out there to cover the length of the causeway.

When both teams were ready, the fire support element put both direct and indirect fire on the Germans. When he was satisfied that they had done all they could to suppress the enemy, Creek gave the signal, and Lieutenant Ames led ten men in a rush over the bridge and down the causeway, where they grenaded and fired into the German foxholes. Five Germans tried to escape across the causeway to the west but were cut down by Ames's men.

Finally, nearly twelve hours after Lieutenant Colonel Ed Ostberg led his scratch force in a rush at the enemy, the paratroopers held both sides of the Chef du Pont Bridge and the entire eastern end of the causeway. It would be up to some other force to push all the way to the western side, but Roy Creek and his determined little band had held on to the important gateway and were now, as the sun began to set on D-Day, in a position to keep the Germans from crossing in an assault aimed at Ste. Mère Eglise or Utah Beach.

Creek dragged himself back to his command post at the creamery, where his medics were treating the wounded as best they could with their limited supplies. There were dead GIs and Germans in various spots throughout the area, including inside the courtyard walls where the wounded lay. Creek had his men move the dead outside, where the wounded didn't have to look at them, and cover the bodies with parachutes. There were thirteen Americans and forty-three Germans lined up, all alike in death.

Now that he had time to pause, Creek began to wonder about the beach landings and if help was going to come, and if he'd be able to evacuate his wounded to the field hospitals near Utah Beach. He had no word about the invasion and no communication with his own headquarters, which, he figured, was with Art Maloney somewhere up near La Fière and Ste. Mère Eglise.

It had been dark for just over an hour when a runner told Creek that there were vehicles approaching from the direction of Chef du Pont. The visitors were American, part of the forward reconnaissance element of the 4th Infantry Division, which had come ashore at Utah Beach that morning. This was the first hard news they'd had from outside Chef du Pont, and as Roy Creek would say later, Chef du Pont is a very small town. The recon soldiers brought news that the Allies were ashore, and their presence told Creek that help would soon be on the way. Most important, perhaps, they dropped off several cases of rations for the hungry paratroopers.

Though they still had to maintain a security perimeter throughout the night, Creek's men could now get some rest, their first in nearly forty hours. Creek, tired as he was, saw to the distribution of rations, made sure that his men were on guard, and that the wounded were as comfortable as possible.

By this time it was nearly June 7. Lieutenant Ames, who had come in with the pathfinders before 0200 on June 6, suggested to his commander that they take turns getting some sleep. Roy Creek took his turn standing watch, and as June 6 gave way to June 7, he sat pondering his first day in combat.

"We had done some things badly," he would say later. "But overall, with a hodgepodge of troops from several units who had never trained together as a unit, [who] didn't even know one another and were engaged in their first combat, we had done OK. We captured our bridge and held it."

As the minute hand on his watch passed twelve, Creek marked the end of his first day in combat and thought that it was going to be a long way to Berlin.[11]

• • •

Roy Creek and his understrength band of tired troopers anchored one corner of the 82nd Airborne Division's position late on D-Day.

The division "airhead" was the shape of a rough triangle, two miles to a side, its corners at Ste. Mère Eglise, Chef du Pont, and La Fière. One German regiment, the 1058th Panzergrenadier, had been delayed at Turnbull's blocking position north of Ste. Mère Eglise but was back in the fight at the northern end of that town. These troops put up a heavy curtain of fire when the Mission Elmira gliders came in on the drop zones just before dusk. Another regiment, the 1057th Panzergrenadier, on the west bank of the Merderet, had been repulsed at La Fière and was preparing to have another go at the important causeway. Although the individual German commanders had acted aggressively, coordination between these units suffered because their overall commander, General Wilhelm Falley, was killed in an ambush of his staff car by members of the 508th PIR of the 101st Airborne Division. These troopers, also badly misdropped, had simply reacted to the sight of a military vehicle with German soldiers in it. They had no idea of the identity of their victims until the shooting was over and they examined the bodies.[12]

Finally, a battalion of the 6th Parachute Regiment, the Fallschirm-jäger, moving north from Carentan, had reached the crossroads village of Blosville, some three miles south of Ste. Mère Eglise. Had this unit pushed farther and harder, it might have linked up with the besieged Germans on Hill 20, also south of Ste. Mère Eglise, who had held up the Raff force.[13] But they stopped short and so did not bring their full weight to bear on the paratroopers in Ste. Mère Eglise.

Inside the airhead, Matt Ridgway had control of about twenty-five hundred men (out of more than seven thousand who arrived in France by parachute and glider that day).[14] And while most of these were the veterans of the 505th, the 1st Battalion leadership—commander, executive officer, and operations officer—had all been killed; the 2nd Battalion commander had a broken leg, and the 3rd Battalion commander was in the aid station with a minor wound.

The poor success of the resupply and reinforcement by glider (Mission Elmira) left the paratroopers scrambling for critical items, especially ammunition, antitank guns and artillery, and medical supplies. But the downed pilots also brought welcome news to Ridgway: they had flown over Utah Beach and could report that the invasion forces were ashore and moving inland. This meant that help was on the way, although Ridgway did not know how long it would take to arrive. In addition, a 2nd Battalion patrol had run into a patrol from the 4th Division near Beuzeville au Plain, just under two miles to the northeast of Ste. Mère Eglise, during the afternoon. The two patrols didn't exchange much information; the handful of paratroopers didn't know the status of their entire division, but they knew enough to recognize good news, and sent back word that the 4th Division was ashore.

Ridgway wanted more substantive communications with the 4th Division. In particular, he wanted to ask Major General Raymond Barton for support in the form of antitank guns and ammo and medical supplies. Ridgway chose his talented assistant G3 (operations officer), Lieutenant Colonel Walter Winton, to make contact with Barton's headquarters.

By the time Winton reported to Ridgway's headquarters for his orders, he had been awake for nearly forty hours and was having a difficult time moving. He got his instructions from Ridgway and a Benzedrine "stay-awake" pill from Assistant G4 (logistics officer) Bill Moorman. He moved out alone to find Vandervoort's troopers, the same dog-tired patrol that had just come from Beuzeville.

The troopers accompanying Winton were as exhausted as he was, and he soon outpaced the main body. He and a smaller contingent eventually ran into soldiers of the 12th Infantry Regiment of the 4th Division, southeast of Beuzeville. These troops took Winton to Barton's command post, near one of the Utah Beach exits, by midnight. This was the first hard information Barton had about the 82nd: the bad drop, especially of the 507th and 508th, the poorly executed glider resupply missions, and the fact that the Raff force had not reached them yet. In addition, Winton reported, the division was under pressure from the north and west, and had some enemy to the south as well. Barton promised to send help at first light; then he sent a message to Joe Collins, commander of the VII Corps. The exhausted Winton, meanwhile, found a spot to lie down and immediately fell into a deep sleep.

All across the division's area, exhausted troopers wrapped themselves in parachutes against the chill night air and tried to get some rest. Staff officers and noncoms worked through the night in shifts, trying to get an accurate picture of where everyone was, where the enemy was, and where he would strike next. The medics and surgeons worked too, short on everything from bandages to morphine. They told the wounded—the ones who needed hope—that the next day would bring evacuation to a field hospital, to a hospital ship with clean sheets, and, for some, to a real hospital in England with clean nurses. They comforted the dying as best they could, and then moved the bodies out of sight of the still-living.

Out amid the hedgerows, infantrymen ran patrols to keep the enemy at bay. Sometimes the patrols crossed paths with German infantry doing the same thing, and there would be a brief burst of light and fire, there would be chaos and confusion, then withdrawal, and a few more names to add to the tally of dead and wounded.

COUNTERATTACK

At La Fière, the men of A Company rested fitfully. They could hear German armor moving up and down the narrow country roads on the west side of the Merderet, could even hear the Germans talking to one another from time to time. Some of the riflemen had expended nearly all of their ammunition shooting at the panzergrenadiers in the first attack, and they hoped for a resupply before the Germans made another push.

Dolan positioned himself right in the middle of the narrow frontage. It didn't take much imagination for the German mortar and artillery crews to figure out where the paratroopers were located, and the fire kept up all night. The tree-burst shells (which exploded twenty to thirty feet above ground and sprayed shrapnel down into foxholes) were the worst and inflicted more casualties on the battered company.

All during this intermittent fire, the small unit leaders on the American side kept moving, adjusting the defense. Dolan positioned some men from B Company inside his own perimeter to act as a reserve force. A squad from B Company of the 307th Airborne Engineers came up to lend some firepower as riflemen, as did two machine guns and crews from the 1st Battalion's Headquarters Company. Dolan and First Sergeant Robert Matteson repositioned the men to get the best coverage of the bridgehead. Lieutenant Wayne Presnell pushed his line to the south a few yards past the manor's buildings to try to get an angle for flanking fire on the causeway.

Private Richard Reyes braved the incoming artillery and mortar fire to search for parabundles containing ammunition. He made several trips to the area of the drop zone, returning with bandoliers of M1 ammo, bazooka rockets, and boxes of machine gun ammunition.[1] But all the moving around came with a cost. Staff Sergeant Lawrence F. Monahan was mortally wounded during A Company's reorganization.

Dolan had plenty to be frustrated about. His company had suffered heavy casualties, but there was no sign that they would be reinforced anytime soon, much less relieved by the more heavily armed troops of the 4th Division. He had lost his executive officer, Lieutenant Tom Furey, who had moved to take over C Company when Captain Stefanich was wounded; and his first sergeant was wounded, though still serving up front. On top of that, when the 507 and 508 men had been pulled out to form a reserve and blocking force back near the railroad, the crew of the 57 mm antitank gun that had been with him all day pulled out, too. He was sure Mark Alexander—who had taken command of 1st Battalion—or Jim Gavin would have the gun moved forward again, but in the meantime it made for some unnecessary worry for the already beleaguered commander.

Around 0200, the GIs hunkered down deep in their foxholes overlooking the bridge heard vehicles out front. Even in the daylight, it was hard to get a clear look at the entire length of the causeway because of the undergrowth and trees. In the deepest part of the night, even with a sliver of moonlight, it was almost impossible to see anything at a distance of more than a few yards. But the sound woke them up, and word was passed from one jumpy sentry to another: "The krauts are back."

One of the squads clinging to the hillside outpost was led by Sergeant William D. Owens, a former drill press operator from Detroit. At thirty-eight, Owens was old for a paratrooper, but he was extremely competent and looked out for his men. Young soldiers like the eighteen-year-old Bob Murphy looked up to him almost as a father, and Owens took care of them accordingly.

Owens heard the vehicles and decided to do something about this newest threat. He stuffed a couple of Gammon grenades in his pockets, then shuffled and crawled through the wet grass and shell holes forward of the A Company lines. The bridge was close, no more than twenty yards, its low arch just visible in the dim light. In the darkness it was hard to make out exactly what was happening on the narrow roadbed amid the tangle of knocked-out tanks A Company had destroyed earlier. All the shapes simply melded together in the gloom. He was safe, for the moment, from German snipers, who couldn't see him any more than he could pick out shapes on the road. But he was also exposed to enemy mortars and artillery, and the company had already suffered heavy casualties due to incoming fire.

When Owens judged that one of the approaching vehicles was close, he removed the cap on the grenade and threw it toward the sound. In the brilliant white flash of the explosion, Owens realized he had only hit one of the tanks that was already wrecked. But the advancing Germans, whoever they were, got the message: the paratroopers were awake and waiting for them. The enemy withdrew back toward Cauquigny, Owens crawled back to his hole, and the men got what rest they could as they waited for the sun to come up on the second day of the invasion.

By the time June 7 broke over Normandy, the Allies had put ashore some 156,000 troops, thousands of vehicles, and tons of the critical supplies needed to sustain a push inland.

On the far left of the Allied lodgment, British paratroopers had seized critical bridges and secured the Allied flank against German panzers to the east. In a brilliant coup de main, Major John Howard's D Company, Oxfordshire and Buckinghamshire Light Infantry had landed almost on top of their targets, seizing the bridges over the Orne River and Caen Canal. The operation secured the left flank of the entire invasion area.[2]

British and Canadian troops coming ashore at Gold, Juno, and Sword beaches had overwhelmed the defenders, who fought from heavily fortified emplacements amid the beachfront communities. By nightfall on June 6, one Canadian armored unit had managed to cross the coastal highway near Caen. Field Marshal Bernard Montgomery wanted British and Canadian forces to seize Caen on D-Day, as the road network through Caen was the door to Paris. Allied airmen also wanted the airfield at Carpiquet, just west of Caen, so as to get their aircraft closer to the fight. Unfortunately for the Allies, the Germans would hold Caen for six weeks.

Omaha Beach, some fifteen miles east of Ste. Mère Eglise, was the scene of horrific slaughter for the first hours of D-Day. Troops of the veteran 1st Division and the untested 29th Division hit one of the most heavily and cleverly defended stretches of coast in France, which the Germans had turned into a killing zone. Hundreds of machine guns and larger-caliber artillery pieces were sighted for plunging fire, enfilading fire, and grazing fire. GIs coming ashore were stopped at the water's edge, then had to negotiate an open stretch of sand to make it to the relative safety of a stone escarpment, where they huddled while German mortar crews dropped rounds on top of them. For nearly two hours, men and equipment piled up on the beach, until a handful of junior leaders took charge of their own little section of the war and made inroads, knocking out a single German machine gun here, climbing a cliff there.

Brigadier General Norm Cota, the assistant division commander of the 29th Division, personally led a few squads of willing men through minefields and deadly fire. The tiny breach they created was one hole in the dike that held back the Allied advance. All along the killing zone that was Omaha Beach, small groups of men, acting on their own initiative and independently of one another, forced cracks in this part of the Atlantic Wall.

Once the Americans reached the tops of the steep cliffs at Omaha Beach, they cleared out the German defenders from the rear. Soon men and vehicles from the follow-on waves were crossing the sandy stretch and moving inland. All around them was evidence of the indescribable violence: the wrecked tanks and trucks and jeeps, the body parts rolling in the surf, the dead lying in rows, the wounded awaiting evacuation.

At Utah Beach, just east of the 82nd Airborne Division's drop zones, the 4th Division had come ashore with relative ease. This was due in part to the fact that the Navy put the first wave ashore a mile or so from where they were supposed to be. (The original invasion beaches, as it turned out, were much more heavily defended than the ones eventually used.) With the paratroopers of the 101st Airborne Division tying up German counterattacks on the left flank of Utah Beach, and with Matt Ridgway's All Americans holding off the armored assaults launched by the Germans west and north of Ste. Mère Eglise, the Utah Beach forces managed to get off the beach fairly rapidly. But the untested infantry units took too long to move inland and tended to hesitate at any sign of resistance. This threw off the timetable for the relief of the paratroopers.

On the morning of D+1, Lieutenant General "Lightning Joe" Collins, whose VII Corps was moving inland from Utah Beach, came ashore and began to shake things up. He committed a reserve tank battalion to break through to the paratroopers at Ste. Mère Eglise and drove his subordinate commanders to get moving. The 8th Infantry Regiment, which had stalled near Les Forges, just south of Ste. Mère Eglise, managed to pierce German resistance there, though the green troops were still slow.

Amazingly, it was not the Shermans of the 746th Tank Battalion, or even the 4th Division infantrymen, who first reached the paratroopers in Ste. Mère Eglise. It was a short, thin, fifty-seven-year-old arthritis sufferer who arrived in a jeep with no armed escort and no personal weapon.

Brigadier General Theodore Roosevelt Jr., the son of the twenty-sixth president, the assistant division commander of the 4th Division, had cajoled his boss, Major General Raymond Barton, to allow him to go ashore on Utah Beach with the first wave of troops. Roosevelt was thus on the spot when the first-wave commander realized they'd been put ashore in the wrong place. Roosevelt is credited with the decision to stay put and the remark, "We'll start the war from right here."

Now Roosevelt, who'd been assigned to the 4th Division by Bradley because his presence would inspire the troops, was once again in front of the action, riding through no-man's-land, armed with a cane, and looking for the fight. Ridgway would later say that Roosevelt came rolling in on June 7 "as if the bullet that could kill him had not been made."[3]

Roosevelt represented relief and resupply, but of course he carried none of that with him, and Ridgway knew it would still be some time before the actual ammunition, food, and medical kits arrived. For the moment, he had to count on the planned arrival of reinforcements by glider and resupply by air drop.

The first wave of reinforcements, approximately one hundred gliders carrying the 1st Battalion of the 325th Infantry, plus some engineers and artillerymen, took off from England at 0430 on June 7. They arrived over the Cotentin around 0700—in broad daylight—and were immediately taken under fire by German ground troops. The gliders were released too early—none of them hit the planned landing zone—and many of them crashed in the short Norman fields. Seventeen men (out of just over seven hundred) were killed outright, with another ninety-eight injured. Among those hurt badly enough to require evacuation was Lieutenant Colonel Klemm Boyd, the 1st Battalion Commander, who was evacuated to England. (Boyd was the sixth infantry battalion commander, out of twelve in the division, lost in the first thirty hours of the invasion.)[4]

The second wave, carrying two battalions of infantry, reached the Cotentin around 0900 and released for Landing Zone W, which was between Ste. Mère Eglise and the slow-moving advance of Raff's force and James Van Fleet's 8th Infantry Regiment. Those landing closest to the German lines, at the north end of the landing zone, were hit hard.

In spite of the casualties and injuries, most of Colonel Harry Lewis's glidermen were on the ground, organized, and ready to move by 1100 hours, though many were dazed from the rough landings. (The British-made Horsa glider—huge, unwieldy, and prone to splintering on impact—was deemed useless by the Americans and never again used to bring GIs to the fight.)[5] Lewis set out on his original mission, moving the 325th Glider Regiment westward from Les Forges toward the Merderet River, then toward Chef du Pont.

Ridgway did not receive any great weight of reinforcements on D+1, though Raff's tanks did eventually make it to the town. His artillerymen managed to salvage a handful of 75 mm pack howitzers from the crashed gliders, giving Ridgway fewer than ten tubes of artillery with which to repulse the German attacks he expected on June 7. He had Bill Ekman's veteran 505th PIR holding the northern side of Ste. Mère Eglise, and Ben Vandervoort's 2nd Battalion had been reinforced with a smattering of strays from the 507th and 508th PIR. Mark Alexander was in charge of holding the bridge at La Fière, and Gavin was helping to oversee that fight. He had Lewis's fresh 325th Glider Infantry Regiment at the eastern end of Chef du Pont, in case the Germans tried to hit him across that causeway. He had wounded piling up in a schoolhouse on the northern side of Ste. Mère Eglise, and German artillery was falling regularly on the troopers and civilians in town. The town's water supply had been badly damaged, and many of the residents had retreated to a spring just north and west of the town square, where a statue of the town's patron saint, Saint Meen, overlooked a shallow pool of water that was not enough to supply the civilians and still satisfy the wounded, whose cries for water were pitiful.

Meanwhile, the German 1058th Regiment prepared another assault along the N13 from the north, and the 1057th Regiment prepared for another attack across the deadly causeway at La Fière.[6]

The two battalions of the 1058th Regiment that were north of Ste. Mère Eglise in the vicinity of Neuville au Plain had run out of steam by the time they pushed Turnbull's platoon out of its roadblock on D-Day. Though small elements tried various points along the line during the night, the paratroopers of Vandervoort's 2nd Battalion managed to hold their ground.

The German division commander ordered the 1058th to renew its attack from the north on the morning of June 7, and he reinforced the regiment with two motorized heavy artillery battalions and a company of self-propelled guns, as well as a special unit known as the Sturm Battalion, which was part of German 7th Army Headquarters. After some initial confusion, the German advance sorted itself out and the Sturm Battalion moved south toward Ste. Mère Eglise on the west side of the N13, supported by the self-propelled guns. Meanwhile, the 1st Battalion of the 1058th Regiment advanced along the east side of the highway.

The Sturm Battalion, which had not been engaged on D-Day, made some progress, pushing back some of the outposts held by Vandervoort's D Company. The self-propelled guns—which can be easily mistaken for tanks by infantrymen hunkered down in foxholes while dodging incoming direct and indirect fire—got close to the American lines. Then an H Company soldier, Private John E. Atchley, saw an opportunity. The former artilleryman had volunteered to stick by the 57 mm antitank gun that had been put in place by Vandervoort on D-Day. Alone and under fire, he single-handedly knocked out two of the self-propelled guns and stalled the German attack.

The Sturm Battalion commander decided to wait until the 1st Battalion of the 1058th, which was supposed to be advancing on the east side of the road, pulled up even with him. The Germans could bring a lot more firepower to bear by attacking on a two-battalion front.

Captain Taylor G. Smith, whose D Company had thwarted several attacks during the night and had held after being pushed back by the Sturm Battalion, recognized that the situation on the north side of Ste. Mère Eglise was becoming critical. He sent his Executive Officer, Lieutenant Waverly Wray, back into town to find Vandervoort and ask for help.

Wray was one of the original officers in the 505th, a veteran of Sicily and Italy known for his devout ways. Dark-haired and sturdily built, the young Mississippi native did not smoke, drink, curse, or chase women. His troops called him "the deacon," but it was out of respect. Whenever he was questioned about his ways, the self-effacing lieutenant said he merely tried to "walk with the Lord." Wray was an accomplished woodsman and a crack shot, and once said he "never missed a shot in his life that he didn't mean to."[7]

Vandervoort told Wray that there was no help available, and suggested that the lieutenant use the D Company platoon that was not engaged and hit the Germans before they could hit D Company again. Wray hustled back to his company command post and briefed Smith on the plan. Smith, who had a badly injured back, agreed to let Wray lead the patrol.

By this time Wray was familiar with the area, having occupied it for the better part of two days. He decided to do a leader's reconnaissance before he moved the patrol forward of friendly lines, and set out by himself toward the advancing Germans, planning on coming at them from the flank. (Wray was on the east side of the N13 and thus in front of the 1st Battalion of the 1058th Regiment.) He suspected that the highway and some smaller, parallel roads would be their main axis of attack, so he used the concealment offered by the ubiquitous hedgerows to move north before turning to come at the highway and the enemy from the flank.

As Wray closed in on the road, he could hear men speaking German. Moving closer, he saw what looked like a command group gathered in the roadway and talking over their plan for attacking the American positions. They didn't have a single man on guard.

Wray held his rifle in the firing position and stepped to where he could see and be seen by the Germans, calling out, "*Haende hoch!*"

All but one of the Germans raised his hands; the eighth one reached for his pistol, and Wray shot him dead. In the momentary confusion the other Germans thought they could get the drop on this GI, who seemed to be alone. They also reached for their weapons, and Wary shot them each in rapid succession.

Two Germans in a foxhole nearby, hearing the commotion, stood up and opened fire on Wray with their machine pistols. A bullet hit the front rim of Wray's helmet and nicked his right ear. The American lieutenant dived for cover, reloaded his rifle, then moved forward and killed the last two Germans with a shot apiece.

Wray's reconnaissance had become a one-man combat patrol, and though he didn't know it yet, he had decapitated the 1st Battalion of the

1058th by killing most of the unit's leadership. Wray made a quick round-trip to the D Company position, returning with an undersized platoon and a 60 mm mortar. Since he now had a good idea where the Germans had staged for the attack, he moved into a position from which he could observe the impact of the rounds. He passed the commands to the crew, then called back with corrections until the rounds were coming in on target, just as fast as the crew could remove the safety pins and drop them in the tube. Wray spotted the rounds himself and walked the mortar fire right onto the enemy positions. A large segment of the German battalion, without leadership or direction, broke cover and ran northward, with the D Company men firing at their backs.

A German medical officer, seeing the imminent destruction of the entire command, waved a white flag and called out in English: he wanted a cease-fire. By this time the D Company commander, Captain Smith, had come up, and along with Staff Sergeant Paul D. Nunan, he went forward to see what the German might have to say.

The medical officer said he would leave behind his wounded and his own medics, along with an American glider pilot they had captured. But he meant to let the infantrymen retreat. Smith refused these terms, demanding the compete surrender of the Germans who were cut off. The two officers could not come to an agreement, so they each returned to their positions. However, the Germans had used the lull to prepare a withdrawal, and as soon as Smith was out of sight, German artillery began crashing down on the D Company men. Under the cover of this fire, the rest of the 1st Battalion of the 1058th Regiment pulled back to the north again, but they had left up to 50 percent of their men killed, wounded, or missing, and had lost their leaders.

The withdrawal left the Sturm Battalion, on the west side of the highway, with no support on its flank. This unit, too, pulled back. D Company moved up to its original positions astride the N13, and the situation stabilized there, although the troopers were still hit by indirect fire throughout the day on June 7.

Shortly after Waverly Wray and D Company turned back the attack on the north end of Ste. Mère Eglise, help arrived at the 82nd Airborne Division command post. The GIs of Van Fleet's 8th Infantry Regiment reached the southern end of the town, creating a real link to the beach forces. Even better, several Sherman tanks of the long-delayed Raff force rolled in. Just behind the tanks came Lieutenant General Joe Collins himself, riding with Van Fleet through a German artillery barrage in an armored vehicle. Ridgway greeted them warmly, and they immediately began making plans to push north while the Germans were reeling.

The new plan called for Van Fleet to move his regiment forward with two battalions abreast, through any remaining German resistance on the Fauville-Turqueville Ridge (Hill 20) south of town. These two relatively fresh battalions were then to move northward toward Neuville au Plain, one on either side of the N13.

But the advancing battalions sidestepped east to avoid German artillery fire, and the result was that both units were not only too far east of the highway but east of Ste. Mère Eglise and almost missed making any contact at all with the 505th PIR.[8]

Meanwhile, an increase in small arms fire at the north end of town convinced the paratroopers that the Germans would counterattack again as soon as they could organize, as their doctrine called for. Ridgway, seeing that Van Fleet's men were not moving fast enough to be of any help, ordered Vandervoort to come up with a hasty plan for an attack north, using the newly arrived tanks for firepower. There were not enough paratroopers on the American line at the north end of Ste. Mère Eglise to withstand a determined German assault, so the paratroopers elected to attack first.

Lieutenant Theodore Peterson had a more-or-less intact 1st Platoon of E Company in position facing north and centered on the main road, the N13. Lieutenant James Coyle had a scratch platoon made up of ten men from E Company headquarters and twenty-five or so misdropped men of the 101st Airborne Division, poised to the left of Peterson and parallel to the road. A platoon from D Company was supposed to be on the right side of Peterson, but this platoon had been sent by its battal-

ion commander, Lieutenant Colonel Ed Krause, out to the east looking
for the missing battalions of the 8th Infantry Regiment. The plans originally hatched by Collins, Ridgway, and Van Fleet for the attack northward called for more than two battalions of relatively fresh infantry, or
nearly a thousand men. As the afternoon wore on and it became apparent that the Americans needed to attack first, the undermanned point
of the spear consisted of one platoon and one scraped-together group,
most of whom did not know one another. The paratroopers would lead
with fewer than seventy-five men.

Lieutenant Coyle moved forward to scout the route his slapped-
together team, now named 2nd Platoon of E Company, would take. The
ground in front of his hedgerow was mostly open, all apple orchards and
grassy fields, and he could see incoming small arms fire clipping the
leaves from the trees. He scampered to his right, looking for a more
concealed way to move forward. He found a small country lane, lined
on both sides by trees and leading generally northward. He sent word
back that he had slightly altered the plan.

Just before the attack jumped off, Lieutenant Eugene Doerfler, Vandervoort's intelligence officer, showed up at the command post. Doerfler had a habit of going out on patrols, sometimes alone, to find out
what the enemy was up to. It made Vandervoort think that he would
soon have to replace his intelligence officer, but in the meantime Doerfler produced an up-to-date picture of enemy action. Doerfler said that
the German buildup in front of E Company was heavy and indicated an
attack very soon. There could be no waiting for further reinforcements;
Doerfler seconded the idea that the paratroopers had to strike first.

Two Sherman tanks from the Raff group reached Vandervoort's command post at the same time, and the infantry officers and tank commanders quickly determined that they could do an end run and hit any
German advance on the flank. The tankers only needed someone to
show them the way forward. Doerfler, who had a penchant for being out
front, said he'd just come from there and would guide them.

Lieutenant Coyle was ready to advance up the little country lane
when Doerfler and two of his section men from the S2 appeared, walk-

ing ahead of the tanks. Doerfler and Coyle agreed that they should split the ad hoc rifle platoon into two sections, putting one tank with each. Since Coyle did not know the 101st Airborne Division men and had no way of knowing how they'd react to an officer they did not know, he put them in the rear with one tank and prepared to lead the advance himself with the other tank and his E Company headquarters men.

To Coyle's right, on Peterson's side of the advance, an unlikely series of events brought help to the American advance.

The 746th Tank Battalion, which had been ordered forward by the Corps commander, Collins, raced through Ste. Mère Eglise with a handful of paratroopers—who'd been sent to guide the tanks—on board. Lieutenant Colonel D. G. Hupfer, leading this charge, slowed his tanks down just long enough to let the paratroopers jump off before he continued the drive to the north end of town. Peterson's E Company men, who had been in France for nearly forty hours and had seen no reinforcements that didn't arrive by air, were overjoyed at the appearance of all this steel and firepower. They were even more surprised when the Hupfer column didn't stop to coordinate an attack but sped right through the E Company line heading north and looking for Germans.

Just a few hundred yards north of town, Hupfer's lead tank commander spotted a column of German vehicles; these were the surviving self-propelled antitank guns that had been added to the German assault just that morning. The German guns had the advantage when it came to killing power in a face-to-face slugfest, but the Shermans were faster and more maneuverable. The Shermans leaped into a one-sided gunfight, knocking out three or four of the German guns and losing one U.S. tank to enemy fire.

The remaining self-propelled guns raced north toward Neuville au Plain, looking for cover and a place to make a stand. Hupfer, who didn't want to give them time to find defensive positions, skirted to the right along the country road to Baudenville, then hooked left to hit the Germans in the flank. When he got close to Neuville, he saw that the enemy had not gone into defensive positions to face his assault but were still intent on getting out of the fight by moving north. The American tanks pushed forward aggressively, destroying most of the remaining guns but losing three more Shermans in the vicious, close-quarters fight in the small fields and shady lanes around Neuville au Plain.

Meanwhile, back on the line of departure for the infantry attack, the two platoons from E Company began their move forward. They had been cheered by the appearance of the tanks (two of which were still with Coyle on the left, or west, side of the road), but they were also alone. The D Company platoon that was supposed to be on Peterson's left had not returned, and there was no contact with either of the battalions from the 8th Infantry that were supposed to be on the far left and far right of the American attack. They would be going north on a tiny frontage, with their vulnerable flanks in the air.

On the left, Coyle moved north on a sheltered lane that ran parallel to the N13, made good progress, and took no fire. At one point he halted his column so that they could move the body of a dead paratrooper out of the road; he didn't want the tank to run over it. Coyle moved cautiously; he had the lead tank fire a couple of main gun rounds into hedgerows where he thought a German ambush might wait. The tank commander also made good use of the mounted .50-caliber machine gun to flush out any Germans hiding in the undergrowth.

About two hundred yards north of their start line, Coyle's patrol came upon a hedgerow running perpendicular to his advance. Coyle pressed through the foliage and looked to his right, expecting to see an empty field behind the barrier. Instead, he saw that there were two parallel hedgerows (he had passed through the first one), and between them was a small sunken lane. The area was crammed with German soldiers, obviously waiting for the order to attack south and hit the position the paratroopers had just left behind. Coyle had beaten them to the punch by a matter of minutes.

Coyle gestured frantically to the tanks. The lead Sherman swung left to protect Coyle's exposed flank, and the second tank pressed forward quickly and turned its guns down the length of the lane, where it had perfect enfilading fire on the hapless Germans. The tank commander opened up with the powerful .50-caliber machine gun, and Coyle's men poked their weapons through a hole in the brush and joined in the killing madness, firing into a tightly packed mass of men trapped in the sunken lane. The firing continued for several minutes, until Coyle spotted a white flag and called for a cease-fire.

Amid the terrible noise and the frantic close-quarters killing, it took a while for Coyle to get the firing under control. When it had finally stopped, Coyle and another officer, Lieutenant Frank Woolsey, stepped into the lane to accept the German surrender and organize the prisoners.

Every combat veteran knew this was a critical moment, the moment of maximum danger for men on both sides, but particularly for those trying to surrender. Two groups of men, all of them nearly overcome with adrenaline and fear, all of them armed and intent on rapidly killing as many of the enemy as possible, must suddenly stop and come back under the control of their officers and noncoms. How could an individual German soldier know that, once he threw down his weapon, the Americans would stop shooting? How could an individual paratrooper, caught up in the bloody killing and desperate to destroy these men who were also trying to kill him, suddenly trust that they did, in fact, want to surrender?[9]

Some of the Germans in the lane were ready to surrender; others were not. When Coyle and Woolsey pushed through the hedgerow and stepped into the lane, they were met by two German grenades, which landed almost at their feet. The two GIs jumped for the ditches alongside the path, one on each side.

Then the paratroopers opened fire again, pouring a deadly hail into the enemy, many of whom had already thrown down their weapons. Some of the survivors pushed through the hedgerow on the north side of the lane, got out into the open field there, and raised their hands. They had moved into an even more exposed position, hoping that the paratroopers would see that they were not armed. It was a desperate move by terrified men.

Coyle thought that a hundred Germans moved into the open field, and that these men, at least, were intent on surrendering. He once again called for a cease-fire, and once again moved toward the enemy to organize the surrender. He stepped into the clear and was immediately shot through the buttocks by a German hiding in another hedgerow. By this time a paratrooper had grabbed a German machine gun, and he used it to spray the area where the last shots had come from. Even with their lieutenant down a second time, most of the GIs held their fire.

Just a few hundred yards away, Peterson's platoon had been reinforced by a D Company platoon under Lieutenant Thomas J. McClean. As the two units advanced, they suddenly saw Germans running across their front, from east to west. (These men were probably escaping the fire from Coyle's platoon.) The troopers opened fire in a setting that resembled nothing more than a shooting gallery, with targets running through an exposed area from right to left. German casualties were heavy.

Meanwhile Doerfler, the S2, and the wounded Lieutenant Coyle, who was bleeding heavily from the wound to his buttocks, became concerned that the enemy might start fighting again if they realized how few paratroopers had taken them captive. Many of the Germans had not put down their weapons, and the ones that had were within arm's reach of plenty of other weapons lying about the grassy field. And for all the Americans knew, there could be another German force just beyond the next hedgerow, waiting to counterattack.

Coyle did not speak German, and his efforts to get the prisoners disarmed and organized did not go well. What's more, some of the tankers had dismounted to help with the roundup (and perhaps to gather coveted souvenirs, like the distinctive Luger pistol). But Coyle needed the tankers manning their weapons, especially the machine guns. The situation was deteriorating and had the lieutenant more than a little nervous when a German officer stepped forward and said, in perfect English, "May I help you?"

Coyle agreed, and, with just a few sharp commands, the German officer had his soldiers disarmed and lined up in a neat formation, ready to be marched to the rear. E Company estimated that Coyle's understrength platoon alone captured 160 prisoners, while Peterson and

McClean, off to the west, took nearly as many. Hundreds of German dead and wounded lay on the field, along with other detritus of battle: abandoned weapons and jackets, mess kits and helmets, all strewn along the edge of the hedgerow that the German soldiers had hoped would give them cover. Lieutenant Doerfler, in the S2 after-action report, estimated that the hasty attack by the E Company platoons and McClean's D Company platoon, augmented with the terrible firepower of the tanks, had killed as many as four hundred enemy soldiers.

Whatever the horrible count of bodies in the fields just north of Ste. Mère Eglise, the 2nd Battalion of the 1058th Regiment effectively ceased to exist. Generalleutenat Karl-Wilhelm von Schlieben, commander of the 709th Division, had two battalions severely mauled and one destroyed in the repeated attacks on the north end of Ste. Mère Eglise. He pulled his remaining soldiers back to a defensive position some fifteen hundred yards north of Neuville au Plain, where they dug in, assessed their losses, and waited for the inevitable advance of the American Army that was pouring ashore on Utah Beach.

Coyle stayed on his feet until the prisoners were taken care of. Then the medics stopped the bleeding as best they could and helped Coyle up onto the deck of one of the tanks, where he lay facedown for the ride back to Ste. Mère Eglise.[10]

NO BETTER PLACE TO DIE

Eighteen-year-old A Company pathfinder Bob Murphy was wet, cold, and shivering as he watched dawn break over La Fière on June 7. The cool, moist air off the floodplain in front of him and the Channel some miles behind him had soaked everything with a heavy dew. Some men had recovered and had wrapped up in parachutes, while some used the GI raincoats they'd carried in their musette bags. Others were crammed, two men to a narrow hole, where body warmth helped fight off the chill. Many had eaten all their rations, and there was no prospect of more anytime soon. Others had drained their single one-quart canteen during the D-Day fight, and while there was probably a well somewhere around the yard of the manor house, no one was ready to get out of his hole to go searching.

Murphy took stock of his meager supply of ammunition. Although daring paratroopers had spent the entire night cruising the drop zones for errant bundles of ammunition (while trying to avoid German patrols and incoming fire), there wasn't much to distribute that morning. Murphy worried that more Germans would come across the causeway than the company had bullets for.

Then the artillery and mortar fire started again, more tree bursts sending jagged shrapnel straight down into the foxholes. Murphy was helpless to do anything but press himself deeper into the dirt and wonder, *Is this the day I get it?*

He could feel the fear gnawing at him and knew it would not go away until he could concentrate on stopping the enemy, until he could raise his rifle to his cheek and squeeze off the rounds. Find a target, aim, pull the trigger one, two, three times until the enemy soldier went down; find another. The act of firing would bring some relief from the terror of the incoming artillery.

The mortars fell most heavily on the positions nearest the bridge. Farther back, Murphy could hear the larger explosions of incoming artillery, as the Germans aimed to cut off resupply or reinforcement. As he looked around, something rammed Murphy's face down into the dirt. He checked his helmet and found that a large piece of shrapnel had hit him low on his neck. The helmet saved him, but only because he had it pushed so far back on his head.[1]

Then the Germans appeared on the causeway, visible to the GIs only sporadically through the trees and the brush. The Americans quickly counted four more of the light Renault tanks and perhaps two companies of infantry—two hundred men moving grimly forward along the narrow lane.

If all the division's assets had been in place, or if the beach assault units had come up with their weapons, John "Red Dog" Dolan would have been able to reach out with artillery and choke off the enemy approach. As it was, he had just one antitank gun, a handful of light mortars, and not much ammunition for either. He would conduct this fight with what he had on hand.

As unsettling as the view from the hill above La Fière Bridge was for Bob Murphy and his tired, hungry comrades, the view across the long causeway must have been just as frightening, or more so, for the panzergrenadiers of the 1057th Regiment who were trying again to punch through the American defenses. For the lowly infantrymen walking out onto the causeway, holding their rifles and peering through the breaks in the trees, the world was reduced to a few terrifying facts: they would attack on a narrow front—almost a column—against an enemy that was dug in, knew they were coming, and had killed many of their comrades the day before.

In fact, the men advancing across La Fière causeway on June 7 had to walk by and step over the bodies of other German soldiers who had tried the same thing less than twenty-four hours earlier. Even to veterans of many hard-fought battles, this attack must have seemed particularly foolish. But the only hope of stemming the tide of the invasion was to hit the Channel beaches, and the direct path to those beaches lay over the tiny bridge at La Fière.

There was nothing to do but move forward.

The view of the causeway from the hillside was obstructed by trees that lined the road and by the detritus of the previous day's battle: the truck that the Americans had placed on the bridge as a roadblock, as well as three tanks knocked out by the bazooka teams of A Company. The lead German tank tried to use this twisted mass of charred steel for cover as it approached.

The A Company bazooka men—Bolderson and Pryne, Peterson and Heim—had moved forward again to get the deadly flank shots that had stopped the German assault on D-Day. But the attackers knew where the teams had positioned themselves the day before, and so directed sheets of small arms fire at the bazooka men.

Up on the hill, the paratroopers manning the 57 mm antitank gun watched and waited. Lieutenant Gerald Johnson of C Company was there with a few volunteers, looking for the line-of-sight shot that might kill the lead vehicle. Below them, just a few hundred yards away, the small tank nosed forward. It certainly didn't look like the tank had much chance of pushing its way through the debris, but if the panzer broke into the clear on the east side of the bridge, it would race toward the antitank gun, and hitting it would be difficult. A German breakthrough might quickly overwhelm the exhausted troopers of A Company who made up the center of the thin line. Once out in the open on the east side of the Merderet, even a small force of tanks could spell danger for the paratroopers.

The lead Renault appeared and disappeared amid the tree branches as it moved. The last few hundred yards on the approach to the bridge were a straight line, and when the tank appeared there, Johnson's team of volunteer gunners opened fire, as did the bazooka teams below them. Something—either the gun or the bazookas—scored a hit that rocked the tank to a standstill and soon set it on fire.

The difference on this day was that the German infantry had kept close to the lead panzer, so that even though the tank stopped, the infantrymen had reached the bridge and the cover offered by all the wreckage. From this close-in position the panzergrenadiers fired down into the holes where the bazooka teams lurked, forcing the GIs to abandon these forwardmost positions.

Now the two groups of soldiers were engaged in an intense firefight from a distance of no more than forty or fifty yards. The panzergrenadiers used the cover well, and the paratroopers could not dislodge them. But the open ground just east of the bridge was swept by fire from the Americans, so the Germans could not move forward.

Murphy poked his head above the lip of his hole, looking for targets. His only thought was to knock down as many of the enemy as he could before they reached A Company's thinly held line. The noise was simply tremendous: the Americans fired machine guns and rifles, and the Germans answered back. It seemed to Murphy that the mortar barrage increased in intensity. (The Americans had a grudging respect for the German mortar crews, who could drop an accurate barrage on the A Company position only forty yards from their own men.) Around him, the wounded screamed; there were cries of "Medic!" and unintelligible curses, groans, pleas for ammunition.

The desperate, close-range fight left some men feeling isolated, their world shrunk to the few feet of grass or hillside they could see around them, and the fields of fire they had picked out for themselves. A man in one foxhole might feel encouraged by what he saw, while a few yards away, another soldier despaired that the battle was falling apart, that the enemy was upon him, that he was breathing his last.

The fight at La Fière had become a battle of small units and individuals. Dolan's company was down to about half strength; he'd lost two platoon leaders the previous day, and he had squads that had gone from twelve men to five. If A Company was to survive, the junior leaders would have to hold it together.

Lieutenant William Oakley was one of those leaders. He had marked himself as a fighter on D-Day, moving among his men in the defensive position as they fought off the first German attacks. Now, on this second day of the invasion, he was up to the same. In spite of incoming mortar, rifle, and machine pistol fire coming from the tangle of wrecked vehicles on the bridge, Oakley managed to function as a platoon leader. He moved about, shored up his line when men went down, directed fire, distributed what little ammunition could be spared or taken from the dead and wounded.

He was above ground when he was hit, and he went down with a gaping wound in his lower back, the blood pouring out in a dark stream. A couple of GIs pulled him back behind a hedgerow and called for Sergeant Bill Owens, who was now the ranking man in the platoon. Owens took one look at Oakley, gave him a shot of morphine to make his last moments free of pain, and moved forward again to assume command of the battered platoon. There in the grass and weeds behind the hedgerow, with the sound of his platoon's fight all around him, with bullets cutting through the grass and leaves, William Oakley bled to death.

The fire pounding the hillside was so intense that Owens could not see how many men were still capable of fighting. In spite of what had just happened to Oakley, he began to crawl as rapidly as possible from hole to hole, dragging behind him slings of M1 ammo that he removed from the dead and wounded. He distributed the ammo, and kept mental track of who had what left, who was wounded and still fighting, who was barely holding on.

Private William Ross had the platoon's walkie-talkie, its only link to Dolan and any kind of higher headquarters. Ross was hit by an 88 round, which disintegrated the soldier and the radio at once, leaving Owens's platoon out of contact. Even though the sergeant knew that Dolan was nearby, it was impossible to communicate with him in the midst of the firestorm.[2]

Bob Murphy was amazed by what he saw: his squad leader, this man too old to be a paratrooper, moving among the platoon's positions when any motion drew fire from no more than forty yards away. Owens's platoon, located in the center of the line, took the brunt of the enemy attack and concentrated fire. More than half of his platoon was dead or wounded. Yet amid the carnage Owens appeared calm, and he reassured his men that he was with them, that they were holding on, that they would make it through this.

Then Murphy noticed other men moving above ground, moving to the rear. They were the stray paratroopers from the other regiments who had been added to the A Company position to strengthen the line. Many of these men had been part of the provisional B Company sent across the causeway on D-Day, only to be driven back under heavy fire. Many waded across the wide floodplain with the German fire picking them off. They spent the chilly night soaking wet, without their own leaders around them, with no resupply of ammunition or food. Demoralized and isolated, some of them cracked under the onslaught now facing them; they got out of their holes and trotted away from the fight.

The problem was that they didn't know Owens, didn't know the men to their right or left, and so did not share those intimate bonds that held a unit together at a time like this. Owens didn't have time to do anything about it, and a handful of paratroopers simply disappeared from the line. Owens was much more concerned that the sight of the men leaving would shake his own troopers, so he moved about even more so that his own soldiers could see him. He risked his life to reassure them in what might be their last moments.

Behind Owens's position, First Sergeant Robert Matteson of A Company saw something that surprised him: a lieutenant was among those pulling out without orders. When Matteson challenged him, the frightened officer said that the enemy was advancing with hundreds of men.

"We can't stop them and it's time to get out," the officer said. Matteson couldn't get him to stay.[3]

Amid the head-splitting noise, Dolan noticed that the antitank gun had stopped firing. He made his way through the hedgerows and across the Ste. Mère Eglise road, where he found the gun abandoned. He tried to operate it by himself, but the firing mechanism had been removed. With the gun out of action and his bazooka teams unable to get off a shot, the defense was seriously compromised. There was nothing between the German tanks and his line but a pile of wrecked equipment.

Dolan acted quickly, rounding up five or six men from his sketchy reserve and putting them near the top of the hill behind a hedgerow. He armed them with as many Gammon grenades as he could gather; they would be a last line of defense if the German tanks broke through. It was hardly an effective defense against a tank assault—a handful of infantrymen hurling plastic explosives—but it was all he could do at the moment.

While Dolan was improvising, the gun's volunteer crew reappeared. They had been driven off by the heavy mortar fire—much of it directed at this gun—but had returned and gone back into action. At least two of these troopers, Dolan saw, were teenage replacements who had just joined the regiment. No one had ordered them back, and no one led them into position. They returned because they knew the gun was critical to the defense.

During this fight, Staff Sergeant Edwin F. Wancio, A Company's supply sergeant, was on the move constantly, running back and forth to the drop zone and to any spot where a trooper thought there might be a bundle of ammunition. With no vehicle to use, Wancio hauled the heavy boxes of ammo forward, crawling the last few yards to the firing line, burrowing through grass and hedgerows to get ammunition to the guns.

The machine guns, in particular, ate up a lot of ammo. And because they were central to the defense, German mortar crews targeted the machine gun positions. When a gun crew was wounded or killed, other paratroopers crawled forward to man the weapon. Because they fired almost continuously, the guns overheated; even when the gunner released the trigger, the weapon kept firing. With no spare barrels to switch out, there was a danger that the overheated guns would simply quit, leaving Owens and his men without their critical firepower.

Lieutenant John Otto of A Company dragged together two guns that had failed, broke them down, and put the pieces together to get one working gun. After handing the gun over to some GIs, Otto climbed to a dangerous spot near the center of the hill behind A Company's position; from there he spotted the fall of the American mortar rounds and called back adjustments to the crews.

In the midst of this chaos, the wounded crawled to the rear, as the unwounded men couldn't leave the line to help them and the medics were struggling to save those already in the aid station.

The Germans seemed close to a breakthrough. Owens had only fifteen men—some of them badly wounded—holding the center of the line. The bazookas were out of action, and the machine guns were failing. A couple of the men called out to Owens. Maybe it was time to withdraw.

"No," Owens said. "We'll wait for orders. We haven't been told to go yet."

But the squad leader, now in command of the most critical part of the American line west of Ste. Mère Eglise, wanted some confirmation that they should stay. Because he was out of radio contact, he called Murphy, who often acted as a runner, and told the young soldier to find Dolan and ask for instructions. Should they fall back? Was there another line of defense?

The run to find Dolan wasn't far, although it was certainly risky. Murphy asked for instructions. Dolan scribbled a note on a scrap of paper, then added verbal instructions.

The young pathfinder made it back to Owens in one piece, which amazed both of them, as the mortar and artillery were coming in like machine gun fire. Murphy found the sergeant and passed him the note.

Dolan had scrawled, "I don't know a better place than this to die." Owens looked at Murphy, who repeated the verbal order. Stay where you are.[4]

Owens turned to the fight and manned a position on the line, firing one machine gun until it overheated and stopped working. He seized a BAR left behind by a wounded trooper and fired that at the Germans until he ran out of ammunition. Then he moved to another position, where a machine gun crew had been killed by an artillery or mortar round. Seizing that gun, he found it had no tripod to hold it steady, so he rested it on a pile of dirt in front of the foxhole and pulled the trigger. The entire defense was down to two machine guns, some sporadic mortar fire, and a few riflemen. It seemed to Owens that he was only a casualty or two from collapsing, and that the Germans would burst onto the east side of the bridge at any moment. Maybe Dolan had seen the future: this is where he would die.

Then, incredibly, the Germans stopped firing. Owens saw a Red Cross flag, the kind used by medical units to mark their location, waving near the bridge. He called out to his few remaining men to cease fire. Lieutenant Otto, spotting for the mortars, saw what was happening and also called for a cease-fire. When the shelling stopped, Owens stood up.

For the first time in hours he had a wider view of the causeway. He estimated that there were two hundred or so wounded and dead Germans along the stretch that he could see, an incredible density of pain and suffering on the narrow road. There were other bodies barely visible in the water along either side of the causeway. Owens yelled for someone to fetch Dolan.

After a few minutes of quiet, the German waving the flag stepped out into the open and, still carrying the banner, walked to where the truck and destroyed tanks lay. Owens watched as an American officer, backed by a couple of GIs, walked down the hillside to the east end of the bridge, where he could talk to the German. The men on the line couldn't hear what was being said, but they were grateful that the firing had stopped, even if only for a short time. The officer came back up the hill and told Dolan that the Germans wanted a cease-fire to pull their wounded back off the causeway.

This was obviously a big job that would take some time. Dolan conferred with Mark Alexander, the regimental exec who had come to take over the battalion after Kellam was killed. Dolan could use the time to move his own wounded, reconstitute his position on the hillside, tie in with the skeleton units from B and C Companies on his flanks, maybe even bring up reinforcements—if any were to be found—and a resupply of ammunition. Dolan and Alexander agreed to the terms, and the Germans began the grim work of carrying their wounded back toward the west end of the causeway and Cauquigny.

It took several hours for the Germans to remove their casualties, and Dolan made use of the time to tighten up his own defense. Some of his exhausted troopers managed to get some sleep during the lull, although after they'd cleared their wounded the Germans began lobbing artillery and mortar fire on La Fière. But this time the incoming fire was not constant and so did not seem the prelude for another attack. The paratroopers looked down at the mangled tanks and bodies, and surveyed the hillside pockmarked with shell holes. They could now count their squadmates on one hand, and they prayed the Germans had had enough.

Dolan got one good piece of news during the afternoon: he now had access to American artillery that had come ashore with the landing forces. If the Germans came again, he'd be able to call for fire that might stop them before they even reached the bridge.

Behind them, in Ste. Mère Eglise, the 2nd and 3rd Battalions of the 505th were also licking their wounds, preparing for another day of combat. The division hadn't broken out of its initial position, but it had not been overrun. At La Fière the GIs clung to their foxholes, listened for incoming rounds, and watched the causeway for signs that the Germans might try again.

During the afternoon of June 7, the 2nd Battalion of the 325th Glider Infantry Regiment moved into a reserve position to the rear of the 1st Battalion, 505th PIR, at La Fière. Along with this force came a platoon of Sherman tanks from the 4th Division, which had come ashore at Utah Beach. Mark Alexander, still in command at La Fière, held the tanks in reserve around the bend of the Ste. Mère Eglise road, just out of sight of the enemy.

During the night, the exhausted troopers of 1st Battalion were pulled out of the line and replaced by the glider troops. They walked a little more than a mile to a spot just west of Neuville au Plain, where troopers from their sister battalion had stopped a German advance from the north. The decimated companies pulled into a defensive position, and the men dug shallow holes to protect them from any incoming German fire. They collapsed, exhausted, for their first real sleep since the restless night of June 4 back in England, which seemed a lifetime ago. Company A, which had left England with 147 men, now mustered just 80 souls, 20 of whom were walking wounded. Dolan's company had suffered 45 percent killed or seriously wounded in less than forty-eight hours of fighting.

Later, the men would be visited by Brigadier General S. L. A. Marshall, the official U.S. Army historian, and Marshall's team of interviewers. The A Company men gave credit for the defense of the bridge at La Fière to Sergeant Bill Owens, the reserved and undistinguished-looking former drill press operator who was well past the age for a paratrooper. It was his example, the men said, his cool under fire that made them stick it out well past the point where the position looked lost.

Owens, in turn, gave credit to his leaders. In front of the assembled company, he told the interviewers, "We stuck because our leaders stuck, and we knew that they were sticking. Captain [then Lieutenant] Dolan was with us the whole time, and Colonel Alexander kept coming up to the fight. We knew what we were doing and that they would give us all the help they could. That did more to give us confidence than the power of our weapons."[5]

FIRST ASSAULT

As bloody June 7 gave way to June 8—D+2 in Normandy—Matt Ridgway still did not have complete control of his division or of his area of operations. He had accomplished his major missions: secure Ste. Mère Eglise and defend the back door to Utah Beach. Company A of the 505th PIR, under Lieutenant John Dolan, had distinguished itself in the brutal fight for La Fière, and Captain Roy Creek of the 507th PIR, with a handful of men he did not know, had managed to secure the eastern end of the Chef du Pont causeway.

Ridgway had a firm hold on Ste. Mère Eglise and a defensive line at the Merderet that, while it wasn't rock solid, had managed to throw back the best enemy attempts to bull across it. But there were still paratroopers isolated on the west bank of the river, and some of these groups were in dire circumstances for lack of medical supplies. More than that, Ridgway's original mission had called for him to have a foothold on the *west* bank of the river, to control the area as far west as Amfreville and as far south as the crossings of the Douve River. This secured lodgment would provide VII Corps with a stable platform to cut the Contentin Peninsula and move on the port of Cherbourg.

Conventional thinking was that the lightly armed paratroopers should be relieved by heavier forces after forty-eight hours. Ridgway's resupply problems seemed to validate this thinking, as did the fact that many of his wounded still had not been evacuated to field hospitals.

But the division commander still wanted to push west to gather his scattered forces and establish a bridgehead on the far bank.

At the same time, Joe Collins, commander of the VII Corps, was concerned that his attack northward had bogged down. The 4th Division, which had come ashore at Utah Beach, was to turn right and head up the east side of the peninsula for Cherbourg. But the green regiments had run into determined German resistance and had all but stopped. Collins told Ridgway he wanted the veteran 505th PIR to join the fight alongside the infantry regiments of the 4th Division. Ridgway gave the mission to Bill Ekman, the regimental commander who was getting his first taste of combat.

Ekman had a tough start in Normandy. Knocked out by a hard landing, he spent a good bit of time wandering around the countryside north of Ste. Mère Eglise trying to find his regiment. By the time he joined the main body, his three battalion commanders and their aggressive subordinates had already begun their missions. There simply was not much of a chance for Ekman to shine during those first two days. The attack northward would change all that.

On the morning of June 8, the 505th was to take the left flank of the advance northward, hugging the eastern bank of the Merderet as they moved toward Le Ham and Montebourg. Since Vandervoort's 2nd and Krause's 3rd Battalions were in the best shape, they led the initial assault, with Mark Alexander's battered 1st Battalion (which included the devastated A Company) bringing up the rear.

Ridgway had three battalions of the 325th Glider Infantry Regiment that had not yet been involved in heavy fighting. The 2nd Battalion was attached to Ekman's 505th for the attack north. When Ridgway turned his attention to forcing a crossing to the west side of the Merderet, he had at his disposal two of his three parachute regiments (the 507th and 508th PIRs) and two-thirds of his glider infantry: the still-fresh 1st Battalion, 325th Glider Infantry Regiment, under Teddy Sanford; and the 3rd Battalion, 325th GIR, under Charles Carrell.

Sanford's unit had seen a few weeks of combat in Italy, and Ridgway put them on the line alongside the Merderet north of La Fière. Carrell's battalion had been part of an independent glider unit and had been grafted—not very successfully—to the 82nd Airborne Division for the Normandy invasion. The men still referred to themselves as the 401st GIR (their old designation), and there was resentment between Carrell's officers and the leaders of the 325th.

In the early morning hours of D+2 Ridgway made Carrell's battalion the division reserve and chose Roy Lindquist and his 508th PIR for an attack west across the Chef du Pont causeway. Lindquist's mission was to rescue a group of paratroopers who were surrounded on Hill 30, across from Chef du Pont.

The 508th PIR was as badly scattered as any regiment in the invasion. Early on June 6, Lindquist landed near Gavin, on the west side of the river. Isolated and unable to find his men, he crossed to the east side of the Merderet early on D-Day and so was on the opposite side of the river from his objectives and many of his troops. All three of Lindquist's battalion commanders landed near Picauville, on the west side of the river. Louis G. Mendez, who had the 3rd Battalion, jumped from more than two thousand feet, thus giving the Germans plenty of time to shoot at him—his equipment bag was shot through at least three times. He was isolated and almost alone for five days. First battalion commander Herbert Batcheller (who had been relieved as regimental commander of the 505th PIR) and his executive officer, Shields Warren, flew through heavy flak and were dropped near the Douve, well south of the drop zone. Batcheller was shot to death on D-Day; Warren managed to round up about fifty paratroopers and make his way north toward the DZ.

Thomas J. B. Shanley, commanding the 2nd Battalion, landed closer to the 508th's drop zone than any other senior commander and managed to collect about thirty-five paratroopers. He set out toward the Douve River to blow up the bridges there (part of the effort to seal the division's flank), but the small band did not have the firepower to break through determined German resistance. Shanley headed north, away from the Douve and toward a piece of high ground that sat south of Cauquigny and between the two major causeways at La Fière and Chef du Pont. Shanley was able to contact Shields Warren by radio, and Warren brought his small group to join forces with Shanley on Hill 30. When the hundred or so men began digging in on D-Day, they had no idea how long it would take the regiment and the rest of the division to reach them.

The mission of Colonel George "Zip" Millett's 507th PIR was to land near Amfreville and seize that small crossroads town as well as the western end of the La Fière causeway. Millett and about forty men actually hit their drop zone (the westernmost of the division DZs), and on D-Day he had rounded up one of the largest single groups of paratroopers assembled by any of Gavin's commanders—some 425 men. But Millett's position was also closest to the area of greatest German strength in the area, the 91st Air Landing Division, headquartered at St. Sauveur le Vicomte. Millett attacked Amfreville on June 6, but the Germans counterattacked vigorously, leaving Millett's group isolated and surrounded.

Charles Timmes, commanding the 2nd Battalion of the 507th, landed about a mile from the drop zone and quickly determined that he was in a better position to attack toward Cauquigny and the western end of La Fière causeway than he was to move on Amfreville. But he had only fifty men when he struck out, and the Germans soon pushed him back up against the river, close to a large château overlooking the floodplain that the GIs dubbed the Gray Castle. Timmes was eventually joined there by Ben Schwartzwalder, the aggressive company commander who fought his way through La Fière on D-Day. By the end of June 7, Timmes was low on everything: medical supplies, water, ammunition, and food; and his injured and wounded men were suffering terribly from the lack of care. Although the overworked medics did what they could, their meager supplies of bandages, sulfa powder, and morphine were soon exhausted.

Ridgway's plan called for an attack by Roy Lindquist and the 508th PIR on the morning of June 8 (the same day the 505th was to join the 4th Division's drive north) across the Chef du Pont causeway to relieve the Shanley-Warren force and seize the western end. Lindquist managed to contact Shanley by radio and told the battalion commander to send a patrol to clear the road between Picauville and Pont l'Abbé. In this way, Shanley would uncover any mobile German force that might speed east across the causeway and run into Lindquist's men coming west.

The two junior officers Shanley named for this task, Lieutenants Lloyd L. Pollette and Woodrow W. Millsaps, leading a group of fewer than twenty-five troopers, not only cleared the road near the causeway but then doubled back and fought their way east across the Chef du Pont causeway to link up with Lindquist. But German artillery observers watched these movements, and soon the causeway was under fire from guns located south of the Douve River. With the long, exposed road turned into a gauntlet, Lindquist abandoned his plan to push across. Still, Shanley's aggressive lieutenants maintained control of the western end, having driven out some Germans who had arrived the day before.[1]

During the afternoon of June 8, Shanley put out a radio call for blood plasma: his wounded men were dying. Another group of paratroopers isolated on the west side of the river heard the call. Remarkably, they had some blood plasma, but they were surrounded by Germans who were pressing them on all asides, as was the Shanley group. Three men volunteered to attempt a breakthrough.[2] Lieutenant Roy Murray, Corporal James Green, and a PFC Circelli strapped bottles of plasma to their bodies and, after dark, set out to cross the flooded approaches to Hill 30.

The Germans had established positions on the banks of the floodplain around Hill 30, and the three men ran into heavy fire. They withdrew into the swamp and tried again from another angle, with a German patrol now following them. This time, they ran into fire from an American outpost to their front, as well as from their German pursuers. Lieutenant Murray was killed, and Green and Circelli were badly wounded. The wounded men on Hill 30 did not get the blood plasma.

The supply situation was also critical for Lieutenant Colonel Charles Timmes and the men isolated north of Cauquigny. Timmes sent out a patrol under Lieutenant John Marr, who had fought so well at La Fière on D-Day, to find an alternate route across to the east side of the river. In his first effort, Marr took a patrol of ten men to the north, but they attracted the attention of the Germans, who were watching for the paratroopers to attempt an escape. In the firefight, several paratroopers were killed, and Marr withdrew to the orchard and the defensive perimeter. But he was determined to try again, this time with just one other man along.

Marr and Private Norman J. Carter set off again, staying close to the edge of the flooded area. Through a mixture of persistence and good luck, the two men were near the ford that the Germans had intended to use to cross the Merderet on D-Day, and which the Americans still knew nothing about.[3] (The approach to the ford was blocked by the Timmes force, whose choice of defensible ground just happened to put them in the path the Germans wanted to use.)

Carter found the ford by stumbling across its raised stone bed. The two men moved east into the open and came under fire from a machine gun in the vicinity of the Gray Castle, but it was too far away to do any damage.[4] The two soldiers reached the railroad (which is in the middle of the floodplain at this point and lies west of the Merderet channel) and followed it until they reached dry ground. French civilians pointed out where they could find other Americans, and Marr climbed to the roof of a building to wave an orange panel, the recognition signal for U.S. forces. Someone waved an orange panel back at him.

Marr and Carter hurried to the lines of the nearest American unit, the 1st Battalion, 325th GIR. There Marr borrowed a jeep to take him to Ste. Mère Eglise and the division command post. Along the way, he ran into Major General Ridgway and told him about the ford, which offered exactly what the commanding general was looking for: an alternate way to cross the river, relieve the besieged troopers on the west bank, and secure his original objectives west of the Merderet. Ridgway immediately passed the word to Colonel Harry Lewis, commander of the 325th: he would put a battalion across that night to seize Amfreville and secure the western end of La Fière causeway at Cauquigny. Teddy

Sanford's 1st Battalion of the 325th GIR was in the right place and had seen some combat in Italy, so they got the nod. Jump-off time for the attack was 2300 hours.

Zip Millett's group, meanwhile, was ordered (by radio) to move east and link up with Timmes and the glider troops, all in preparation for a push south to Cauquigny and the western end of La Fière causeway.

Not only had Marr and Carter found a way across the river; they were the men who could find it again and lead Sanford's glider troops in the attack. Marr sent Carter back to Timmes with a message to remove the mines on the northern approach to the orchard, and to inform the GIs on the perimeter that other Americans would soon be coming in. One of the most dangerous maneuvers an infantry force can make at night is to attempt to pass through friendly lines. Timmes's men, in particular, were jumpy: low on ammo, aware that they were surrounded, exhausted by the constant strain of watching for the German attempt to overrun them. It would be dangerous for the glidermen to approach in the dark; Carter's message might save some confusion and deaths by friendly fire.

Carter and two infantrymen from the 325th—sent along as security—and some engineers went along to mark the approaches to the ford with white tape so that the glidermen could stay on the ford.

Marr reported to the 1st Battalion, 325th GIR, command post around 1800 hours. The exhausted lieutenant thought it would be a good idea to try to get some sleep before the attack jumped off in a few hours, and so he collapsed on the ground. Meanwhile, Sanford briefed his company commanders on the plan: the battalion would split up when they reached the far shore, with some of them swinging west toward Amfreville, the rest going south to link up with Timmes and continue the move on Cauquigny.

The column was already en route when Ridgway sent a change to the order. He wanted the glidermen to disregard Amfreville and instead capture a bridgehead at Cauquigny before dawn. The commanding general wanted to control both ends of the La Fière causeway before he undertook the bigger job of capturing towns on the west bank.

Teddy Sanford took about four hundred soldiers across the ford discovered by Marr and Carter, and they received no German fire while
they were out in the open and at their most vulnerable. Marr was relieved that they made it across, but he was still concerned that
Timmes's jumpy and exhausted paratroopers might open fire on the
325th column as it approached. He had no way of knowing if Carter
had gotten through with his message. When they reached the western
bank, the column paused long enough for Sanford to put his men in
fighting formation; Marr moved forward on his own to make sure
Timmes knew they were coming. Although Marr had anticipated a
problem and taken steps to avoid a nasty friendly fire incident, his departure also left Sanford without his most knowledgeable guide just
when he needed him most.[5]

Having reached the west bank, Sanford now had to turn south, find
Timmes, and move on Cauquigny. But this meant he would be crossing
in front of any enemy force near Amfreville, presenting his flank to a
quick attack. When his C Company troops took some automatic
weapons fire from the Gray Castle, Sanford became convinced that his
exposed flank was in danger. He diverted C Company to pivot north
and west, attack the château, and clear it of Germans. While this gave
him some protection on the flank, it also diverted one third of his combat strength from the main mission.

Sanford was also concerned that German units near Amfreville
would hit this same exposed right flank as he moved south. He had reason to be concerned: the Germans had been in this area for a while and
could be expected to know every road and lane. Since they were professionals, they would have prepared defensive positions, sighted artillery
and mortar targets, and might even have rehearsed counterattacks in
the area. Finally, the Germans on the west bank of the Merderet had
not relinquished control to the invaders as had their comrades on the
eastern shore. Indeed, they had bottled up hundreds of paratroopers
and kept the Americans from accomplishing any of their missions.

Sanford directed A Company to the tiny crossroads of Le Motey to
stop any enemy thrust from that direction. His B Company now had

the lead in the move toward Timmes and, farther south, Cauquigny. C Company would follow Company B when the Gray Castle was secured. This sudden change from a concentrated attack by an entire battalion on a single axis to a three-pronged night offensive made control very difficult. Sanford, who was the battalion executive officer when the unit left England (the commander, Klemm Boyd, was one of the many glidermen injured in the landing), may have been in over his head.

Sanford and Timmes managed to link forces in the orchard that had been Timmes's refuge since D-Day, but there was no sign of Millett, whose force had run into heavy resistance in its move east. (Millett's group became separated in the night movement, and Millett was captured, though Timmes and Sanford didn't know it at the time.) Sanford told Timmes that they were to press on to Cauquigny, with the relatively fresh glider troops leading the way. But Sanford was worried that his C Company was taking too long to eliminate the German outpost in the Gray Castle, and he didn't want to go into the fight with only one of his three companies. (A Company was still guarding the flank at Le Motey.) Sanford sent the ubiquitous Lieutenant Marr back toward the crossing to find C Company and hurry them forward.

Marr, who spent the previous night searching for the crossing and got only a few hours' sleep before beginning this movement, turned back once again to find C Company. The glider troops had not killed the Germans in the vicinity of the Gray Castle but had merely forced them to withdraw. When C Company began its move south to link up with B Company, the Germans followed, in growing numbers, pressing C Company in the rear and along the western flank with harassing fire. The Germans knew the land here. All the overgrown lanes that were dark even in the daytime became infinitely more difficult to navigate at night, and only Marr had been over this ground before. He tried to hurry C Company, tried to get them to catch up with B Company, which was already moving toward Cauquigny from the Timmes orchard. But the jumpy, exhausted troops were too concerned about what was lurking on their flanks in the dark, and they moved slowly.

Meanwhile Sanford left the orchard with B Company, headed toward Cauquigny. (Lieutenant Levy, who had been the first to hold Cauquigny, went with B Company as a guide.) By this time the Germans on the western bank of the Merderet knew exactly what was going on, and they fought a series of delaying actions from cleverly concealed positions, shooting up the Americans who were advancing through unfamiliar countryside in the middle of a dark night.

Sanford wanted to approach Cauquigny from the west, and he struggled to get his companies up and on line along the road from Amfreville. Marr managed to guide C Company into position alongside B Company and generally oriented toward Cauquigny, but when the glider troops started moving forward, they veered off course. Marr was convinced that they were now headed too far south.

The nighttime, cross-country movement proved very difficult. The fields were small and cut through with black walls of hedgerows that did not run in straight lines, tiny tracks that turned into cart trails and then back into meandering footpaths. Hand signals were useless, and sergeants couldn't identify their own men from more than a foot or two away. And always, out there in the dark, perhaps just a few feet away, the enemy waited for the unwary GI who was the first to stick his head around a corner or through some underbrush. It was frustrating and nerve-racking, and the penalty for a mistake was death.

The C Company men, working hard to stay in sight of each other as they advanced, finally ran into the German defensive line around dawn. The Americans might have waited until they could tie in with B Company on their flank; a coordinated attack would have been more powerful, but it also would have squandered the initiative. Instead, C Company pressed forward and even achieved a penetration of the German line.

But the Germans did not buckle, and they held the shoulders of the penetration and soon had enough fire on the Americans—at least two light machine guns—that the advancing glidermen were pinned down. One C Company platoon had advanced farther than the others and now, with the forward movement stalled, was in the most exposed position. The men took what cover they could find in a shallow roadside ditch. Instead of attacking, they were now on the defensive, and the amount of fire from the glidermen fell off. Now the Germans began to achieve fire superiority: that is, there was so much fire coming from the German position that the Americans were forced to keep their heads down and could not move.

One platoon of C Company was caught in a forward position, exposed to fire from three sides, unable to maneuver as its men sought any cover they could find. In order to pull back, the entire platoon had to filter through a single opening in a hedgerow behind them. The Germans, of course, knew exactly where the opening was, and so concentrated their fire there. Any move the glidermen made would have to run this gauntlet of fire. The situation deteriorated quickly, and the glidermen knew they were about to be cut off completely. Unable to pull back or maneuver, they'd all be killed or captured.[6]

Private First Class Charles N. DeGlopper, a twenty-two-year-old BAR man from Grand Island, New York, was one of the GIs pinned down with the forwardmost platoon. DeGlopper—who stood six feet six inches tall and weighed nearly 240 pounds—had no problem handling the 19.4-pound weapon. Carrying a BAR exhausted soldiers of average size; in DeGlopper's hands, the big gun looked like a rifle.

DeGlopper knew that he had to achieve some sort of fire superiority with his automatic rifle: he had to force the enemy to take cover so his buddies could move. He began firing from a roadside ditch, and the Germans, who saw the muzzle flash from the big weapon, began to concentrate their fire on the lone infantryman. DeGlopper saw an opportunity. If he could get enough of the Germans shooting at him, the rest of his platoon might just be able to back out of the killing zone.

DeGlopper yelled for his comrades to pull back, then stood up and stepped from the ditch onto the road and into the open.

He now had better targets; the Germans shooting at his buddies gave away their positions with the muzzle flashes of their weapons. DeGlopper, holding his big BAR at the shoulder, raked the enemy positions. The Germans, perhaps startled by the sight of this big man stepping into the open, concentrated their fire on him. DeGlopper's buddies started moving back, but several of them lingered long enough to see DeGlopper get hit. He went to his knees but kept shooting and prevented the Germans from maneuvering to cut off the escaping American platoon. DeGlopper finally fell and lay bleeding in the Norman dirt, having purchased survival for his buddies with his own life.[7]

The C Company glidermen recoiled from the German advance, falling back one field to regroup. Lieutenant Marr, crawling below the incoming fire, found two wiremen from the communications section of C Company. The three men administered first aid to some of the wounded before Marr led them back toward the main road between Amfreville and Cauquigny to see what was going on. He heard shooting from the direction of Le Motey and thought that perhaps A Company, sent there by Sanford to block a German counterattack, was engaged. Marr and the two soldiers crawled out beside the main road, where they were once again pinned down by fire coming from the Germans at the Cauquigny end of the road.

Incredibly, when they hit the ground, one of the wiremen put his hand directly on some communications wire he had laid earlier, during the first assault. The soldier had a sound-powered telephone with him, and after he spliced into the wire, Marr was soon talking to Lieutenant Willard E. Young, who commanded the mortars back in the orchard with Timmes and the surrounded paratroopers. Marr called for fire on the road, a registration round from which he could adjust to hit the German machine gun covering the road. The first round came, and Marr made some quick adjustments, which he relayed back to Young. The mortar barrage drove the enemy machine gunners from their position.

During this temporary lull in the shooting, Marr crossed the road to the north and found the flank of B Company. The commander, whose attack had never been coordinated with C Company's on the south side of the road, had ordered his men to withdraw. All Marr could do was to cover the withdrawal with mortar fire from Young's helpful crews. When the glidermen got back to the orchard near the Merderet, they reported that the attack on Cauquigny had failed. Timmes sent word to Ridgway by radio that he and Sanford had been unable to reach Cauquigny from the west.

The news was not welcomed by Ridgway. Although most of the division had performed splendidly, even when handicapped by terrible drops and lack of supplies, Ridgway was keenly aware that he had not achieved his D-Day objectives of securing the west bank of the Merderet. On the morning of June 9, Ridgway felt the pressure from higher headquarters.

Omar Bradley knew, through radio intercepts, that the Germans were sending reinforcements north toward Cherbourg through the city of Ste. Sauveur le Vicomte, which was some six or seven miles west of the 82nd Airborne's westernmost advance. Bradley, the overall commander of U.S. forces in Normandy, was concerned that the German reinforcements would make it difficult to seize the port at Cherbourg. That failure, and the resulting logistic strain, had the potential to throw off the entire Allied timetable for breaking out of the invasion area. It would be difficult, if not impossible, to deliver the tens of thousands of tons of supplies, fuel, and ammunition, not to mention the follow-on divisions waiting in England, over the beaches. The Allies needed Cherbourg, and that meant that Joe Collins's VII Corps had to get across the Merderet.

Collins's 90th Division, unblooded but more heavily armed than the 82nd Airborne, was unloading at Utah and would soon be available for the fight. Collins's plan was to pass the 90th through the paratroopers at Ste. Mère Eglise and throw them at the troublesome La Fière crossing to crush, by sheer weight of numbers, the stubborn German resistance that had the Americans bottled up on the east side of the river.

Ridgway's men had captured Cauquigny on D-Day, only to have the tiny occupying force (Lieutenant Levy and fewer than two dozen men) driven out. The 1st Battalion of the 505th managed to capture and hold on to La Fière, in spite of furious German attempts to force a crossing to the east. But the 1st Battalion, 325th GIR, attack across the ford had failed, as had the unimpressive effort made by the 508th PIR to take the entire Chef du Pont causeway. On the morning of June 9, Ridgway still had a large number of paratroopers holding out in encircled positions on the west bank. The wounded men there were in desperate need of medical attention, and there was always the threat that the Germans might overpower the besieged troopers.

Although Ridgway could have asked to be relieved by the 90th Division and other VII Corps units, he was not ready to leave the field without having carried out his mission completely. He wanted to force a crossing of the Merderet, and he decided it would be at La Fière. Gavin agreed wholeheartedly, and Ridgway gave him command of the operation.

THE GAUNTLET

The only fresh unit available to Gavin on the eastern bank was the untested 3rd Battalion of the 325th Glider Infantry Regiment.[1] The men of this battalion, formerly part of the independent 401st Glider Infantry Regiment, were outsiders in the division. The officers, starting at the top with the commander, Charles Carrell, did not feel a part of Harry Lewis's 325th Glider Infantry Regiment. Carrell, a thirty-four-year-old West Point graduate, didn't think much of Lewis as a commander, and he scarcely knew Ridgway or Gavin.[2] When he looked at the long causeway with its piles of ruined equipment and the putrefying bodies of Germans and Americans strewn along its length, he decided that the mission was suicidal, and that he and his men had been chosen for it precisely because they were outsiders.

Ridgway and Gavin spent the morning of June 9 gathering whatever artillery support they could get for what was sure to be a difficult attack on a narrow front, right into the teeth of some determined German defenses. Of his own division's artillery, Ridgway had access to seven 75 mm pack howitzers of the 319th Glider Artillery, and eight 105 mm snub-nosed howitzers of the 320th Glider Artillery. He was also counting on another ten more of the smaller guns—the trail element of the 456th Parachute Field Artillery—due to arrive via Utah Beach sometime that day. Some Shermans from the 746th Tank Battalion came forward, and Gavin's aide, Captain Hugo Olson (who had been one of the first scouts to swim the flooded Merderet Plain early on D-Day), placed them behind the paratroopers. From there, the tanks could put cannon fire on the German positions across the river.

Most important, Brigadier General John M. Devine, a West Point classmate of Ridgway's who commanded all the artillery assets of the 90th Division, came up to see what help he and his twenty-four cannon—some of them large-caliber 155 mm guns—could offer. Devine brought with him one of his subordinate commanders to register the guns (that is, zero them in on a target). Frank W. Norris, who commanded the 345th Artillery Battalion, was a West Point classmate of the 505th PIR's commander, Bill Ekman. Like Ekman, he was in combat for the first time.

When the artilleryman Devine reached Ridgway, he told the airborne commander that five of his twelve howitzers were ready to fire right then, but that he would have all twelve ready if Ridgway could give him about an hour. There was tremendous pressure on Ridgway to get across. Collins was waiting to send the 90th Division into the fight, and if Ridgway was going to accomplish the mission first, he had to strike quickly.

In spite of the pressure, Ridgway turned to his staff officers and said, "The attack is delayed."

Then he turned to Gavin and told the one-star general to personally take Devine, Norris, and Norris's executive officer, Lloyd Salisbury, forward to see the targets. The artillerymen were surprised that Ridgway told Gavin—who had command of the assault and a lot of work to do in preparation—to help the artillerymen spot the targets. But the artillery support might mean the difference between success and failure, and neither of the paratrooper generals wanted any misunderstandings.

Norris was even more surprised at what he saw when he came up behind La Fière: the narrow causeway stretching into the distance, the wreckage of men and vehicles, the forbidding fields of fire the GIs would have to cross. An American assault would be channeled; there would be no maneuvering right or left, no surprises for the Germans. It was as if the glidermen were going to charge down a long, narrow alley, and waiting for them at the other end were a bunch of men with auto-

matic weapons. Norris thought that two well-defended German machine guns could stop an entire attacking regiment, and considered the
task "appalling."[3]

Gavin led Norris and Salisbury closer to the front, where German artillery and mortar fire still landed all around the manor house, bridge,
and intersection, making the personal reconnaissance risky. Gavin's foxhole was located just beside the road, about two hundred yards back
from the bridge.

"You two get in there and I'll show you what we want to hit," Gavin
said, indicating his foxhole.

"General," Norris said. "That's your foxhole."

Gavin replied, "You look like you need it more than I do, and besides,
I want you to do the shooting."

Norris and Salisbury jumped into the hole and began zeroing their
batteries, calling for marker rounds, and adjusting so that the guns
would know exactly where to shoot.

Gavin had his artillery, and he had his assault force (3rd Battalion of
the 325th GIR under the reluctant Carrell); he still had to put together
a reserve. He turned to Art Maloney, now commanding the patched-
together elements of the 507th PIR. Maloney had assembled three
scratch companies of troopers from the remnants of his regiment on
the east bank. He simply designated them by the names of the officers
he put in charge: Robert Rae, of Service Company; Roy Creek, the
commander of E Company who had taken and held Chef du Pont on
D-Day; and Morgan A. Brakonecke of the regimental Headquarters
Company.

Maloney called his officers together and told them about the upcoming attack across the La Fière causeway. The regimental intelligence officer, John H. Wisner, noticed that the men turned pale when it became
clear what Maloney was asking for: they were to make the same assault—in reverse—that had slaughtered so many Germans on June 6
and 7. And those German panzergrenadiers, whose bodies still littered
the causeways and lay soaking in the flood, had been supported by
tanks.

"Colonel, it will be a slaughter," one of the officers said. "They can fire on us from three sides for five hundred yards."

"I know," Maloney said. "But Timmes is over there and we must go to his help."[4]

Maloney told the men that the glidermen of the 325th would lead the attack, and that the paratroopers of the 507th were to support the attack if it faltered, and to take advantage of a breakthrough on the far side. Whatever else happened, he wanted the men to know that they were going across.

Wisner waited for someone to make a counterargument, but no one could; they could not deny that they owed it to Timmes and his men to try to break through. Wisner had spent three days contemplating the river and could think of no other way to get through to the besieged paratroopers on the other side. Roy Creek and his men had been in position behind La Fière since early on June 7, and he had seen very clearly what kind of fight was possible on the narrow causeway. He knew they had to undertake the mission, and even believed that they'd be successful. He was skeptical only about his ability to survive, and wondered which of Maloney's companies would be chosen to go first.

During this time of incoming fire and organization for the attack, Maloney was knocked down by the explosion of an artillery or mortar round. The artilleryman Norris saw Maloney flat on his back, with a lot of blood coming out of his head, and thought that he was dead. Norris and some others went over and saw Maloney's eyes flutter open as he regained consciousness. A fragment of a shell had pierced the top of Maloney's helmet and struck him in the head, giving him a slashing wound that bled profusely but wasn't deep. The medics moved him a few yards away and patched him up as best they could with a big bandage. When the medics were done, Maloney put his helmet, which now had a big hole in it, back on his head and moved forward again to help oversee the advance.

Gavin wanted Maloney, who was a big man—over six feet four inches tall, 240 pounds, and broad at the shoulders and chest—to act as a kind of backstop for the advancing infantry. Maloney was to stand at the east end of the bridge and stop any GIs who faltered and tried to escape to the rear. Maloney armed himself for the task with a large tree branch. He had dried blood all over his face and streaked through his three-day growth of beard. He looked like exactly the kind of man who would use the big stick—if not a pistol—to enforce battle discipline.

While Gavin was finalizing his plans and getting his artillery support ready, Lieutenant Colonel Carrell issued his orders to his company commanders. Most of his unit was located behind Le Manoir la Fière and would actually make their run at the bridge through the yard and front gate of the manor.

Carrell transmitted his pessimism to his subordinates, which was understandable, but inexcusable in a combat commander. His men, who would make the assault no matter how Carrell felt about it, deserved every bit of support they could get, and that included the moral support of their commander.

Around 0930 hours, Gavin called Carrell forward for a final discussion. The battalion commander, worried about the attack and his chances of success—if not his own prospects for survival—was clearly troubled.

"I don't think I can do it," he told Gavin.

When Gavin asked why, Carrell protested that he was sick.

Gavin said simply, "You're through," and dismissed Carrell.[5]

Gavin told Harry Lewis, the commander of the 325th GIR, that he had just fired one of Lewis's commanders. The next man in line was the battalion executive officer, Charles Moore; but Lewis instead named his own regimental operations officer, Major Arthur W. Gardner, as commander of the 3rd Battalion. It could be that Lewis had more faith in Gardner (the commander and operations officer would have worked very closely during the buildup to the invasion), but the soldiers did not know Gardner, nor did most of the officers. This stranger was forced on them at a most delicate and dangerous moment.

Gavin had been confident that the assault would succeed if the attackers were determined and quick enough to reach the enemy just as the American bombardment lifted. But with this sudden shake-up in command of the 3rd Battalion, Gavin became deeply concerned. He prepared a backup plan.

Gavin tapped one of Maloney's commanders, Captain Robert Rae, and told the young officer that he and his men would be the reserve force for the glider troops going across the causeway. Gavin told Rae that the glider troops might hesitate, or lose their momentum, once they encountered the full force of German fire and saw how far it was to the other side.

"At that instant I'm going to wave at you," Gavin told Rae. "I want you to jump up with all your men yelling their heads off and go right through them [the glider troops] and take them with you."

Rae and his men had been under indirect fire since relieving Bill Owens's A Company platoon, but they were ideally situated at the east end of the bridge and could jump into the fight quickly. What's more, Rae had shown exactly the kind of initiative Gavin and Ridgway expected of their junior officers.

Rae had spent most his first hours in France alone, having been dropped far off course, in the 101st Airborne Division sector. After sunrise, he found a group of men from the 82nd and moved with them toward the sounds of a fight close by. They arrived just as another group of paratroopers was driving some Germans out the back door of a farmhouse. The Germans never saw Rae's newly arrived troopers, and Rae's men cut them down as they raced to get clear of the building.

Later, Rae ran into a Frenchman who was fleeing the fighting with his wife and two little children. The man couldn't speak English, but when Rae got out his map, the man was able to tell the paratrooper where he was. Soon Rae and his men made it to a collection point in the 101st Airborne Division sector, where they found ninety other troopers from the 82nd. Rae got them organized and moving toward Ste. Mère Eglise, arriving late on D-Day. On June 7 Art Maloney sent Rae and his men down to the bridgehead at La Fière.

• • •

The American barrage started around 1030 hours, with the artillery concentrated on the far shoreline and the little crossroads of Cauquigny. The Germans answered with their own artillery and mortars.

Captain Roy Creek was up and moving about, checking on his own "Creek Company" (as Maloney named it), when the German fire began. He had nowhere to go as the incoming fire increased, so he ran for the nearest hole he could see and dived in. The foxhole, built for one, was already occupied by a frightened young private Creek did not recognize. The two men squeezed in as tightly as possible, trying to make sure that every part of them was below ground.

They had to yell to be heard, even though they were practically embracing each other. Still, they tried to reassure one another that unless a shell had your name on it and landed right in the hole, you were sure to survive. When the firing at last seemed to die down, Creek pulled himself free to go back to his men. He bent down to thank the soldier for sharing the foxhole. It was only then that Creek saw the GI had been killed by a shell fragment that had punctured his helmet. Creek trotted off to rejoin his company; he had never learned the soldier's name.

Company G of the 3rd Battalion, 325th GIR, had been chosen to lead the assault, and they moved out onto the road east of the bridge, which was concealed from German view. Incoming artillery fire drove them into the ditches beside the road, and there they waited for the smoke screen that had been promised them.

Captain John B. Sauls, commanding G Company, examined the approach to the bridge. Several paratroopers had been killed by German artillery, and their bodies were in plain view on the road. This meant that the area had no cover, which concerned him. But he also knew that seeing and having to step over the dead GIs might rattle his men, who were going into their first fight. Sauls looked for a more covered approach,[6] and he found one in the yard of the manor house, where a stone wall ran along the western end of the Manoir property to a point just seventy-five yards from the foot of the bridge. The wall was shoulder high and so would provide cover for the men, except for a large gap where a German shell had blown a hole in the stone.

Some of Rae's men were well forward of the wall and yard, all the way down near the bank of the river where they were safe from direct German fire. Sauls asked one of Rae's sergeants to come back and help him move the bodies of the troops who had just been killed, so that his men won't have to step over them when they began the assault.

Once the bodies were moved, Sauls went back through the manor yard and led his men between the big stone buildings to this new, covered approach to the bridge. One by one they dashed across the open area of the gap in the wall. Soon a German machine gunner spotted the movement and hit the area with bursts of fire. The dash across the open space, no more than a few yards, became another dangerous stretch on the way to the bridge. Sauls managed to move two of his platoons to the side of the gap nearest the bridge, where the men huddled with their backs to the wall, protected for a moment from the fire. They caught their breath, checked, and rechecked their weapons. They prayed, and they waited for the order that would soon have them running across the open bridge.

Meanwhile, the 90th Division's heavy artillery pounded the west bank. Gavin, who had seen plenty of artillery barrages, was still amazed at the tremendous noise, the big shells screeching overhead, the *bang bang bang* of explosions on the far shore, the close-in firing of automatic weapons and tank cannon.[7] As Gavin watched, some of the Germans who were getting hammered by this merciless fire started across the causeway, bleeding from ears and mouths, hands up, dazed, and in shock.

The Germans knew what the barrage meant: an attack was coming. They responded with their own indirect fire, hoping to catch the attacking troops forming at the east end of the causeway.

The glider troops watched for the smoke that had been promised. It was nowhere in sight; the Germans still had a clear view of the length of the causeway. When their new battalion commander, Arthur Gardner, came up to check on G Company, some of the men yelled, "Where's the goddamned smoke?"

The jump-off for the infantry attack was 1045 hours, smoke or no smoke. Gardner checked his watch, checked the far shore once more, where the American artillery was still landing, then shouted, "Go! Go! Go!"

At the front of the G Company column were Staff Sergeant Wilfred L. Ericsson and Lieutenant Donald B. Wason; they would lead the attack. The plan was to cross the bridge and then peel off right and left once they reached the far shore.[8] The roadbed was thirty yards wide in some spots, narrower in others. Some places had a sheer drop of a few feet into the water on either side, and there were dead soldiers and destroyed tanks in the grass, in the water, amid the shrubbery, so that a man running for his life, trying to make his best speed, would have to dodge and leap and try not to trip over a dozen obstacles in his path.

The G Company men ran flat out, weapons and equipment banging against their bodies, their pockets full of grenades, heavy rifles held across their chests. It was a fear-driven dash along a five-hundred-yard corridor that seemed to go on for miles.

This first group made it across the causeway while American artillery was still coming down; when they reached the west end, U.S. shells were falling just a few yards up the road. Because the incoming fire kept most of the Germans down in their holes, Sauls did not encounter the deadly machine gun fire he expected.

When they got to the far side, Sergeant Ericsson turned left, running down a little trail that paralleled the edge of the flooded area. Lieutenant Wason pressed straight ahead, bypassing the right turn that led to the bombed-out stone church. Up ahead, a large house sat hard by the road, some hundred yards back from the end of the causeway, and Wason headed for the roadside ditch there. As he ran, he could see the winking muzzle flash of a German machine gun situated just behind the corner of the house.

Wason yelled to one of the riflemen with him, Private Frank Thurston, the company runner. "Stay back; I'll get that gun," Wason said. He threw his grenade as he ran directly at the gun. The Germans shot him dead in the dusty road, but his grenade exploded on its target, killing the crew and knocking out the gun.[9]

Meanwhile, Captain Sauls had stopped where the dirt roads and waterside trail intersected, then turned to look for the rest of his company, the rest of his battalion. But the troops behind him had faltered, and their initial rush had been followed only by a lone BAR man and a couple of riflemen. He and his handful of men, just a little more than a rifle squad, backed up by a single BAR, now were the entire western bridgehead at La Fière.

After seeing Wason go down, Thurston went back to the intersection and reported to Captain Sauls, saying he thought there was another German machine gun position near the same house. He asked permission to go after it.

Thurston was more cautious in his approach, and he crawled toward where he thought the German gun was located, taking his time to push through the hedgerows. His approach worked, and he got the drop on the German gun crew, killing them with rifle fire. He reported to Sauls once again that he'd taken out the gun.[10]

Meanwhile, Sergeant Ericsson and his squad moved south on the narrow lane that ran along the edge of the flooded plain. He figured that the Germans firing across the flooded area at the manor must be in foxholes just on the edge of the water. He positioned a BAR man to the right side of the lane, thinking that any Germans he flushed from their fighting positions would run away from the flood and right toward the ambush.

Ericsson's squad fired into the hedgerows and threw hand grenades at likely spots. Many of the German defenders, who had been heavily shelled for nearly forty minutes, were ready to give up. They came out of their positions with their hands up, their weapons already discarded. Ericsson merely motioned toward the causeway, telling them to move along. He did not have any extra men to guard them.

Ericsson and his small force pushed south for about 150 yards along the edge of the water. All the firing had left them low on ammunition, so he called his squad to pull back to the main road, where they could dig in and help hold the bridgehead. He was nearly to Cauquigny when a bullet punched him hard in the back and knocked him down.

When Captain Sauls saw Sergeant Ericsson go down, he called another of his lieutenants who had just made it across to take over Ericsson's squad and secure the left side of the road. He put a few other men just off the main road, oriented to the north, where the small stone church was tucked behind a bend in the road. He had reached his objective, but with less than a platoon to keep the foothold.

On the causeway, many of the Germans who surrendered to Ericsson were killed by their own fire—coming from behind them—as they made their way east to the American lines and captivity. Ericsson, seeing this, determined that he'd rather chance bleeding to death on the west bank than crossing the causeway again, so he found a ditch and crawled in. He was found there hours later, weakened but still alive.

Back on the east side of La Fière, many of the glidermen had hesitated at the breach in the stone wall.[11] Private Melvin L. Johnson said to the men around him, "Here I go," just before he dashed across the space. But the German machine gunners were waiting, and Johnson went down, his head torn by machine gun fire. His body lay in the gap, a psychological barrier to the men just a few feet behind him.

Another G Company platoon leader, Lieutenant Frank E. Amino, managed to coax a handful of men to follow him across the open area and onto the bridge. Some men from the company weapons platoon made the dash, because their comrades on the far side needed the firepower if they were going to stay in place on the west end. But when the men got out on the causeway, they could not run the entire length, weighed down as they were with the heavy machine guns and mortars. Their periodic stops to catch their breath left them strung out and disorganized; their weapons did not, at first, lend much help to Sauls.

All the while the German gunners sprayed the causeway with automatic weapons fire, eager to avenge what the paratroopers had done to the panzergrenadiers on June 6 and 7. Many of the G Company men were wounded, and some were simply too frozen in fear to move forward. Soon the narrow causeway was clogged with the bodies of the dead, the dying, and those too frightened to move.

Gavin, watching the attack falter, ordered one of the tanks to bull through the wreckage near the bridge, to clear a path for the armor to move forward and provide support for the infantrymen. The Sherman drove down the hill and crossed the short span to the other side of the clutter of destroyed German armor the GIs had dragged out there on D-Day. The tank tried dodging around one of these wrecks but ran over an antitank mine that A Company had placed on the road. The mine only disabled the tank, but the blowback from the explosion wounded seven more men, including Staff Sergeant George F. Myers, mortar section leader. Myers took a piece of shrapnel in the eye. The wound bled heavily, but Myers continued moving west, calling for his men to follow. He made it to the far end, where he passed out from blood loss.

Company E was to follow G Company and clear the area around Cauquigny church, which sits just a little west and north of the western end of the causeway. Lieutenant Richard B. Johnson ran off ahead of his platoon to find a place where his men could join the fighting. He arrived just as Sauls was trying to reinforce the left, or south, side of the road, where Ericsson's men had cleared the Germans out. Johnson turned right, toward the church, crawling through the hedgerows to get a look at what might be out there. The church was wrecked, with a large hole in its roof and a huge chunk of the ancient stone wall knocked lose. The tiny churchyard, with its few dozen headstones, was churned up by the American artillery barrage. The good news for Johnson was that he saw no German infantry; the bad news was that there was no sign of his platoon.

Company E was stalled out on the causeway, held up by the G Company stragglers lying in the ditches or crawling back for help, and by the German prisoners, who took cover rather than walk straight into the American advance. Wounded men from both sides crawled or limped eastward, and even some men who were unhurt suddenly found excuses to return to the jump-off point. But the E Company men finally pushed through, prodded by their company executive officer, Lieutenant Bruce H. Booker. (The E Company commander was wounded in his run across the causeway.)

Booker also went down with wounds to both legs, but he crawled forward along the causeway to the western end and exhorted his men from there. The remaining platoon leaders and squad leaders led their men to Cauquigny, from which they fanned out and cleared the area around the church and just to the north, gathering prisoners as they went. Another element overran a German mortar position dug in some two hundred yards west of the causeway's end. Lieutenant Johnson's platoon finally reached him, and he had them dig in near the church.

By this time almost forty-five minutes had passed since Captain Sauls crossed the bridge. Although the 325 glidermen who made it to the west side were doing the right things—rooting out German mortar and machine gun positions, killing off their gun crews, digging in a defensive line—no word of these successes reached the east side, where Gavin watched nervously. He did not even see the German prisoners sent back by the glidermen, as these unfortunates were cut down by their own fire as they tried to cross. Those who were not hit took cover amid the dead and wounded on the causeway.

From Gavin's point of view, the situation looked desperate. The foliage, trees, and smoke obscured his view of the west bank. He did not have radio contact with the few leaders who had crossed, and was getting no reports back. All he could see was the stream of wounded and broken men trickling back.[12]

Captain James M. Harney's F Company was next in line, with a mission to shore up the bridgehead and provide stability in the event of a counterattack. Like Gavin, Harney could see very little from his jump-off point by the bridge, and what he could see was not encouraging: the causeway was choked with men moving west, men moving east, and wrecked vehicles, and the German fire was still coming in.

Harney pushed off from the bridge and had not gotten far when some of his men began to hang back amid the confusion and the cover offered by the wrecked vehicles. Harney cursed at them, pushed and shoved and kicked them until he got some of them moving. But he could not linger and drag each man, so he forged ahead with the men who would follow him.

Gavin couldn't tell what was happening on the west side, but he could see that the manpower needed to expand and hold the bridgehead was piling up just past the bridge, amid the wrecked German and American tanks and the milling wounded. He turned to Maloney, who had stationed himself nearby to relay the order for Rae's advance. After Gavin gave the order,[13] Rae moved across the causeway by fits and starts: running, doubling back to cajole men forward, grabbing and dragging, and always in plain view where his men could see him.

The west end of the causeway had become a collection point for walking wounded who wanted to head back to La Fière but did not want to brave the gauntlet of fire again. Men lay sprawled and bleeding in the ditches around the little intersection, some of them hurt very badly. No American vehicles had yet come across to reinforce the bridgehead or evacuate the wounded; the medics did what they could with their tiny aid bags, and the wounded men tried to hang on.

After Rae crossed, Gavin, Ridgway, and Maloney waded into the mess at the bridge and moved among the men on the eastern end of the causeway, pushing and pulling and yanking them clear of their hiding places, all amid the falling mortar and artillery and incoming machine gun fire. Ridgway, carrying his World War I vintage rifle, moved to the recently disabled American tank, which blocked the roadway and kept Gavin from sending reinforcing armor across. While German fire shrieked around him, Ridgway began rigging the tow cable on the Sherman so that another vehicle could pull it out of the way. Men who had been hiding in the ditches came out at the sight of the division commander out in the open, doing the work of a tank crew. Several men pitched in. A mortar round landed just ten feet away from the tank, killing one man and wounding several others. Lieutenant Joe Shealy took steel fragments in his head, arm, and leg. But Shealy, a platoon leader in the Heavy Weapons Company, could not very well give up when his forty-nine-year-old division commander was out there. Shealy led a group all the way to the west bank before he collapsed from blood loss.[14]

While Ridgway cleared the wreckage off the roadway, Gavin went back to where the Sherman tanks of the 746th Battalion were firing in support of the assault, and he got them ready to make a run across the causeway. The tanks clattered out onto the dusty road at the foot of the bridge and began pushing across, though they had to pause often while dead and wounded were pulled from their paths. Those walking across also had to be careful not to step on the bodies of the dead glider troops, who were stretched, Gavin would later write, "head to foot" across the causeway.

Lieutenant Wisner, an intelligence officer who went with Rae's troops, thought the causeway looked like an escalator, with two streams of men moving west on the outside and a steady stream of walking wounded moving east on the inside.

When they reached the other side, Rae and Harney pushed through the jumbled GIs there, moving straight ahead toward Le Motey and beyond the Amfreville road. The road was lined on either side with numerous hedgerows, many of which hid German positions. Moving forward, the glidermen and paratroopers had to fight for every field, sometimes in gruesome, hand-to-hand struggles, while runners trotted back and forth to the western end of the causeway, begging ammunition. It was a completely decentralized fight, with very little direction from above. Instead, individual soldiers and small teams fought to hack out a bridgehead for the massive VII Corps advance.

The Shermans rolled out onto the causeway after the wreckage of the bridge was cleared, using their big .50-caliber machine guns to clear any Germans still clinging to foxholes on the edge of the flooded area. Unfortunately, the tankers came upon a field where the 3rd Battalion, 325th GIR, command post was just being set up under Captain Lewis Mentlik.[15] The American tankers killed or wounded five of the headquarters men in a brief burst; Mentlik was killed later in the battle after taking his men back for medical help.

When Gavin arrived on the west side, the fighting was still hot and heavy close by Cauquigny, which limited his freedom of movement. But he did see that he had underestimated the German strength on the west side. In a field just a hundred yards from the end of the bridge he found a dozen mortars dug in deep, square positions. There were armored half-tracks and self-propelled guns, either destroyed or abandoned by the Germans. There was horse-drawn artillery (the norm in the German Army) and, all around, dead and dying horses still harnessed to the guns.

Gavin turned left on the west bank, following behind a U.S. armored car as he moved south toward where Shanley was holed up with his paratroopers at Hill 30. The armored car surprised a German mortar squad and mowed them down to a man, leaving them lying in a ditch, head to foot, knocked over as they'd been walking. At the head of the column, Gavin spotted the body of a German lieutenant, who was carrying a map. Thinking that the map might have information about the German positions on the west bank, Gavin took it from the dead man's still-limp hands. While it did not show the German defenses, it was interesting for another reason. On the back side of the La Fière map was a map of England; Gavin figured it had been prepared years earlier, as part of the German plan to launch a cross-Channel invasion. Before he left, Gavin took the lieutenant's watch, as his had been torn off in the D-Day jump.

A little farther to the south, Gavin came across a German command post, also littered with hastily abandoned equipment. Nearby he found a paratrooper, still in his harness and suspended in the apple tree in which he had become tangled on June 6. The Germans had shot him as he hung in his harness, without giving him a chance to surrender. As the afternoon wore on, Gavin stayed on the west side until his troops had contacted Shanley and he felt that the bridgehead was secure; then he headed back to La Fière to find Ridgway and learn how the rest of the division was faring.

Meanwhile, Colonel Harry Lewis, commander of the 325th GIR, crossed the causeway from La Fière with his executive officer, Herb Stitler, and the regimental staff. The command group made its way to the crossroads of Cauquigny, with its shattered church, smoking shell holes, and litter of dead and wounded. The hard-fighting men who pressed across the causeway had handed Lewis a tremendous opportunity to secure a bridgehead for the advancing 90th Division. He was in the right place at the right time, and though his troops were battered and exhausted, he had momentum on his side. But at this critical moment, he failed.

Lewis was already suffering from the cancer that would kill him in less than a year. In addition, many of his own officers thought him too old for a combat command at the front. He may have succumbed to combat fatigue, and perhaps the sight of so many of his dead and wounded troopers, lost in the tough frontal assault, unnerved him. Shortly after he reached Cauquigny, he stopped functioning as a commander: he could not give any orders, could not grasp the situation, could not fight. He was evacuated back across La Fière causeway and eventually to England.[16]

Le Motey, the next little crossroads to the west, seemed to be a good jump-off point for a German counterattack. Gavin, studying his map and the terrain, was concerned that the Germans would shelter amid its stone buildings as they prepared for an attack against the Americans west of the river, who were neither consolidated nor dug in. When he returned to the east bank, Gavin asked for artillery fire on Le Motey from the dedicated 155 mm battery that had supported the push.

But the little crossroads village also appealed to the GIs on the west bank, who were moving forward and looking for defensible terrain. Robert Rae and his paratroopers headed west toward Le Motey, followed closely by James Harney and his glider troops of F Company. The American fire Gavin requested fell at the crossroads just as the first infantrymen were closing in. Several of Rae's paratroopers were killed before the rest of the men found shelter amid the buildings in town. Harney and his troops were caught in the open by this friendly fire, and several were killed. Although wounded, Harney stayed in command, sending a runner back to tell the artillery to stop firing. Harney made his way to a tank that was behind the advance and tried to use its radio to call for a cease-fire, but the shells kept coming in.

When the fire eventually lifted, Harney pulled his men back to some high ground just short of Le Motey, while Rae and his paratroopers went all the way back to the damaged church at Cauquigny, where they were put in reserve.

A patrol sent north to contact Timmes's group in the orchard was also brought up short by the American artillery fire. Harney had moved closest to Le Motey, but his flanks were in the air. He had fewer than one hundred men with him, not nearly enough to cover his frontage and tie in with the units to his left and right. He soon began drawing fire from Le Motey. Although it did not look like the enemy was trying to flank him, it was only a matter of time before the Germans—who had not lost their aggressiveness—figured out that he was too far extended. A well-executed attack could easily turn him or cut him off from the bridgehead at Cauquigny.

When he attempted to readjust his line and move closer to Le Motey, the Germans ambushed one of his platoons from buildings that Rae had already cleared. The enemy was moving forward again to re-occupy lost ground. Harney went back to the church in person to get some help.

By the time Harney returned, the Germans had retaken more of the buildings that had been cleared by Rae and his men. More unsettling, the enemy had found the gaps in the American positions and began to push between the overstretched units. Harney had no support from behind, no one on his flanks, and an enemy trying to get behind him. The wounded captain had to undertake one of the most difficult tactical moves, a movement to the rear while in contact with the enemy.

Harney picked out a position a couple of hundred yards back from Le Motey, a slight elevation where he thought he could make a stand until more help arrived from the east side of the river. He ordered his mortars to withdraw first, to be followed by his riflemen and machine gunners.

Harney's withdrawal started smoothly enough, but the Germans followed him closely and managed to put enfilading fire on another unit of glidermen that was moving to support Harney. Some of these men bolted for the bridgehead, and Harney was concerned that his own men, already under pressure, might do the same. He stood up so that his men could see him and, by force of his presence, kept them calm and their movements controlled.

The men received some much-needed ammunition when a lieutenant persuaded one tank commander to convert his Sherman into a supply vehicle. Lieutenant Sturm loaded the deck of the tank with ammunition, and the tankers ran it up the road to Harney's position under intense direct and indirect fire. When Harney had enough ammunition to make a stand, the Sherman pulled up to provide direct fire support to the glidermen.

Harney was in command of the situation in the center of the bridgehead, but it didn't look that way from back at La Fière, where Gavin got the word that the bridgehead was collapsing.[17]

Gavin found Stitler in a stone farmhouse, where Stitler told the general that the bridgehead was collapsing and that he was preparing to withdraw. Gavin was livid. The men of the 82nd had been through three days of hell to control the causeway, and the men of the 325th Glider Infantry Regiment had paid dearly for this foothold on the western bank. They would not give it up.

Gavin ordered Stitler to gather every available man, clerks, runners, signal men, and any man who could carry a weapon, including Stitler himself, and prepare a counterattack. Gavin then sent an armored car south to find the Shanley group to tell them of the planned counterattack and, more important, to let them know the Americans were not withdrawing back across the causeway. Then the general went forward, personally spreading the word to every man he saw that they were attacking. As Gavin moved toward Le Motey, he saw the grass around him being cut down by the intense small arms fire, and he got down on his hands and knees to crawl forward. He found Captain Robert Rae and told the paratrooper to push back into Le Motey. Rae and his men advanced alongside Harney, and the Americans retook Le Motey in the dying light of day.

●   ●   ●

During this advance Second Lieutenant Leo J. Fitzmartin walked through a gap in a hedgerow and was cut down by German machine guns firing from the corners of the field. Four riflemen who followed him were killed, and Fitzmartin was badly wounded, his right leg smashed. The rest of his platoon saw the whole thing and assumed that all their comrades had been killed, but the lieutenant merely played dead so as not to draw more fire.

Fitzmartin was conscious through the night, stranded under the guns of the Germans just a few yards away. Later he heard vehicle engines off to the east, and he hoped that meant reinforcements were coming. He had no way of knowing how the larger battle was playing out—few combat soldiers in the 82nd Airborne Division had any idea of what was happening more than a few yards from whatever hole they were in. But they shared a common hope: that the vast Allied war machine would move out inexorably from the beaches, terrible and unstoppable. In the meantime—until reinforcements arrived or the German defenses cracked or they were ordered out of the line—they held on. Those who struggled and clawed their way forward did so not to serve some grand plan, and not because the generals were tracking their progress on a map. Like soldiers everywhere, in the end they fought for the guy on the right and the guy on the left.

Fitzmartin was hopeful as he lay bleeding in a dark field, surrounded by the bodies of his soldiers. If the Germans nearest him withdrew, he might avoid capture. He might survive.

During the night, Fitzmartin heard the Germans talking in the hedgerow just thirty yards away, and he prayed they were discussing their own retreat. Shortly after dawn, the Germans pulled out, leaving Fitzmartin stranded and alone. Less than an hour later, glidermen from his own company moved forward again and found him. They carried him across the causeway on a litter as fresh troops of the newly arrived 90th Division moved west and up to the fight, across ground won at such a high cost by the All Americans.

Food, water, and ammunition came up to the paratroopers and glidermen by truck from the vast supply dumps being created just inland from the beach. The wounded who required hospitalization made the return trip on the same vehicles. The dead were wrapped in parachutes or blankets and laid in shallow holes to await the Graves Registration details. The exhausted living soldiered on, wrestling pieces of France from her occupiers, buying fields and crossroads, villages and rivers with their blood, paying for her freedom with their sweat, their dreams, their youth.

EPILOGUE

Matt Ridgway's 82nd Airborne Division was not relieved by the beach assault forces on D+7 as planned, but instead was called upon to bolster and even lead attacks that would cut off the Cotentin Peninsula in the weeks following D-Day.

The 505th PIR, with the 2nd Battalion of the 325th GIR attached, attacked north from Ste. Mère Eglise beginning on June 8, just as soon as the paratroopers were able to catch their breath after the initial battle. Bill Ekman, who had no combat experience when he took over the regiment in England, found his stride in this fight and developed into one of the premier combat commanders of the division. The 508th PIR moved south and established a bridgehead across the Douve River. On June 14 the 507th PIR and the 325th GIR, moving west, passed through the still-struggling 90th Division toward St. Sauveur le Vicomte, which was the center of the division's original drop zones in Normandy. Finally, in early July, the 82nd attacked south and west toward La Haye du Puits. A map overlay accompanying the division's official after-action report offers this summary: "33 days in action without relief, without replacements. Every mission accomplished, no ground gained ever relinquished."[1]

All during June and July, the fighting raged across the expanding Normandy battlefield. Allied advances were slowed considerably by the almost impassable hedgerows, which the Germans cleverly integrated into their defensive positions. The Allied failure to anticipate the diffi-

culties of moving through this country was one of the significant intelligence missteps of the campaign.

Mistakes also dogged German efforts at closing off the landing areas.
Field Marshal Gerd von Rundstedt was the only high-ranking German
officer who correctly sized up the threat on D-Day. Within hours of the
parachute assault, Rundstedt alerted the two panzer divisions that were
set aside as the strike force for Normandy. The morning of June 6 was
overcast, and the Germans might have been able to move their armor
formations in spite of Allied air superiority. But Rundstedt was reminded that Hitler controlled all the panzers in France, and Hitler was
not to be disturbed. The Führer slept until noon and did not release the
panzers until almost 1600. By then the skies above Normandy had
cleared, Allied fight-bombers were on the prowl looking for targets, and
the German armor formations were unable to move. Hitler remained
convinced that the landings in Normandy were a diversion to cover the
main assault in the Pas de Calais, and kept critical reserves tied up and
waiting for this ghost attack.

In the British sector Montgomery failed to take Caen—his principal
D-Day objective—until August. George Patton, whom the Germans assumed would command American, if not all Allied, ground forces, was
not brought to France until July 6. His massive 3rd Army used those
weeks to move men and equipment into France for a major breakout.
Patton had been preparing for this battle for his entire life. He had even
reconnoitered the area south of Cherbourg while he was a student at a
French military school in 1913, and again when he was training his tank
corps during World War I. Finally turned loose on 1 August, Patton
sliced through German defenses, sweeping south and east into Brittany, occupying one town after another, and allowing the fleeing Germans no chance to rest or regroup. He kept relentless pressure on the
retreating enemy and was halted only by a shortage of fuel for his
tanks.

By the end of the Normandy campaign in August the Allies had suffered a total of 209,672 casualties, including 36,976 killed. The 82nd
Airborne Division, which committed 11,770 men to the battle, lost

1,142 killed in action or died of wounds, 2,373 wounded, 840 missing or captured. Estimates of German losses for the campaign were much harder to gauge, since these units sometimes just disintegrated in front of the Allied steamroller. The numbers approached 200,000 killed and missing, and another 200,000 captured.

Three temporary cemeteries were established near Ste. Mère Eglise as soon as the battle moved away from the town, and nearly fourteen thousand American soldiers killed in the campaigns across Europe were interred there. After the war, the families of the dead were given the option of having the bodies returned to the United States for burial. In 1948, two-thirds of those laid near Ste. Mère Eglise were shipped back home, and the rest were moved to the U.S. Military Cemetery at Colleville sur Mer. Nine thousand, three hundred eighty-six military personnel (307 of whom are unknown) are buried on the plain above Omaha Beach, on a site beautifully maintained by the U.S. Battle Monuments Commission. Each of the white, government-issue headstones faces west, toward home.

Captain Roy Creek, the New Mexico native whose quick actions on June 6 grabbed the causeway at Chef du Pont for the Americans, survived the war. In 1948, as a student at the Infantry School at Fort Benning, Georgia, he wrote a paper on the airborne fight during the period June 5–7, 1944. In the report, Creek described the cold calculus that Eisenhower used in his decision to send thousands of paratroopers into battle in spite of Leigh-Mallory's dire predictions.

Warned that casualties among the airborne forces might approach 75 percent, Ike determined that "support by the airborne troops was essential": "I ultimately took upon myself the heavy responsibility of deciding that the airborne operation against the Cotentin [Peninsula] be carried out. The decision, once taken, was loyally and efficiently executed by the airborne forces, and it is to them that immeasurable credit for the subsequent success of the western operation belongs."

"The bridge was ours," Creek wrote about the end of D-Day at Chef du Pont, "and we knew we could hold it, but like all victories in war, we shared a let-down feeling. We knew it was still a long way to Berlin."

Fred Caravelli, the rifleman whose train was met by General Ridgway in the middle of a rainy night in Ireland, also survived the war and returned to Philadelphia and his wife, Marie. He adjusted to civilian life, landed a good job, started a family, and seemed to have put his war experiences behind him. One day, he was taking a break at work and reading the *Saturday Evening Post*. A writer told of meeting a former paratrooper who was haunted by a wartime memory: the veteran had been fighting in the hedgerows and had come upon another GI who was horribly wounded, his face shot off, gasping for air, and clearly dying in great pain. An officer asked the paratrooper to shoot the wounded man and put him out of his misery.

Caravelli recognized the details: he had also been there and had been asked to extend the same brutal mercy to the dying man. Caravelli had refused, but when the officer later asked the man in the story to do the same, he complied, and was now haunted by what he had done. Caravelli closed the magazine and his office door and cried, for the wounded paratrooper who knew he was dying, for the man who had shot him, for what all of them had lost.

The bazooka men Marcus Heim, Leonold Peterson, John Bolderson, and Gordon Pryne were each awarded the Distinguished Service Cross—second only to the Medal of Honor—for their actions in stopping the German tanks on La Fière Bridge on D-Day.

In 1945 Heim returned to the United States and met his pen pal, a seventeen-year-old high school girl named Gloria Eckert, with whom he had been corresponding for nearly two years. The couple met at her home on a Tuesday, and on Saturday of the same week Heim proposed. They had been married for almost sixty years when Heim passed away—painlessly—over breakfast after his morning walk.

Gloria Heim said her husband did not speak of the war for forty-five years, until he was asked to address the local schoolchildren in their hometown of Middleburgh, New York. It was while he was talking about the actions at La Fière, recalling the men who died that day, that she first saw him shed tears over the war. He grieved, he told her later, for all those young men "who never got to have a family, or own a home, or get married, or have any sort of life."

Dean McCandless, the communications officer who had doubts about his selection of a command post until Jim Gavin came walking through the mortar fire, became a physician after the war. In an interview Mc-Candless recalled moving through a hedgerow later in the Normandy campaign and coming across the body of a German officer. "He was very young, blond haired, handsome, and clean looking. Even his uniform was clean, except where there was blood. He looked waxy, from the loss of blood," McCandless said. "And I thought, 'What a waste this all is.'"

Arthur "Dutch" Schultz, who got religion before every campaign, landed a federal job at the Frankford Arsenal in Philadelphia after the war. There was another 505th PIR vet there named Bill Donnelly, who had been badly wounded in Holland. Donnelly liked to talk about his experiences—brag a little bit—and even carried around a newspaper photo of Gavin. The way Schultz saw things, Donnelly had earned the right to brag. But Donnelly had some trouble getting along with his supervisors, whom Schultz referred to as "toy soldiers who wouldn't know combat from close-order drill," and was in danger of losing his job. Schultz knew that Donnelly had some emotional problems stemming for his war service, but he always performed his job at the arsenal. Schultz wrote to Jim Gavin, then the U.S. ambassador to France, for help. Gavin replied with a letter on State Department stationery.

●　　●　　●

Dear Schultz:

Thank you for your letter of 2 March. I was distressed to learn of Donnelly's situation and have written to him at once. I will also write a note to the Commanding Officer of the Arsenal and I hope that he will be in a position to take a personal interest in the case.

As the years go by, and the war recedes in the past, many of our Veterans will develop war-induced conditions. They are entitled to more than routine consideration and I certainly want to do all that I can to be sure that they receive it.

Later, Schultz had some difficulties of his own. He avoided going back to Europe and did not stay in touch with his former comrades. He married a woman he hardly knew and soon descended into alcoholism, losing his career and his family. Schultz moved to California to be near his elderly parents, and once told his mother that he did not feel he had been a brave soldier. His mother, aware of the demons her son wrestled with, told him that bravery on the battlefield is instantaneous, but bravery in life, day in and day out, is really heroic.

Schultz eventually went back to France, and in the cemetery above Omaha Beach he confronted his past. He broke down amid the headstones, amid the thousands of graves, and let his grief pour out of him. Although the change was not immediate, the experience was cathartic. Schultz stopped drinking and became a counselor in alcohol abuse and drug prevention programs, eventually earning a doctorate in the field.

On June 6, 2004, the sixtieth anniversary of D-Day, Dutch threw out the first pitch at a California Angels game where World War II veterans were honored. He passed away in 2005.

Dennis O'Loughlin, who joined the paratroopers to get away from crowds, went back to Montana after the war. According to his friend Otis Sampson, with whom he remained in touch for six decades, O'Loughlin never lost his bellicose streak and remained "a man you didn't want to cross." On one occasion, O'Loughlin found a trespasser on his property, panning for gold in a stream. When the man refused to leave, O'Loughlin pulled one of the two pistols he carried in holsters, gunslinger style, and fired a round past each side of the man's face. When the police came and said, "You could have killed the guy," O'Loughlin answered, "I only hit what I'm aiming at."

Sergeant James Yates and Lieutenant Robert Ringwald, who were gravely injured on the jump and had to be abandoned by Wheatley Christensen on June 6, were captured by the Germans on D-Day and spent the rest of the war as prisoners. Liberated by the Allied advance into Germany, the two men stopped briefly at the camp where the 505th PIR was resting in the late spring of 1945, but could not stick around long enough to reunite with their G Company comrades.

Lieutenant Colonel Edwin Ostberg of the 507th PIR, who was wounded leading the first charge across Chef du Pont on the morning of D-Day, survived the battle and was awarded the Distinguished Service Cross. He was on hand to meet the unit when the 82nd Airborne arrived back in England in July 1944. Hit again during the Battle of the Bulge, he died of his wounds in February 1945. He was thirty years old.

Anthony Antoniou, who was saved from jumping with a shredded parachute by the copilot of his C47, and who was surrounded for three days with other lost troopers, rejoined B Company near Ste. Mère Eglise around 10 June. During the fighting near St. Sauveur le Vicomte on 15 June, he was wounded by shrapnel in the backs of his legs. For several days he walked with his legs splayed, enduring teasing by his companymates. On 25 June he was wounded again by artillery or mortar fire and was evacuated to England. By the end of the war he had been wounded five times. His five Purple Hearts gave him the second-highest point total in the company (points were awarded for campaigns, awards, and wounds) and made him one of the first men from B Company to receive orders sending him home.

Fred Morgan, the A Company medic who was reported buried alive on D-Day, survived the war and later became an officer in the U.S. Air Force. He did not speak of his wartime experiences for fifty years. In 1994, with public interest rising for the fiftieth anniversary of D-Day, one of Morgan's sons—also an Air Force officer—convinced his father to share the story of his service in World War II. The elder Morgan was invited to speak to schoolchildren on Martha's Vineyard, where he grew up and lived after retirement. He was surprised to find some healing in the effort and has given many talks over the years. Morgan encourages other veterans to speak about their experiences as therapy for dealing with wartime trauma.

In August 1944 Matt Ridgway became the commander of the newly constituted XVIII Airborne Corps, which consisted of three airborne divisions (the 82nd, the 101st, and the newly formed 17th). Ridgway commanded this corps through the end of the war in Europe.

In December 1950 the commander of the U.S. 8th Army in Korea was killed in a jeep accident, and Ridgway became his replacement. Eighth Army had been reeling from repeated onslaughts by the Chinese Army, which entered the war in November and pushed UN forces back some seventy miles south of Seoul. American units had been cut off and surrounded so often that commanders spent as much time worrying about their routes of retreat as about their advances. Ridgway changed that. He personally visited every unit command post down to regimental level. He forced commanders to leave their dugouts, get out on the ground, and conduct personal reconnaissance. He stressed the need for aggressive patrolling and good planning of fire support (in which U.S. forces had a distinct advantage). Above all, he demanded that leaders and soldiers perform their duty. Ridgway made the Eighth Army a fighting unit again.

When General Douglas MacArthur was fired by President Harry Truman in January 1951, Ridgway became the commander of all UN forces in Korea and fought the enemy to a standstill along the 38th Parallel. In June 1952 Ridgway took Eisenhower's place as the Supreme Commander of Allied Forces in Europe, and in 1953 he became the Chief of Staff of the Army. His time in the Pentagon was marred by almost constant clashes with President Eisenhower and Secretary of Defense Charles E. Wilson, both of whom thought U.S. defense policy should rest on massive retaliation—nuclear weapons delivered by bombers—instead of large conventional forces. Even after his retirement in 1955, Ridgway continued to fight for the Army he so loved and which he had served for nearly forty years.

In 1986 he was awarded the Presidential Medal of Freedom. The citation read: "Heroes come when they are needed. Great men step forward when courage seems in short supply. WWII was such a time, and there was Ridgway."

Jim Gavin took command of the 82nd Airborne Division in August 1944, becoming—at thirty-seven—the youngest division commander in the U.S. Army since the Civil War. He led the division in the invasion of Holland, the Battle of the Bulge, and the assault into Germany in 1945. Gavin's troops were selected to be America's Honor Guard in Soviet-occupied Berlin, and they represented the entire Army in the Victory Parade in New York City in early 1946. Gavin retired as a three-star general and later served as the ambassador to France under President John F. Kennedy. During Gavin's time in Paris, the irascible Charles de Gaulle decided he no longer needed a U.S. military presence in his country. He summoned Gavin and told the ambassador he wanted all American soldiers out of France. Gavin, mindful of the American boys resting in cemeteries from the English Channel to the German border, said, "Yes, Mr. President. Does that include our dead?"[2]

Gavin was an early critic of American involvement in Vietnam. After a 1967 visit, he urged negotiations to end the war "by any means available."[3]

Gavin remained active with veterans organizations—particularly those of the 82nd Airborne and especially his beloved 505th Parachute Infantry Regiment—until his death from Parkinson's disease in 1990. He is buried at West Point.

Bob Murphy, who was an eighteen-year-old pathfinder on D-Day and fought with A Company at La Fière, returned to Boston and law school after the war. He wrote a book in 1999 because he noticed a shortage of detailed memoirs from the most junior soldiers.

"Many of the details [about past battles] come from officers that [sic] made personal notes and official entries in order to refresh their recollection years later when writing books or assisting military historians.

"But it was the low ranking soldiers, the privates, the sergeants and the junior officers who fought the war in the front lines. These were the men who fired the rifles, bazookas and cannons and who were wounded and bled. They endured the cold or fever and lived from hour to hour, rather than from day to day. These young combat soldiers were not taking notes or keeping diaries. They weren't writers or correspondents. Most were in their early twenties with no more than a high school diploma.

"These men did not write about history, they made it."

Lieutenant Waverly Wray, who single-handedly destroyed the leadership of a German battalion and thus thwarted a massive counterattack on Ste. Mère Eglise on D+1, was killed by a sniper during Operation Market Garden (the invasion of Holland) on September 19, 1944. Ben Vandervoort, Wray's battalion commander, recommended Wray for a Medal of Honor, calling him the "Sergeant York of World War II." The award was downgraded to a Distinguished Service Cross.

Lieutenant General (Retired) Jack Norton, who was the regimental operations officer of the 505th PIR in Normandy, tried for years to track down enough corroborating evidence of Wray's exploits to have the Medal of Honor awarded. But the battle had been too fluid, too much time had passed, and many potential witnesses did not survive the war.

The current headquarters of the 505th Parachute Infantry Regiment, which is still a part of the 82nd Airborne Division at Fort Bragg, North Carolina, is located in Wray Hall.

The communications man Ed Misencik, who was rescued from drowning in the Merderet by his quick-thinking sergeant, was still with the division in July when they moved to the Channel coast for evacuation. When they stepped out onto Utah Beach, Misencik and his buddies were struck dumb by the vast number of ships, the tons of supplies, the sheer spectacle of the Allied armies still pouring ashore more than a month after D-Day. Misencik saw a German prisoner of war standing nearby, also waiting, also dumbfounded. He looked at the paratroopers and said in English, "Hitler lied. He said we could push you back into the sea, but he lied. It was never possible."

Ed Misencik married Anna Hornyak in 1946 and became a police officer in Cleveland, Ohio. For years, Ed suffered dreadful nightmares. He would roll off the bed in the middle of the night, yelling warnings about the artillery and gunfire that had killed so many of his friends, that still chased him in his dreams. Anna sat on the floor and held his sweat-soaked body until the nightmares passed. Later, their son wrote, "It took years for those dreams to disappear [but] her love and tenderness finally won."

John Dolan, who commanded A Company of the 505th PIR in Normandy, returned some thirty years later with one of his former soldiers. Dolan had traveled thousands of miles to visit the bridge at La Fière, where his company was savaged by German artillery and tanks, where the wounded and dying lay in their foxholes because nothing could move above ground.

"Let's go," Dolan said, turning to leave after a minute or two. "Too many bad memories." He never went back.

AUTHOR'S NOTE

In late spring, the Merderet River moves slowly and quietly under the arched stone bridge at La Fière. To the west lies a wide plain that floods with the winter rains. To the east, the road climbs a wooded hill before ambling toward the village of Ste. Mère Eglise, with its ancient stone church and lovely shops crouched shoulder to shoulder around the square.

On the gentle slope of a hill fifty yards from the river's edge stands a statue of an American paratrooper. He clutches his weapon as he peers out across the plain to the west, as if still on guard.

This is the place the veterans told me about, where, for three days in June 1944, a few hundred American paratroopers placed themselves in the enemy's path to protect the still-vulnerable landing beaches. It was across this picturesque bridge that their comrades attacked to enlarge the foothold the Allies had gained in France.

I expected something grand, something larger, that befit the events that took place here. But you can walk to every corner of the battlefield in an hour, and you might not see another person. I'd studied the battle from the generals' point of view, but I wanted to know about the individuals who fought here. What did they see as the sun rose on June 6? Were they still wet from being dumped onto the flooded plain? Were they hungry? Were they frightened? Did they put on brave airs because they saw the men around them acting bravely? Did they pray?

Those are the stories I wanted to learn and tell.

This work is based on interviews with World War II veterans of the 82nd Airborne Division. I have yet to speak to one of these men who considers himself part of the "Greatest Generation." To a man they told me, "I was just doing my job." They wanted to get the war over with, get home, and get on with their lives. Many of them did not make it, and my interview subjects lent their time and effort to this project to honor the comrades they lost.

It is obvious that memory fades over sixty years. It is also evident to these combat veterans that no two men—even if they shared the same foxhole—will remember a particular incident in the same way. I have used my own research and the work of other historians to develop the larger framework of this story, and I am solely responsible for any errors. I have relied on the veterans' memories to give the portrait color, to capture the emotions, to portray the terror, the fortitude, the humor, the creativity, and the unbearable sadness of so many lives cut short.

My special thanks go to these veterans: Roy Creek, Bob Murphy, Fred Morgan, Robert Franco, Wheatley Christensen, Dean McCandless, Arthur "Dutch" Schultz, Jack Norton, Ken Russell, Otis Sampson, Berge Avadanian, Anthony Antoniou, Bill Blank, Francis Buck, Fred Caravelli, George Clark, Chuck Copping, Les Cruise, Larry Dudley, Bill Dunfee, Harold Eatman, Bob Fielder, John Gallo, Joe Tallet, Bob Gillette, George Jacobus, Gerald Johnson, Bob McGee, Bob Piper, Ed Ryan, Walter Winton, Ed Sayre.

I am also indebted to the following people for their generous help and advice: Phil Nordyke, Mike Ekman, Nick Springer, Martin Morgan, Mark Bando, Jim Blankenship, Katie Troccoli, John Sparry, Gloria Heim, Star Jorgensen, Annie McIlvoy Zaya, Barbara Gavin Fauntleroy, Rick Misencik, Keith Schneider, Jennifer Pouchot.

Merci to ICL Graphics, Valognes, France; Office of the Mayor, Ste. Mère Eglise, France.

And thank you, Marcia, my best friend, my wife, and a truly generous soul.

Ed Ruggero
Wallingford, Pennsylvania
January 2006

NOTES

My first book about World War II paratroopers, *Combat Jump: The Young Men Who Led the Assault into Fortress Europe, July 1943* (New York: HarperCollins, 2003), was based mostly on interviews with veterans of the 505th Regimental Combat team. When I began writing this book, my intention was to use the same methods and write only about the 505th PIR in Normandy. Sadly, many of the men I had come to know had passed away. I widened the scope of the book to include the entire 82nd Airborne Division and thus widened the pool of likely interview subjects. In addition to the interviews, I have relied upon published and unpublished histories, memoirs, and letters to help me re-create the months before D-Day and those crucial first three days in France. Unless otherwise indicated, stories that appear in this book are drawn from my interviews. My goal was always to note the tremendous sacrifices made by these soldiers, without ever glorifying war.

PROLOGUE

1. Headquarters, 82nd Airborne Division. *82nd Airborne Division Operations in Normandy, France, June–July 1944,* Fall 1944.

2. Ibid., Annex 1 C.

3. James M. Gavin, *On to Berlin* (New York: Viking Press, 1978), 106.

4. Covering up insignia of rank was a practice in the Pacific but had not been in the 82nd. To his credit, Gavin admitted in his memoir *On to Berlin* that he should have discovered this in training, not after they arrived in Normandy.

5. Otis Sampson, who made all five combat jumps with the 505th, said that after a combat jump, soldiers had a tendency to spend time reliving and sharing stories about the jump, as if the jump (and not the ensuing combat) was the biggest challenge. Alan Langdon, the 505th PIR historian (who would be wounded at La Fière), attributes some of this business of a slow start to the quick

transition from a no-shooting training environment to one in which soldiers are expected to kill. Incoming fire, Langdon noted, usually got the men focused. (Langdon, quoted in Clay Blair, *Ridgway's Paratroopers: The American Airborne in World War II* [Garden City, N.Y.: Dial Press, 1985], 233.) Roy Creek was satisfied because the men immediately around him responded when he ordered them. Gavin, trying to assert authority through layers of disorganized command, had more difficulty. Thus the two men had different impressions of how cooperative the soldiers on the bank were that night.

6. Roy E. Creek, *The Operations of a Mixed Group from Units of the 507th Parachute Infantry (82nd Airborne Division) in the Invasion of France, 5–7 June 1944 (Normandy Campaign): Personal Experience of a Company Commander,* Advanced Infantry Officers Class No. I, 1948, 6.

7. Gavin, *On to Berlin*, 106–8.

8. Clay Blair, *Ridgway's Paratroopers: The American Airborne in World War II* (Garden City, N.Y.: Dial Press, 1985), 234.

CHAPTER 1. THE GATHERING HOST

1. While the movie *Sergeant York* does address York's religious doubts about taking human life, it does not portray his efforts to convince Americans that the United States should stay out of the European war. Before the Japanese attack on Pearl Harbor, York had changed his mind, and he saw the Axis, particularly the Nazis, as an evil that had to be eradicated. The plainspoken celebrity even visited his old division, suggesting to its commander, Omar Bradley, that the soldiers practice marksmanship in a wooded setting, to better prepare them for the kind of shooting they would have to do on the battlefield.

2. Quoted in Clay Blair, *Ridgway's Paratroopers: The American Airborne in World War II* (Garden City, N.Y.: Dial Press, 1985), 30.

3. Colonel (Retired) Ed Sayre telephone interview.

4. Ridgway did not accompany the division to Ireland but was called back to the States by George Marshall for meetings on how the airborne forces would be employed in the invasion of France. Ridgway put Ralph "Doc" Eaton, his Chief of Staff, in charge during his absence. Eaton later wrote: "Ridgway gave me three important tasks: 1) Get the division to Ireland; 2) Get his Cadillac staff car—an old rattletrap—to Ireland; 3) Get that wine and brandy cache from the secret room in the Naples hotel suite to Ireland. I loaded the Caddy and the booze, packed under a tarp in a trailer, on board our ship. A high-ranking Army staff officer said, 'What the hell is that Caddy doing on this ship!' I said it was Ridgway's staff car. He said, 'Well get it off right now!' So I lost his car. One day off the coast of Ireland there was a great hullabaloo in the Merchant Marine crew. They were all drunk! I thought, 'Uh-oh' and rushed down into the hold to the booze trailer. Sure enough, it was completely empty. They had stolen it all. But I got the division there!" Quoted in Blair, *Ridgway's Paratroopers*, 170–71.

5. Allen L. Langdon, *"Ready": A World War II History of the 505th Parachute Infantry Regiment* (Indianapolis: 82nd Airborne Division Educational Fund, 1986), 35.

6. Northern Ireland was then, as it is now, part of the British Empire. The Republic of Ireland, to the south, was officially neutral during the war.

7. Paul Fussell, *Wartime: Understanding and Behavior in the Second World War* (New York: Oxford University Press, 1989), 200–1.

8. Dennis G. O'Loughlin, "Fierce Individualists: U.S. Paratroopers in WWII," unpublished memoir.

9. Quoted in Blair, *Ridgway's Paratroopers,* 170.

10. James M. Gavin, *On to Berlin* (New York: Viking Press, 1978), 78.

11. Ibid., 83.

12. Blair, *Ridgway's Paratroopers,* 74.

13. Matthew B. Ridgway, *Soldier: The Memoirs of Matthew B. Ridgway* (New York: Curtis, 1956). 68.

14. In his memoir, *On to Berlin,* Gavin refutes the claims of several British historians who wrote, after the war, in disparaging terms of the American contribution. Of particular note is Gavin's dissatisfaction with a writer named Norman Lewis, who in 1972 published an article titled "Mafia Wins Sicily for the U. S. Army," in the magazine section of a London newspaper. Lewis claimed that the "Italo-German forces in the area [of the U.S. invasion] had been intelligently pulled back some 30 miles from the American beachhead and had taken up defensive positions." According to Lewis, this was accomplished through the intercession of the American gangster Lucky Luciano, who was in Sicily during the war. Gavin says, "Either this is totally untrue or the Hermann Goering Division and the Livorno Division did not get the word [to pull back and leave the Americans alone]—an unlikely event." Gavin wrote that both the German and Italian commanders in Sicily were "hell-bent on throwing the U.S. divisions into the sea and destroying the U.S. 1st and 4th Divisions, which were ashore." *On to Berlin,* 49.

15. Gavin, *On to Berlin,* 83.

16. On the sixtieth anniversary of D-Day in 2004, visiting heads of state attended an outdoor event at Arromanches, where the French president decorated Allied veterans in the shadow of a German artillery fire direction center that is now part of a monument. Visitors who stand atop this monument can see the whole sweep of beach that was the original landing zone. The German artillerymen who built the post would have been able to see—and cover with fire—the same stretch.

17. Carlo D'Este, *Eisenhower: A Soldier's Life* (New York: Henry Holt, 2002), 461–62.

18. Ibid., 462.

19. Ibid., 467.

20. Ibid., 492.

21. In the United States, a boatbuilder named Andrew Higgins worked tirelessly to perfect a landing craft, later called the "Higgins boat," that was economical to build. Higgins's obsession with landing craft—their numbers, delivery dates, production time, ratio of steel to wood, speed, and draft—paid handsome dividends for the Allies. Tens of thousands of soldiers rode to battle on his boats. Ike called Higgins "the man who won the war." Stephen E. Ambrose, *D-Day, June 6, 1944: The Climactic Battle of World War II* (New York: Touchstone, 1994), 45.

22. Roger Hesketh, *Fortitude: The D-Day Deception Campaign* (Woodstock, N.Y.: Overlook Press, 2000), xi.

23. Allied planners were careful because the Germans had used some of the very same deception tactics on the eastern front, to make the Soviets think that the main thrust of 1942 would be aimed at Moscow, not at Stalingrad. The German effort, code-named Kreml, was similar to Fortitude. Ambrose, *D-Day*, 81.

24. Hesketh, *Fortitude*, xv.

CHAPTER 2. TRAIN THOROUGHLY

1. James M. Gavin, *On to Berlin* (New York: Viking Press, 1978), 89.

2. The British 6th Airborne used this aspect to full advantage in the D-Day assault on Pegasus Bridge at the extreme eastern end of the Allied sector. British glider troops of D Company, Oxfordshire and Buckinghamshire Infantry, landed on top of the German defenders and achieved almost complete surprise. Major John Howard's company seized the bridge, thus securing the right flank of the British lodgment.

3. Captain Al Ireland, a 505 paratrooper who made the combat jumps into Sicily and Italy, went into Normandy on a glider to accompany the critical antitank guns the gliders carried. Asked about the ride and crash landing, he said, "Those guys don't get paid enough." Allen L. Langdon, *"Ready": A World War II History of the 505th Parachute Infantry Regiment* (Indianapolis: 82nd Airborne Division Educational Fund, 1986); 56.

4. Charles J. Masters, *Glidermen of Neptune: The American D-Day Glider Attack* (Carbondale, Ill.: Southern Illinois University Press, 1995), 19.

5. Information on U.S. gliders from ibid.

6. Quoted in Omar Bradley, *A Soldier's Story* (New York: Modern Library [reprint], 1999), 232–34.

7. One result of this back-and-forth was that some glider troops made a beach assault. Bradley wanted the 327th Glider Infantry (of the 101st Airborne Division) available for its missions near Carentan by noon on D-Day, but the restrictions on using gliders in the hours of darkness meant they would have to come across Utah Beach in a follow-on wave of the assault forces.

8. Clay Blair, *Ridgway's Paratroopers: The American Airborne in World War II* (Garden City, N.Y.: Dial Press, 1985), 177.

9. Ibid., 189.

10. Ibid., 544, note 19, letter from Gavin to Clay Blair.

11. Colonel (Retired) Mark Alexander interview.

12. Dennis G. O'Loughlin, "Fierce Individualists: U.S. Paratroopers in WWII," unpublished memoir.

13. Alexander interview.

14. During World War II nearly half a million Axis prisoners were sent to 511 work camps in the United States. There were 27 camps in Florida alone, where ten thousand former German soldiers worked in the citrus and cane fields. Road crews and work gangs of former German soldiers could eat in roadside diners from Florida to Texas, while African American GIs weren't allowed in the front door.

15. Blair, *Ridgway's Paratroopers*, 194.

16. Ibid., 194.

17. Ibid., 198.

18. In a letter written long after the war, Gavin would say that he should have been much harder on the 507th and 508th, who did not have the benefit of combat experience. Ibid.

CHAPTER 3. OPERATION NEPTUNE

1. In a 2003 interview Mark Alexander dismissed all consideration that Bill Ekman did not deserve the command. "He had the experience, and he had the confidence of the division commander. The important thing was to get the troops ready. There was plenty of work for everyone."

2. Photocopies of these cards supplied to the author by Colonel (Retired) Mike Ekman, Bill's son.

3. This form of punishment takes away from cadets their most valuable asset: free time. On weekends cadets on "area tours" march back and forth in the paved barracks area for hours at a time. Missing a formation might net a cadet five hours. A dirty belt buckle during an important inspection might cost an hour of a Saturday afternoon. The practice survives at West Point today.

4. Barbara Gavin Fauntleroy interview.

5. Gavin letter of Dec. 26, 1943, provided by Barbara Gavin Fauntleroy.

6. Gavin letter of Jan. 12, 1944.

7. In *On to Berlin* (New York: Viking Press, 1978), Gavin writes about the postwar interrogation of General Karl Student, who had commanded German airborne forces in Crete. Student claimed that the Germans had drawn up an elaborate plan detailing fictitious preparations for massive antiairborne obstacles throughout Normandy. Gavin never saw the document, meaning it probably never fell into Allied hands.

8. Gavin, *On to Berlin*, 96.

9. Carlo D'Este letter to author.

10. 82nd Airborne Division Headquarters, *82nd Airborne Division Operations in Normandy, France, June–July 1944,* Fall 1944; and Clay Blair, *Ridgway's Paratroopers: The American Airborne in World War II* (Garden City, N.Y.: Dial Press, 1985), 192–93.

CHAPTER 4. COUNTDOWN

1. Dwight D. Eisenhower, *Crusade in Europe* (New York: Doubleday, 1948), 246.

2. Ibid.

3. Schultz is portrayed in the Cornelius Ryan book *The Longest Day* and is one of the featured paratroopers in the 1962 movie of the same name (for which Ryan wrote the screenplay). In both of those stories Ryan portrays Schultz winning a great deal of money in a high-stakes dice game during the waiting period. Then the young private is stricken with thoughts of home. Feeling guilty about gambling, he rejoins the game determined to lose the money. The real Arthur Schultz has steadfastly maintained that the details in the movie were wrong. The game in which he won the money took place back in Quorn, before the 505th left for the departure airfields. Schultz did have a run of luck, breaking everyone in the game with the exception of one staff sergeant, a man Schultz disliked intensely. When the young private saw that his nemesis had only forty or fifty dollars left, Schultz decided to take the rest of the man's money and complete his humiliation. But Schultz's luck had run out, and he managed to lose the $2,500, all in trying to take the last $50 from this man he disliked. After the war Schultz explained to Cornelius Ryan that the details of the card game were wrong, and that there was nothing noble about how he eventually lost the money. In fact, he lost his winnings because of hubris. Ryan explained to the veteran that the book's version made for a better story. Arthur Schultz interview.

CHAPTER 5. ALL THAT BRAVERY AND DEVOTION TO DUTY COULD DO

1. Carlo D'Este, *Eisenhower: A Soldier's Life* (New York: Henry Holt, 2002), 524.

2. Quoted in ibid., 527.

3. Quoted in Paul Fussell, *Wartime: Understanding and Behavior in the Second World War* (New York: Oxford University Press, 1989), 296–97.

4. Quoted in Stephen E. Ambrose, *D-Day, June 6, 1944: The Climactic Battle of World War II* (New York: Touchstone, 1944), 193.

5. Jim Gavin had served with the 25th Infantry Regiment shortly after his graduation from West Point in 1929. (T. M. Booth and Duncan Spencer, *Paratrooper: The Life of General James M. Gavin* [New York: Simon and Schuster, 1994], 47–48.) Bob Sink, who would command the 506th PIR of the 101st Air-

borne Division—the regiment made famous by Stephen Ambrose's *Band of Brothers*—also served with Creek at Huachuca. Roy Creek interview.

6. Creek interview.

CHAPTER 6. A FIRE-LIT SKY

1. The storage building is no longer there but is clearly visible in period photographs. Ste. Mère Eglise enjoys a thriving tourist industry built around the invasion, as does the entire area, called simply Le Debarquement on the highway signs. But the area is not crassly commercial, and visitors, particularly American visitors, still get the sense that the French recognize and appreciate the sacrifices the Allies made here. In 2004, returning veterans of the 82nd and 101st Airborne Divisions were greeted everywhere as heroes. One veteran told me he was touched most not by the many official ceremonies but by a French child, who handed him a flower and said a simple *"Merci."*

2. The house was located on the site of the current museum in Ste. Mère Eglise.

3. Allen L. Langdon, *"Ready": A World War II History of the 505th Parachute Infantry Regiment* (Indianapolis: 82nd Airborne Division Educational Fund, 1986), 49.

4. Murphy vehemently disputes Stephen Ambrose's claim that the air crews were poorly trained. He said a group of C47 Troop Carrier vets even wanted Murphy, a trial lawyer after the war, to sue Ambrose's estate. Bob Murphy interview.

5. Cornelius Ryan, in *The Longest Day*, has Murphy landing in a garden and being accosted by a startled Frenchwoman, who reports to the mayor and pastor. Murphy did not land in anyone's yard and even told Ryan that he had the facts wrong. Ryan replied by smiling and saying, "Well, it's a good story." Murphy interview.

6. The total of 378 aircraft comes from 82nd Airborne Division Headquarters, *82nd Airborne Division Operations in Normandy, France, June–July 1944*, Fall 1944, 3.

7. Ibid., 7.

8. Ken Russell interview.

9. Steele's experience was made famous in the book and movie *The Longest Day*. Steele, who survived the war, often returned to Ste. Mère Eglise for reunions after the war. Because D-Day tourism is big business in Normandy, a dummy paratrooper with a white chute hangs, more or less permanently, from the church steeple in Ste. Mère Eglise.

10. Maughn befriended the family and visited with them after the war. The little girl later told him the story from her perspective.

11. Ed Misencik unpublished memoir and interviews conducted by son, Rick Misencik, February 2003.

12. *82nd Airborne Division Operations in Normandy, France*, Annex 1 D (1).

13. Letter from James Coyle quoted in Otis Sampson unpublished memoir.

14. Langdon, *"Ready,"* 53.

15. Langdon, in his well-researched and reliable history, *"Ready,"* says Krause arrived at the northeast corner of the town, but this seems unlikely, as it would have been a roundabout route from the drop zone and would have required Krause to cross the N13. Since he did not know the extent of any defenses waiting for him, this would have been unnecessary. Even if the Frenchman lived on the northeast corner and was most familiar with that area, it seems unlikely, given that the town is so small, that he would have felt it necessary to go back to that point. He probably would have known the most direct route.

16. Ibid., 54.

17. In *Night Drop*, S. L. A. Marshall has this incident occurring on June 7. Langdon, in *"Ready,"* says that his fact-checking with the men involved puts it early on D-Day.

18. DiTullio was awarded the Distinguished Service Cross for this action, though he did not live to see the medal. He was killed in Ste. Mère Eglise on June 7.

CHAPTER 7. OUR SONS

1. The huge flag Krause carried into France and hung from the Ste. Mère Eglise city hall is on display there at the top of the main staircase. Krause's widow donated the flag to the people of Ste. Mère Eglise after the war.

2. My interviews with Anthony Antoniou took place nearly sixty years after D-Day. He had long ago come to grips with things he had seen and done, but the memory of the dying GI's anguished night struck a chord with him. When I asked if the man survived, Antoniou, who had remarkable recall for an eighty-year-old, said he could not remember.

3. Ibid.

4. Twenty-seven of Vandervoort's thirty-six sticks hit the drop zone or landed within a mile of it, and probably five minutes ahead of schedule. Allen L. Langdon, *"Ready": A World War II History of the 505th Parachute Infantry Regiment* (Indianapolis: 82nd Airborne Division Educational Fund, 1986), 49.

5. Ibid., 55.

6. Otis Sampson memoir, 220.

7. S. L. A. Marshall says the men ran; see his *Night Drop: The American Airborne Invasion of Normandy* (Nashville, Tenn.: Battery Press, 1962). Sampson reports in his memoir that he walked beside and spoke to Turnbull, and that he didn't see anyone running.

8. Sampson memoir, 206.

9. Lieutenant Turner Turnbull was killed by German artillery fire on June 7. The U.S. Army historian S. L. A. Marshall points out that Ste. Mère Eglise not

only gave the 82nd Airborne Division a secure base but helped stabilize the flank of the entire corps struggling ashore that day. The British historian John Keegan says of Turnbull, "He belongs with those who saved the invasion." Quoted in Langdon, *"Ready,"* 57. Many of the wounded men Turnbull was forced to leave behind were rescued by advancing American forces. Private First Class Roy A. Stark, who was seriously wounded in the fight and stayed with the medic James Kelly, was captured and brought to a German hospital in Cherbourg; he was freed when that city fell to the Americans on June 27. Many of the other D Company men were recovered on the night of June 7–8 when an American tank battalion overran Neuville au Plain and paratroopers from the 2nd Battalion of the 505th moved into the area again.

Sergeant Robert Niland, who led the tiny rear guard of Turnbull's platoon, was one of four brothers from the Niland family, of Tonawanda, New York, serving in the military. Three of them became casualties within a three-week span in 1944. Oldest brother Eddie was part of a bomber crew that was shot down in the China-Burma-India Theater on May 16, 1944. On June 8, his mother, Augusta Niland, received a telegram informing her that Eddie was missing in action. Sergeant Robert Niland, D Company, 505th PIR, was killed in Neuville on June 6, after volunteering to cover the withdrawal of his hard-pressed platoon. Lieutenant Preston Niland came ashore at Utah Beach with the 22nd Infantry Regiment, 4th Division, and was killed the next day northwest of the landing area. Sergeant Frederick "Fritz" Niland, H Company, 501th PIR, 101st Airborne Division, was misdropped south of Carentan on D-Day but found his unit and fought beside his comrades throughout the Normandy campaign. He returned to England with his company in July 1944. After learning of the Niland family's losses, Father Francis Sampson, the Catholic chaplain of the 501th PIR, requested that Fritz Niland be sent to safer duty in the States. Fritz wanted to stay in the theater and rejoin the fight but was shipped back to the United States. He served in a stateside post until the end of the war. Oldest brother Eddie Niland survived a stint in a Japanese prison camp and returned home after the war. Bob and Preston Niland are buried beside each other in the American Military Cemetery at Colleville sur Mer, above Omaha Beach. The story of the Niland family served as an inspiration for the 1998 movie *Saving Private Ryan*. From "Saving Sgt. Niland," Mark Bando, www.101airborneww2.com.

10. Marshall, *Night Drop*, 66.

11. One of the riskiest moves a man can make in close-quarters combat is attempting to surrender to an enemy he has been trying to kill. The closer and more furious the action, the less likely the enemy will pause for that critical second or two to determine if the surrender is real or a ruse. Roy Creek, who observed the action on the causeway from close by, was adamant, in a 2004 interview, that the American soldiers' actions were reasonable, given the circumstances and the almost unimaginable tension felt while sneaking up blindly on a

deadly enemy. Creek defies anyone who has not been in combat to understand
how difficult it is for a man already under fire and physically close to his enemy,
in his first combat action and startled by a sudden movement, to do anything but
shoot. "To this day, years later, I don't know if the enemy was trying to surrender
or not. I observed this whole action at very close range, and in my opinion, any
enemy shot during this attack, as close and intense as it was at time, had waited
too long to surrender. He was committed, as the attacker was, to [a] fight for survival."

CHAPTER 8. STE. MÈRE EGLISE

1. Clay Blair, *Ridgway's Paratroopers: The American Airborne in World War II*
(Garden City, N.Y.: Dial Press, 1985), 195.

2. S. L. A. Marshall, *Night Drop: The American Airborne Invasion of Normandy* (Nashville, Tenn.: Battery Press, 1962), 83.

3. 82nd Airborne Division Headquarters, *82nd Airborne Division Operations
in Normandy, France, June–July 1944*, Fall 1944, 3.

4. The major reinforcement by glider on D-Day, called Mission Elmira, used
both U.S.-made Waco and British Horsa gliders. Some 175 gliders landed in a little more than two hours, bringing parts of the 80th Airborne Antiaircraft Artillery,
the division artillery headquarters, A Company of the 307th Airborne Engineers,
the 307th Medical Company, the 319th and 320th Glider Field Artillery Regiments, as well as signals units and jeeps for the division headquarters. One hundred and thirty-seven of the 175 gliders were damaged or destroyed, mostly by
crash landing in the short fields.

5. Marshall, *Night Drop*, 85.

6. Gavin would later write that he had told troopers in the Sicily jump to attack the enemy where they could, but he revised his thinking after Normandy,
where German defenses were better and small groups of paratroopers didn't have
the firepower to take on the enemy.

CHAPTER 9. LA FIÈRE BRIDGE

1. Much of Dolan's story comes from a detailed letter he wrote to Gavin in
1959. The letter was forwarded by Gavin to Cornelius Ryan and is reprinted in
Robert M. Murphy, *No Better Place to Die* (Croton Falls, N.Y.: Critical Hit,
1999).

2. The bridge takes its name from the manor house, not from the nearby village of La Fière, which is called Le Bosc on modern maps.

3. Allen L. Langdon, *"Ready": A World War II History of the 505th Parachute
Infantry Regiment* (Indianapolis: 82nd Airborne Division Educational Fund,
1986), 66.

4. Ibid., 68.

5. In a 2004 interview the owner of Le Manoir la Fière, Monsieur Yves Pois-

son, said that the current manor house dates from the sixteenth century. The berm was the site of a watchtower and dates from the twelfth century.

6. Langdon, *"Ready,"* 72.

7. By D-Day in Normandy the British had quick-release mechanisms on their parachute harnesses. The Americans wouldn't develop them until the jump into Holland in September 1944.

8. This small-unit action at Le Manoir la Fière shows how difficult it is even for participants to keep straight what happened in a firefight. S. L. A. Marshall's account, in *Night Drop: The American Airborne Invasion of Normandy* (Nashville, Tenn.: Battery Press, 1962), and Dolan's account, in a lengthy 1959 letter to Gavin, have Presnell's platoon in the rear of the order of march. But the regimental historian Allen Langdon (himself a C Company soldier that day) says that Presnell set out for the river from the drop zone, in a "preplanned" move to flank the Germans at the manor house. It seems unlikely that Presnell would have been sent toward the bridge on a different track from the rest of the company (i.e., Langdon's "preplanned" flank movement), when Dolan had no idea what he might find at the bridge or on the way to the bridge. In fact, by the nature of A Company's excellent drop, Dolan had achieved what so many paratroop commanders wanted in those first hours: a concentrated force he could control. He had no reason to split his force before he ran into resistance. Sound tactics dictated that Dolan keep his force together until he could develop the enemy situation. Robert Murphy, the A Company pathfinder, wrote his memoir, *No Better Place to Die*, in 1999 and set out, according to his introduction, to correct mistakes he saw in earlier historical works. In an interview Murphy said that two men sitting ten yards apart will have completely different stories about the same action.

9. Murphy, *No Better Place to Die*, 23.

10. Ibid., 28.

11. Schwartzwalder went on to coach the Syracuse University football team to a national championship in 1959.

12. The 505th PIR historian, Allen Langdon, a paratrooper with C Company, 505th PIR, who was later wounded in the fighting at La Fière, believes that Schwartzwalder and company arrived before the main body of A Company, and that the machine gun that engaged Marr was the same one Presnell heard from his position near the lower, river road.

13. Martin K. Morgan, *Down to Earth: The 507th Parachute Infantry Regiment in Normandy, June 6–July 15, 1944* (Atglen, Pa.: Schiffer, 2004), 178.

14. Murphy, *No Better Place to Die*, 43.

15. For all the traffic in the area, Kellam and Lindquist were not in contact with each other and apparently did not speak that day.

16. Marshall's account of the end of the German defense of Le Manoir la Fière is significantly different from that offered by Langdon in *"Ready"* or Murphy in *No Better Place to Die*. In *"Ready"* Langdon (a 505 trooper) gives full credit for

the capture of Le Manoir la Fière to the men of A Company, 505th. Although Marshall was the Army's official historian, Langdon's account should not be discounted. Langdon spent years working on his book, interviewing his comrades, collecting letters and memoirs, and vetting his work with surviving officers (who tended to have more of an overview, since their job was to keep track of what was going on across the whole fight). Marshall also based his account on scores of interviews, many of them done by assistants not long after the action. The yard of the manor house, which is really a complex of stout stone buildings, is large enough for both of these actions to have taken place at nearly the same time. It is plausible that Oakley's platoon, attacking from the north side of the road, took some prisoners, while Schwartzwalder's men, attacking from the east and south, took other prisoners. The number of prisoners (twenty to twenty-five) noted in *"Ready"* may have been a final tally, or it may even have included other prisoners captured by the 1st Battalion, 505th PIR, during those first hours of D-Day.

17. In situations like this, the Americans had a distinct advantage with their semiautomatic M1 Garand, probably the finest infantry rifle in the war. The GI could fire one shot after another simply by pulling the trigger. The German soldiers carried the Mauser, a bolt-action rifle. Every time he fired, the soldier had to remove his hand from the trigger and pull back the bolt to seat another round, which made for a much slower rate of fire. An American GI could get off more shots than his German counterpart in the same amount of time.

18. Mattingly was awarded the Silver Star for his quick thinking and action, and later Lieutenant Marr would say, "It was the best piece of individual soldiering I've ever seen." Quoted in Morgan, *Down to Earth*, 179.

19. Murphy, *No Better Place to Die*, 35.

20. Marshall, *Night Drop*, 62.

CHAPTER 10. UNDER FIRE

1. Anthony Antoniou interview.

2. It has been very difficult, even for the veterans who were present, to agree on what time these events took place. Heim says it was around 1700, S. L. A. Marshall says it was 1730. Bob Murphy puts the time at 1600. Mark Alexander, the regimental executive officer, puts the time around 1400, and the official history of the 505th puts this first attack at around 1200 on D-Day.

3. Robert M. Murphy, *No Better Place to Die* (Croton Falls, N.Y.: Critical Hit, 1999), 45.

4. The tanks were French-built Renault models from the 100th Panzer Replacement Battalion. The infantrymen were from the 1057th Panzergrenadier Regiment, which was part of the German 91st Division.

5. Allen L. Langdon, *"Ready": A World War II History of the 505th Parachute Infantry Regiment* (Indianapolis: 82nd Airborne Division Educational Fund, 1986), 71. Fitt was killed in action on 13 June 1944.

6. Clay Blair, *Ridgway's Paratroopers: The American Airborne in World War II* (Garden City, N.Y.: Dial Press, 1985), 251.

7. Buck was evacuated across Utah Beach on June 8 or 9 and woke up in a troop train in England. Francis Buck interview.

8. During the late afternoon of D-Day, an order came from the division command post that the 507 and 508 men in the bridge area should pull back to the railroad cut along the Ste. Mère Eglise road to form a blocking position, in case the Germans broke through at the bridge. This force, which would be three-quarters of a mile closer to Ste. Mère Eglise, would also form a division reserve. When the word came down to the paratroopers at the bridge, some of the 505 men in adjacent positions thought the order to pull out applied to them as well, and so began moving back. Gavin intercepted some of these men and set them straight, but it was this partial withdrawal that led to a notation in the division log that 1st Battalion of the 505th PIR had lost La Fière Bridge. Langdon, *"Ready,"* 71.

9. Ibid., 71.

10. Mark Alexander interview.

11. Roy Creek interview.

12. These alert troops were under Lieutenant Malcolm D. Brannen, commander of Headquarters Company, 3rd Battalion, 508th PIR. Brannen later reported the incident to Ridgway "with great glee," Ridgway recalled. The American division commander responded: "Well, in our present situation, killing division commanders does not strike me as being particularly hilarious. But I congratulate you. I'm glad it was a German division commander you got." Clay Blair, *Ridgway's Paratroopers*, 277.

13. Ibid., 251.

14. *82nd Airborne Division Operations in Normandy, France, June–July 1944,* Fall 1944.

CHAPTER 11. COUNTERATTACK

1. Robert M. Murphy, *No Better Place to Die* (Croton Falls, N.Y.: Critical Hit, 1999), 56.

2. The drawbridge over the Caen Canal was renamed Pegasus Bridge (after the winged patron of the British Airborne) and became the center of British anniversary celebrations for sixty years.

3. The Roosevelts were a famously bellicose family. President Theodore Roosevelt led his Rough Riders up San Juan Hill in Cuba in 1898; Quentin Roosevelt, another of the president's sons, was an aviator in World War I and was killed in action. Brigadier General Theodore Roosevelt Jr.'s son, named Quentin after the uncle who died in the Great War, was an artilleryman with the 1st Division and came ashore at Omaha Beach on D-Day. Theodore Roosevelt Jr. died of a heart attack in July 1944 while in Normandy. For his actions throughout the campaign, he was awarded the Congressional Medal of Honor. He is buried at

the American Military Cemetery at St. Laurent sur la Mer, overlooking Omaha Beach. His brother Quentin was relocated to the same cemetery, and the two rest side by side.

4. Clay Blair, *Ridgway's Paratroopers: The American Airborne in World War II* (Garden City, N.Y.: Dial Press, 1985), 260.

5. Following the war, the British decided that the Horsa was not even airworthy, and the entire fleet was grounded. When Darryl F. Zanuck was preparing to film his epic 1962 movie about the invasion, *The Longest Day*, the new laws forced him to dismantle the Horsas he found in England and have them shipped to locations in France.

6. Other German assaults were planned to hit Ste. Mère Eglise from the south, but these were waylaid by the 101st Airborne Division and by the advance of Van Fleet's 8th Infantry, which was the only regiment of the 4th Division to reach its D-Day objectives. Allen L. Langdon, *"Ready": A World War II History of the 505th Parachute Infantry Regiment* (Indianapolis: 82nd Airborne Division Educational Fund, 1986), 58–59.

7. Ed Ruggero, *Combat Jump: The Young Men Who Led the Assault into Fortress Europe, July 1943* (New York: HarperCollins, 2003), 100.

8. Langdon, *"Ready,"* 61.

9. Soldiers on both sides traded in stories of atrocities and deceptions committed by the other side. General George Patton, in remarks made to his soldiers before the invasion of Sicily, said the Germans and Italians would feign surrender and then kill their would-be captors. Captain John T. Compton, C Company, 180th Infantry Regiment, 45th Infantry Division, used Patton's remarks (successfully) in his own defense when he was court-martialed for killing unarmed Italian prisoners on Sicily in July 1943. Carlo D'Este, *Bitter Victory: The Battle for Sicily, 1943* (New York: HarperCollins, 1988), 318, 612–13.

10. In *"Ready,"* 65–66, Langdon writes: "[A] number of errors were made by the ETO historian, Colonel S.L.A. Marshall, in reporting the last battle for Ste. Mère Eglise by units of the 2nd Battalion, 505. . . . [T]hese errors have been self-perpetuating in that almost every history, including the official U. S. Army History, 'Cross Channel Attack,' has repeated them. The major error in reporting the 2nd Battalion's fight was to place the 8th Infantry Regiment in it. Every veteran who was in a position to know saw nothing of the 8th Infantry until the fight was over. There is no doubt that unit did carry the fight on to the north as their positions for that night are well documented as being just short of, and east of Neuville au Plain. The possibility remains that they did encounter other German units and fought them, and so the supposition was made by Marshall that it was all one and the same fight. Napier Crookenden, in his excellent (but not error-free) history, 'Drop Zone Normandy,' apparently discovered the error and eliminated it as on page 159 he states 'and Company E went forward without waiting for the 8th Infantry.' In that same paragraph another possible discrepancy crops

up where it says, 'By now a 4th Division Artillery forward observer had reached Vandervoort's CP and a barrage was arranged. At 5:15 PM the barrage fell. . . .' No veteran who participated in this attack recalled or believes that there was a preliminary artillery barrage. If there was it must have fallen on distant targets. Marshall refutes the idea that there was an artillery barrage in his manuscript, 'Regimental Study #6, The Capture of Ste. Mère Eglise,' Page 61, he wrote, 'at first there had been some thought of getting artillery support . . . the opposing lines were drawn too close for such fire to be both safe and effective.' The jeep patrol by Coyle at almost the 11th hour also seems to refute the idea of the artillery observer and barrage. That leads to the questions of why the Germans bunched up in the small lane. This may have been partially answered by a glider pilot who had been captured by the Germans and was with them at the time. He told Otis Sampson, after the fight was over and he had been liberated, that Sampson's first few rounds were 'overs' and that caused the Germans to run for the nebulous shelter of the lane. There are lesser errors by Marshall. One [was] that the charge by Hupfer's tanks and the attack by E company were [part of] a coordinated action. They weren't. Neither unit had any idea of the other. The 'coordinated action' tanks came from Colonel Raff's 'Howell Force' and although they were from the same battalion, they were from different companies [that] made totally different landings on Utah Beach. Also, there were just two of them, not six as Marshall states, which every veteran and especially Eugene Doerfler (Colonel, Retired) who brought them up can attest to. Lastly, General Collins did not witness the attack as reported by Marshall. This is refuted by the General's own autobiography, 'Lightning Joe' . . . Pages 204–205." Author's note: *"Ready"* uses nonstandard punctuation, which I have corrected in the interest of clarity.

CHAPTER 12. NO BETTER PLACE TO DIE

1. Robert M. Murphy, *No Better Place to Die* (Croton Falls, N.Y.: Critical Hit, 1999), 57.

2. Ibid., 59.

3. Ibid., 60.

4. Bob Murphy interview.

5. Murphy, *No Better Place to Die*, 66–67.

CHAPTER 13. FIRST ASSAULT

1. Clay Blair, *Ridgway's Paratroopers: The American Airborne in World War II* (Garden City, N.Y.: Dial Press, 1985), 267.

2. William G. Lord, *History of the 508th Parachute Infantry* (Nashville, Tenn.: Battery Press, 1977), 25.

3. Some French civilians had reported the ford's existence to various units, but the information was either dismissed or not deemed important enough to pass on.

4. S. L. A. Marshall, *Night Drop: The American Airborne Invasion of Normandy* (Nashville, Tenn.: Battery Press, 1962), 117.

5. Ibid., 119.

6. Martin K. Morgan, *Down to Earth: The 507th Parachute Infantry Regiment in Normandy, June 6–July 15, 1944* (Atlgen, Pa.: Schiffer, 2004), 203–6.

7. Charles DeGlopper was awarded the Medal of Honor for his actions. He is buried in the Maple Grove Cemetery, Grand Island, New York.

CHAPTER 14. THE GAUNTLET

1. Both S. L. A. Marshall and Clay Blair call it the 2nd Battalion of the 325th GIR. The 82nd Airborne Division after-action report and Jim Gavin's memoir call it the 3rd Battalion of the 325th GIR, as does Order of Battle marker in France.

2. Clay Blair, *Ridgway's Paratroopers: The American Airborne in World War II* (Garden City, N.Y.: Dial Press, 1985), 270.

3. Ibid., 271.

4. Ibid., 272.

5. In his memoir, *On to Berlin* (New York: Viking Press, 1978), Gavin indicates that this conversation with Carrell took place when he called the battalion commander forward for final coordination, which would have been some minutes before the attack was to jump off. In his note to Clay Blair, author of *Ridgway's Paratroopers*, Gavin writes that Carrell's moment of hesitation came at the very time of the attack. The first explanation is more plausible, since Carrell's replacement, Arthur Gardner, had time to come up and position himself with his troops. Carrell transferred out of the division because, Ridgway wrote, he wasn't battalion command material and "I will not permit him to command one." Carrell transferred to 90th Division, which he had helped mobilize and train. There he commanded a regular infantry battalion and was wounded in combat. But he was forced to retire at his permanent rank of captain in 1947. He said, "This incident was and has been very painful to me. The way it was done. No chain of command and no consideration. . . . This was rather precipitous and brutal since we were recently attached to the 82nd. I was treated very badly. It was unfair to all of us." Carrell died in 1990. Quoted in Blair, *Ridgway's Paratroopers*, 273.

6. S. L. A. Marshall, *Night Drop: The American Airborne Invasion of Normandy* (Nashville, Tenn.: Battery Press, 1962), 138.

7. Blair, *Ridgway's Paratroopers*, 273.

8. Marshall, *Night Drop*, 140.

9. Marshall says Wason was killed in this rush on the gun. Bevrijdingsmuseum, *Roll of Honor: 82nd Airborne Division, World War Two* (Groesbeek, The Netherlands, Nijmegen University Press, 1997), says Wason died of his wounds on June 11. Second Lieutenant Donald B. Wason is buried in New York's Long Island National Cemetery.

10. Marshall, *Night Drop*, 141.

11. The wall is repaired today, but the outlines of the breach are still clearly visible.

12. In *Night Drop*, Marshall takes some pains to make the point that the 325 soldiers who did make it to the western shore pressed the attack and had at least a tenuous hold of the bridgehead from early in the fight. Gavin's memoir, *On to Berlin*, and Blair's *Ridgway's Paratroopers* are written from the point of view of someone standing on the eastern, or La Fière, end of the causeway. Gavin's impression—that the attack was badly stalled and in danger of failing—was informed by what he saw from his end: the men piled up behind the stone wall, the malingerers trickling back, the wounded and unwounded alike hiding in the ditches. He had the painful duty of relieving Carrell, and of watching Sauls and a handful of men dash across the bridge alone. He could not see those same men, like Sauls, Sergeant Ericsson, and Lieutenant Wason, who were attacking aggressively on the far bank. Captain Robert Rae of the 507th PIR, whom Gavin had tapped to make the charge across the causeway, later took his cue on what had happened at La Fière from Gavin. The general told Rae the attack was failing, that the situation was desperate, that Rae and his men had to save the day. Rae did everything that was asked of him, at great risk and at great cost. It was only natural that he believed that he and his men *had* saved the day. But the glider troops on the west end of the causeway were not in the dire straits that Gavin and others thought. Some of them—many of them, even—faltered in the face of what looked like a suicide mission, beginning with their own commander. But others made the run and fought bravely on the other side. This takes nothing away from Rae and his men, but it might be that Rae's paratroopers did not, single-handedly, save the western bridgehead.

13. Marshall says in *Night Drop* that Gavin gave the order directly to Rae, bypassing Maloney and thus giving Rae even more of a sense that things were desperate. Gavin's memoir says he "signaled" Rae (*On to Berlin*, 117) and that Rae and his men—somewhat less than the ninety he'd brought into the position two days before—jumped up and became the latest group to throw themselves into the deadly tangle on the bridge. It is significant that "Rae Company" was not a real unit made up of men who knew one another and had trained together. Instead, it was an ad hoc group of paratroopers put together by Maloney under the command of one of the three ranking officers he found on the east bank. In the kind of deadly situation the men faced on the causeway, they could be expected to perform better for leaders they knew, and beside comrades who knew them, than for a relative stranger from the Regimental Service Company who just happened to be wearing captain's bars. That they advanced at all is a testament to the bravery and selflessness of the individual soldiers, and the pride they felt at being paratroopers. Like Harney's F Company, Rae's men stalled among the wounded men and disabled tanks just east of the bridge. Incoming German artillery fire wounded several troopers. Like Harney, Rae grabbed the soldiers by

their shirts, yelled, and pushed them until most of them got up and started moving again.

14. Blair, *Ridgway's Paratroopers*, 275.

15. Marshall calls him Mentli, but the *Roll of Honor* lists him as Lewis S. Mentlik.

16. According to Blair in *Ridgway's Paratroopers*, Lewis harbored "no bitterness" toward Ridgway and took his relief "philosophically." Lewis wrote to Ridgway from Walter Reed Army Hospital in Washington (where he was operated on in September 1944 for cancer) that he thought Ridgway was the "best division commander in the United States Army and a wonderful man." Lewis died of his cancer in early 1945.

17. There is some confusion among the available historical accounts. Gavin says in his memoir, *On to Berlin*, that when he arrived at the western end of the causeway, the "situation was deteriorating badly," and that Herb Stitler, the executive officer of the 325th, now in command, was preparing to withdraw. From Gavin's perspective, it looked like the whole thing was collapsing, so he pushed Rae back into the action. S. L. A. Marshall, the historian of the theater, is adamant that Harney and his troops were not in danger of collapsing, even if it looked to Stitler like it was time to pull out. One plausible explanation: from Stitler's command post the situation looked lost, while the men in the hedgerows still holding the line were convinced that they could hang on. Marshall wrote that Rae exaggerated the contributions made by his men, not out of any need to grab glory—they had certainly shown courage enough to merit any accolades—but only because he was not in a position to see the whole fight. Marshall believes that it was the glidermen, especially those under Harney, who stabilized the line and held the bridgehead for the All Americans.

EPILOGUE

1. 82nd Airborne Division Headquarters, *82nd Airborne Division Operations in Normandy, France, June–July 1944, Fall 1944*.

2. Related by General (Retired) P. X. Kelley, former commandant of the U.S. Marine Corps.

3. *Time* magazine, March 5, 1990, 69.

WORKS CITED

Albright, Barry E. *Operations of the 2nd Battalion, 508th Parachute Infantry Regiment (82nd Airborne Division) in the Invasion of Normandy, June 5–13, 1944 (Normandy Campaign): Personal Experience and Observation of a Rifle Platoon Leader.* Advanced Infantry Officers Class No. II, 1949.

Ambrose, Stephen E. *Band of Brothers: E Company, 506th Regiment, 101st Airborne from Normandy to Hitler's Eagle's Nest.* New York: Touchstone, 2001.

———. *Citizen Soldiers: The U.S. Army from the Normandy Beaches to the Bulge to the Surrender of Germany, June 7, 1944–May 7, 1945.* New York: Simon and Schuster, 1997.

———. *The Supreme Commander: The War Years of Dwight D. Eisenhower.* Garden City, N.Y.: Doubleday, 1970.

———. *D-Day, June 6, 1944: The Climactic Battle of World War II.* New York: Touchstone, 1994.

Andrews, John. "Airborne Album Normandy." Unpublished memoir, 1993.

Badsey, Stephen. *D-Day: The Strategy, The Men, The Equipment.* London: Salamander Books, 1993.

———. *Normandy, 1944.* Campaign series. Oxford: Osprey, 1990.

Balkoski, Joseph. *Beyond the Beachhead: The 29th Infantry Division in Normandy.* Mechanicsburg, Pa.: Stackpole Books, 1989.

Barger, Allan C. *War and People: A Veteran's Own Story.* Port Orchard, Wash.: Self-published memoir, 2001.

Bernage, Georges. *The Guide: The D-Day Landing Beaches.* Bayeux, France: Heimdal, 2001.

Bevrijdingsmuseum. *Roll of Honor: 82nd Airborne Division, World War Two.* Groesbeek, The Netherlands: Nijmegen University Press, 1997.

Blair, Clay. *Ridgway's Paratroopers: The American Airborne in World War II.* Garden City, N.Y.: Dial Press, 1985.

Booth, T. M., and Duncan Spencer. *Paratrooper: The Life of General James M. Gavin.* New York: Simon and Schuster, 1994.

Bradley, Omar. *A Soldier's Story.* New York: Modern Library (reprint), 1999.

Burriss, T. Moffatt. *Strike and Hold: A Memoir of the 82nd Airborne in World War II.* Dulles, Va.: Brassey's, 2000.

Collier, Richard. *D-Day: 06-06-1944.* London: Seven Dials, Cassell, 1999.

Creek, Roy E. *The Operations of a Mixed Group from Units of the 507th Parachute Infantry (82nd Airborne Division) in the Invasion of France, 5–7 June 1944 (Normandy Campaign): Personal Experience of a Company Commander.* Advanced Infantry Officers Class No. I, 1948.

Crookenden, Napier. *Dropzone Normandy.* New York: Charles Scribner's Sons, 1976.

Davidson, Edward, and Dale Manning. *Chronology of World War Two.* London: Cassell, 1999.

Davis, Larry. *C-47 Skytrain in Action.* Carrolton, Tex.: Squadron/Signal Publications, 1995.

D'Este, Carlo. *Bitter Victory: The Battle for Sicily, 1943.* New York: HarperCollins, 1988.

———. *Decision in Normandy.* New York: HarperCollins, 1983.

———. *Eisenhower: A Soldier's Life.* New York: Henry Holt, 2002.

———. *Patton: A Genius for War.* New York: HarperCollins, 1995.

DeTrez, Michel. *Sainte-Mere-Eglise: 6 June 1944: Photographs of D-Day.* Wezembeek-Oppem, Belgium: D-Day Publishing, 2004.

———. *The Way We Were: Colonel Robert M. Piper, Headquarters Company, 505th Parachute Infantry Regiment, 82nd Airborne Division.* Wezembeek-Oppem, Belgium: D-Day Publishing, 2002.

Devlin, Gerard M. *Paratrooper!* New York: St. Martins, 1979.

Doubler, Michael D. *Closing with the Enemy: How GIs Fought the War in Europe, 1944–45.* Lawrence: University Press of Kansas, 1994.

Duboscq, Genevieve. *My Longest Night.* New York: Seaver Books, 1981.

Eisenhower, Dwight D. *Crusade in Europe.* New York: Doubleday, 1948.

Fowler, Will. *D-Day: The First 24 Hours.* Miami, Fla.: Amber Books, 2003.

Fussell, Paul. *The Great War and Modern Memory.* New York: Oxford University Press, 1975.

———. *Wartime: Understanding and Behavior in the Second World War.* New York: Oxford University Press, 1989.

Gavin, James M. *On to Berlin.* New York: Viking Press, 1978.

Gawne, Jonathan. *Spearhead D-Day: American Special Units in Normandy.* Paris: Histoire et Collections, 1998.

Gilmore, Donald L., ed. *U.S. Army Atlas of the European Theater in World War II.* New York: Barnes and Noble, 2004.

Graham, Martin F. "History of the 463rd Parachute Field Artillery Battalion." Unpublished memoir, 1995.

Grossjohann, Georg. *Five Years, Four Fronts: The War Years of Georg Grossjohann, Major, German Army.* Bedford, Pa.: Aberjona Press, 1999.

Grossman, Dave. *On Killing.* Boston: Little, Brown, 1995.

Headquarters, 82nd Airborne Division. *82nd Airborne Division Operations in Normandy, France, June–July 1944.* Fall 1944.

Hesketh, Roger. *Fortitude: The D-Day Deception Campaign.* Woodstock, N.Y.: Overlook Press, 2000.

Jacobus, George R., ed. *Echoes of the Warriors: Personal Experience of the Enlisted Men and Officers of E Company of the 505th Parachute Infantry Regiment, 82nd Airborne in World War II.* St. Simon's Island, Ga.: Self-published memoir, 1996.

Jorgensen, Starlyn. Unpublished memoir of the 456th Parachute Field Artillery.

Keegan, John. *The Oxford Companion to World War II.* New York: Oxford University Press, 2001.

Kennedy, David M. *Freedom from Fear: The American People in Depression and War, 1929–1945.* New York: Oxford University Press, 1999.

Knell, Hermann. *To Destroy a City: Strategic Bombing and Its Human Consequences in World War II.* Cambridge, Mass.: Perseus Books, 2003.

Langdon, Allen L. *"Ready": A World War II History of the 505th Parachute Infantry Regiment.* Indianapolis: 82nd Airborne Division Educational Fund, 1986.

Lewin, Ronald. *Ultra Goes to War.* London: Hutchinson, 1978.

Lord, William G. *History of the 508th Parachute Infantry.* Nashville, Tenn.: Battery Press, 1977.

Marshall, S. L. A. *Night Drop: The American Airborne Invasion of Normandy.* Nashville, Tenn.: Battery Press, 1962.

Masters, Charles J. *Glidermen of Neptune: The American D-Day Glider Attack.* Carbondale, Ill.: Southern Illinois University Press, 1995.

Mauldin, Bill. *Up Front.* Cleveland: World, 1945.

McCullough, David G., ed. *The American Heritage Picture History of World War II.* New York: American Heritage, 1966.

McManus, John C. *The Deadly Brotherhood: The American Combat Soldier in World War II.* Novato, Calif.: Presidio Press, 2001.

Megellas, James. *All the Way to Berlin: A Paratrooper at War in Europe.* New York: Random House, 2003.

Meyers, James J., and Robert W. Gillette. *Search for Members of the 505th Parachute Infantry Regimental Combat Team of World War II, 1942–45.* Self-published records, 1999.

Michelin Travel Publications. *Bataille de Normandie Map: Juin–Aout 1944.* Watford, United Kingdom: Michelin Travel, 1998.

———. *The Green Guide: Normandy.* Watford, United Kingdom: Michelin Travel, 2001.

Morgan, Martin K. *Down to Earth: The 507th Parachute Infantry Regiment in Normandy, June 6–July 15, 1944.* Atglen, Pa.: Schiffer, 2004.

Murphy, Robert M. *No Better Place to Die*. Croton Falls, N.Y.: Critical Hit, 1999.

Nichols, David. *Ernie's War: The Best of Ernie Pyle's World War II Dispatches*. New York: Simon and Schuster, 1986.

O'Donnell, Patrick K. *Beyond Valor: World War II's Ranger and Airborne Veterans Reveal the Heart of Combat*. New York: Free Press, 2001.

O'Loughlin, Dennis G. "Fierce Individualists: U.S. Paratroopers in WWII." Unpublished memoir.

OREP editors. *Historical Map: Omaha Beach—the Pointe Du Hoc*. Cully, France: OREP, 1999.

Pyle, Ernie. *Brave Men*. New York: Henry Holt, 1944.

Raibl, Tony J. *The Operations of the 82nd Airborne Division Artillery (82nd Airborne Division) in the Airborne Landings Near St. Mere Eglise, France, 6–8 June 1944 (Normandy Campaign): Personal Experience of a Division Artillery Communications Officer*. Advanced Infantry Officers Class No. II, 1948.

Ridgway, Matthew B. *Soldier: The Memoirs of Matthew B. Ridgway*. New York: Curtis, 1956.

Rottman, Gordon, and Ron Volstad. *U.S. Army Airborne, 1940–90*. Elite series. Oxford: Osprey, 1990.

Ruggero, Ed. *Combat Jump: The Young Men Who Led the Assault into Fortress Europe, July 1943*. New York: HarperCollins, 2003.

Rush, Robert S. *US Infantryman in World War II*. Vol. 3, *European Theater of Operations, 1944–45*. Warrior series. Oxford: Osprey, 2002.

Ryan, Cornelius. *The Longest Day: June 6, 1944*. New York: Simon and Schuster, 1959.

Sampson, Otis. Untitled and unpublished memoir.

Shilleto, Carl, and Mike Tolhurst. *A Traveller's Guide to D-Day and the Battle for Normandy*. New York: Interlink, 2002.

Smith, Carl, and Mike Chappell. *U.S. Paratrooper, 1941–45*. Warrior series. Oxford: Osprey, 2000.

Thomas, Nigel, and Stephen Andrew. *The German Army, 1939–45*. Vol. 5, *Western Front, 1943–45*. Men-at-Arms series. Oxford: Osprey, 2000.

Tucker, William H. *D-Day: Thirty-five Days in Normandy: Reflections of a Paratrooper*. Harwichport, Mass.: International Airborne Books, 2002.

———. *Parachute Soldiers*. Harwichport, Mass.: International Airborne Books, 1995.

U.S. Department of War, Historical Division. *Omaha Beachhead: 6 June–13 June 1944*. Washington: U.S. Government Printing Office, 1984.

Webster, David K. *Parachute Infantry: An American Paratrooper's Memoir of D-Day and the Fall of the Third Reich*. New York: Random House, 2002.

Weinberg, Ann. *Stanley Weinberg: World War II Remembrances*. Self-published memoir, 1997.

Winchester, Jim. *The World War II Tank Guide*. Edison, N.J.: Chartwell Books, 2000.

Windrow, Martin, and Richard Hook. *The Panzer Divisions*. Men-at-Arms series. Oxford: Osprey, 1982.

Winterbotham, F. W. *The Ultra Secret*. New York: Harper and Row, 1974.

Yenne, Bill. *"Black '41": The West Point Class of 1941 and the American Triumph in WWII*. New York: John Wiley, 1941.

INDEX

ALSO BY
ED RUGGERO

COMBAT JUMP
The Young Men Who Led the Assault into Fortress Europe, July 1943

ISBN 978-0-06-008876-7 (paperback)

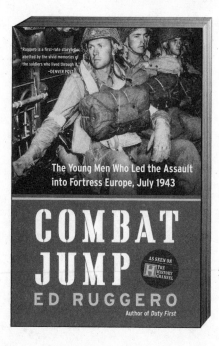

A classic tale of military action—the first American Airborne invasion of World War II and the courageous paratroopers who risked their lives to free Europe from the Nazis.

By the first light on D-day, July 10, 1943, it looked as if their mission to hold the beaches of Sicily for General Eisenhower's landing forces might fail. Inexperienced pilots, lost or blown off course, dropped 80 percent of the troopers miles from their targets. Just a few hundred men—of 3,400—landed near their objective, and soon they discovered that the Germans had tanks. The lightly armed paratroopers, with their rifles and hand grenades, were not equipped to take on the forty-ton panzers. But against all odds, they did—and without Sicily, there might have been no airborne invasion of France in June 1944.

"Ruggero is a first-rate storyteller, abetted by the vivid memories of the soldiers who lived through [World War II]." —*Denver Post*

"A master of the World War II genre." —*Los Angeles Times*